In
Memory of
Norman & Thelma
Schowalter

MINNESOTA GOES TO WAR

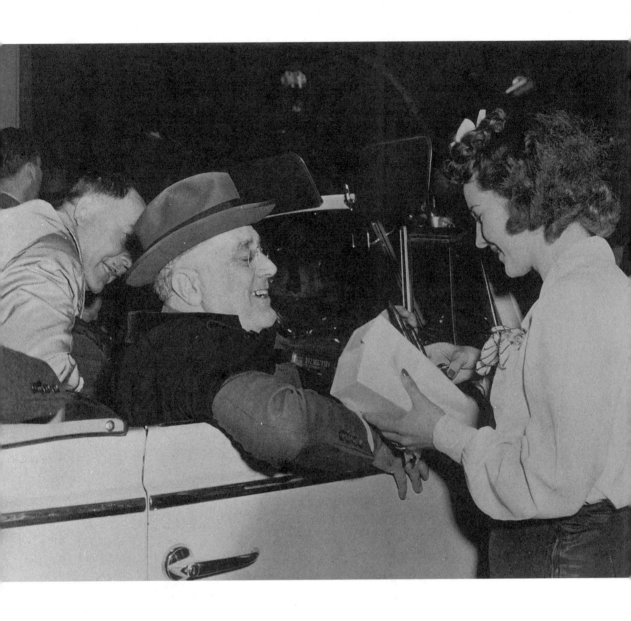

MINNESOTA GOES TO WAR

The Home Front during World War II

Dave Kenney

Foreword by
WENDELL R. ANDERSON
Former governor of Minnesota

M MINNESOTA HISTORICAL SOCIETY PRESS

Publication of this book was supported, in part, with funds provided to the Minnesota Historical Society by the George A. MacPherson Fund, St. Paul, and by the Elmer L. and Eleanor J. Andersen Publications Endowment Fund of the Minnesota Historical Society.

Part of chapter 2, "The Home Front," appeared in a different form in *Northern Lights: The Stories of Minnesota's Past*, 2nd ed. (St. Paul: Minnesota Historical Society).

www.mnhs.org/mhspress

The Minnesota Historical Society Press is a member of the Association of American University Presses.

Manufactured in the United States of America

10 9 8 7 6 5 4 3 2 1

∞ The paper used in this publication meets the minimum requirements of the American National Standard for Information Sciences—Permanence for Printed Library Materials, ANSI Z39.48-1984.

International Standard Book Number
0-87351-506-4 (cloth)

Library of Congress Cataloging-in-Publication Data

Kenney, Dave, 1961–
    Minnesota goes to war : the home front during
    World War II / Dave Kenney ; foreword by
    Wendell R. Anderson.
        p.   cm.
    Includes bibliographical references and index.
    ISBN 0-87351-506-4 (alk. paper)
    1. World War, 1939–1945—Minnesota.
    2. Minnesota—History—20th century.
    I. Title.

D769.85.M6K46 2005

2004008635

For Nancy

. . .

ACKNOWLEDGMENTS

One of my few regrets on this project is that I didn't start sooner. Nearly six decades have passed since the end of World War II, and with each day that goes by it becomes increasingly difficult to find people willing and able to share their memories of those tumultuous war years. For that reason I am especially grateful for the opportunities I had to speak with some marvelous storytellers from that era. Thanks to Tosh Abe, Don Arm, Pernina Burke, Harry Davis, Ancel Keys, Margaret McGillis, Henry Peck, Kenneth Porwoll, Don Samuelson, Henry Scholberg, and Leonard Strobel for helping me fill in so many gaps.

Much of the material I gathered while researching this book lurks in local museums, libraries, and research centers—impervious to those of us who might try to access it without expert help. I spent hours upon hours paging through documents, flipping through photographs, and listening to tape recordings in the collections of such far-flung places as the Charles Babbage Institute at the University of Minnesota; the Crow Wing County Historical Society in Brainerd; the Maritime Collections of the Jim Dan Hill Library at the University of Wisconsin–Superior; the Northwest Minnesota Historical Center at Minnesota State University Moorhead; the Olmsted County History Center Library in Rochester; the Southern Minnesota Historical Center at Minnesota State University Mankato; the Superior Public Library in Superior, Wisconsin; and the West Central Minnesota Historical Research Center at the University of Minnesota–Morris. I owe a great debt of gratitude to Stephen Gross, Laura Jacobs, Julie Kapke, Lucille Kirkeby, Korella Selzler, Terry Shoptaugh, and Daardi Sizemore for helping me make the best use of my out-of-town research time. Others who supplied invaluable assistance from afar include Dave Frederickson, Doris Glick, Davis Helberg, Pat Labadie, Mark Peihl, Bud Nakasone, Jan Stepanek, Bill Tuttle, and Renee Ziemer.

While I depended heavily on assistance from far afield, I actually spent the great bulk of my research time closer to home, at the Minnesota History Center library in St. Paul. Deserving special mention are the reference assistants and copy center staffers who put up with my endless barrage of photocopy requests. Many thanks to Patrick Blaine, Bethany Carlson, Holly Collins, Nick Duncan, Ruth Goerger, Keeley Hanson, Todd Mayberry, Stefan Songstad, and Chris Welter.

I also would like to thank three other essential collaborators from the Minnesota Historical Society: Debbie Miller, who encouraged me to pursue this project; Pam McClanahan, my editor, who turned my manuscript into something that people might actually read; and Greg Britton, who showed more confidence in me than I ever had the right to expect.

My sincere gratitude, also, to former governor Wendell Anderson for lending his considerable prestige to the project.

Finally, my deepest thanks to my family: my parents, Vern and Gail; my daughters, Helen and Grace; and my wife, Nancy Lebens. Without their love and support I could never write another word.

Contents

Foreword

Wendell R. Anderson

Dave Kenney's book, *Minnesota Goes to War: The Home Front during World War II*, is a must read for anyone interested in the most critical period of the twentieth century. I was there. I lived through it. I remember it well.

Two personal experiences greatly influence my reading of this book. My dad was one of eleven children. He was the second youngest of this long line of siblings and he had nephews his own age. His favorite was my cousin Bob. Bob was single and was drafted into the war early. On a Saturday in the summer of 1943 when I was ten, I went with my father to the St. Paul railroad station to pick up Army Private First Class Robert Anderson. We drove home in my dad's 1929 Model A Ford. On the way, we stopped at the Anderson Liquor Store on Payne Avenue to buy a bottle of whiskey. My mother prepared supper: pot roast, mashed potatoes, real gravy. Then, it was cards—a game of whist—and coffee and cake.

Early the next morning, we took Bob back to the railroad station. The Normandy invasion was the sixth of June, 1944. Bob was killed on June 16 in the hedgerow country of France and buried there temporarily. We returned to the railroad station in 1947 to escort his casket to the Lutheran church in White Bear Lake for the memorial service.

On April 9, 1942, I was on our back porch on Edgerton Street when the *St. Paul Dispatch*, the evening newspaper, arrived. Big black headlines read: "Bataan Falls." I brought the paper to my mother, who was having coffee with her cousin Helen. When my mother saw the headlines, she said to Helen, "Ester will be worried." Ester was another of my mother's cousins, and her son Glen Noreen was on Bataan. He never returned.

When I was governor of Minnesota in the early seventies, I visited with a Bataan survivor. I mentioned my cousin Glen Noreen. The man didn't remember Glen, but he said he tried to keep his sanity as a prisoner by recording statistics. The man checked his records and found Glen's name. He wrote me and said that Glen survived the march but ultimately died like so many other prisoners of the Japanese: They would get sick and often got dysentery. They were given no food, no water, no medicine. They were simply left to die.

When one walked through any neighborhood in Minnesota during the war, it seemed as if every other house had a small flag in the window with a white star, an indication that a member of the family was serving in the military. Often, there was more than one flag. When the terrible news came that a loved one was lost, a gold star replaced the white star. Gold stars were everywhere.

The author's description of the impact of the war in Brainerd, Minnesota, was, for me, the most moving. He captures the atmosphere of that difficult period. Brainerd had more men on Bataan per capita than any other community in Minnesota. He quotes from my dear friend, Don Samuelson, former president of the Minnesota State Senate. His father died on December 7, 1942, in China. The Japanese worked him to death at a mine. Samuelson was in the third grade when he got the call to go to his grandmother's house, and Kenney quotes Don's memory of that tragic event:

> "As a little kid, even though you're told he's not coming back, somehow you think it's not true," he said. "He's too strong. He'll be back. So it takes a lot of convincing."

The people of Brainerd were worried about their men who were imprisoned in Japan near Hiroshima. If an American soldier was captured by the Germans, 97 percent survived. If an American soldier was captured by the Japanese, only 53 percent survived. A ship in Admiral Bull Halsey's fleet picked up two Swedish escapees from a Japanese POW camp. They said if the guards at the camp realized that the war was lost, they would execute all the prisoners. A young staff officer to Admiral Halsey, former Minnesota governor Harold Stassen, was given responsibility to rescue the POWs. Although General Douglas MacArthur had given the order that Allied troops should not set foot on Japanese soil until after the surrender, Admiral Halsey ordered the Stassen operation that successfully liberated the camp, and many Brainerd survivors. Only thirty-two of the sixty-two Brainerd men captured by the Japanese survived, and Kenney faithfully tells the emotional journey of the Brainerd men and their families as it unfolds from 1941 to 1945.

As one who grew up in the sixties, when draft avoidance was in and draft-card burning was common, Kenney can be forgiven for not fully appreciating the intense desire most men had to serve in World War II. But Kenney doesn't fail to offer us the heartfelt desire of Hubert Humphrey, who, speaking to the newly formed DFL party that had asked him to run for governor, said: "I want to go into the armed forces if I am acceptable. I want to be with those other young men and women in the armed forces, and you can't deny me that privilege." When Humphrey discovered he had flunked his navy physical, the author describes Humphrey's patriotic torment:

> *Democrat Orville Freeman [later governor of Minnesota and secretary of agriculture under President Kennedy] recalled how hard Humphrey took the news: "I can remember putting him on a train one night when he was just literally crying. He was so frustrated and unhappy and was trying in every way he could to get into the service, and he just couldn't get in."*

Whenever the author tackles an event where I was a witness (or near witness), his descriptions take me immediately back to that amazing time. His account of the merger of the Farmer-Labor party and the Democratic party was a joy to read. The Minnesota Communists view of the war changed as the dictator of the Soviet Union, Joseph Stalin, changed his views. The Minnesota Communists were against the war until Hitler broke his pledge to Stalin and invaded the Soviet Union. The author's vivid accounts of Minnesota's war production, rationing, race relations, and of Ancel Keys' starvation experiments on volunteer conscientious objectors are especially noteworthy.

I had seven first cousins and four second cousins in uniform in World War II. We lost two of them. I never heard anyone in my extended family, in my neighborhood, or among my friends complain about rationing or lack of consumer goods. Our concern was for the safety of the men and women in uniform. Little was said about anything else. The United States lost about 450,000 men and women during World War II. Dave Kenney has written an important book on World War II that increases my respect for what I think is rightly called "the greatest generation."

Preface

Growing up during the 1960s, I always associated World War II with chewing gum wrappers. My parents had both experienced the war as home front children: my father in Oak Park, Illinois; my mother in Minneapolis. As adults, they occasionally regaled me with stories of what it was like to grow up during wartime, but the only anecdote that stuck with me was the one my mother most liked to recount—the one about chewing gum wrappers. As I understood it, my mother and her little friends in Minneapolis single-handedly won the war for the Allies by carefully peeling off leaves of tinfoil from their gum wrappers, rolling the precious metal into balls, and turning it in to the War Department for use in the production of planes, tanks, and atomic bombs. For years, this anecdote constituted the extent of my World War II knowledge. I learned very little about the war in high school—or college for that matter. Perhaps no one bothered to teach me, or I never bothered to learn. World War II was ancient history and I had other, more pressing topics on my mind at the time. None of them had anything to do with troop movements or tire rationing.

It's hard to say when I began taking an interest in the history of the Second World War, but it must have been sometime around the fiftieth anniversary of the attack on Pearl Harbor. I was working as a senior writer at CNN in Atlanta, and we at the network liked to saturate the airwaves with nostalgic, newsreel-like feature stories every time we noticed a significant World War II anniversary on the calendar. ("On this day fifty years ago, Allied troops . . .") At some point during this period, my wife, Nancy Lebens, and I decided to push forward with a project that we had recently begun considering: a television documentary about life in Georgia during World War II. Nancy oversaw the project (she was a public television producer) and I did most of the research and writing. For the better part of two years, I immersed myself in Georgia home front stories—everything from the construction of liberty ships in Brunswick, to the training of paratroopers at Fort Benning, to the race-baiting wartime politics of Governor Gene Talmadge. It was fascinating stuff and I got hooked. But Nancy and I left Georgia a few years after completing the documentary and moved back to Minnesota. I didn't know if I would ever get the chance to revisit World War II again.

By the summer of 2001, however, I was working on a new edition of the Minnesota Historical Society's state history textbook, *Northern Lights*. My colleagues and I had decided to devote one chapter of the book to World War II, and since I already was quite familiar with the period, I figured it would be an easy chapter to write. But I soon learned there were no comprehensive histories covering the World War II years in Minnesota—just a few journal articles about specific wartime events in the state. I had to start from scratch. Fortunately, the Historical Society houses a wealth of primary sources covering the war (including, most notably, the letters of Leland Rowberg and his parents), and I quickly collected enough material for the chapter. A few months later, during a discussion with one of our advisors, Debbie Miller, I mentioned the gap I'd noticed in Minnesota's wartime history records. Debbie's eyes lit up. "You should write a book," she said.

Going into this project, I knew that many historians believed World War II was a watershed event that forever changed the nation's economic, political, and social orders. Others felt many of the changes commonly attributed to the war were well under way before the war began. Still others saw the war's impact as a "mix of change and continuity."[1] While I found the intellectual debate stimulating, I realized that I wanted to write about the fascinating, often forgotten, stories I was discovering—most of which would never have taken place had America not gone to war in 1941. As historian Barbara Tuchman once wrote, "no one could possibly persuade me that telling a story is not the most desirable thing a writer can do."[2]

Stories of Minnesota at war illustrate much that was going on in the nation at that time. But these stories also show what was unique about wartime in Minnesota. The state virtually exhausted its supplies of high-grade iron ore, one of its most highly prized natural resources, to provide raw material for the nation's arsenal. Its companies churned out wartime products with diverse brand names such as Spam and Scotchlite. Its brightest minds conducted extraordinary wartime research using animal and human test subjects. Its three-party political system succumbed to wartime pressures. And one Minnesota city—Brainerd—suffered war casualties greater than most American communities had to endure. Some of the simplest anecdotes have an only-in-Minnesota ring to them. I'm especially fond of Chisholm resident Ruth Dolinar's recollection of December 7, 1941:

We were ice fishing at Pelican and it was very cold. We had our car parked on the ice. When we got through fishing we went into a little shack where a fellow lived on Pelican. And we went there to warm up. He asked us to come in. He told us that the Japanese had bombed the United States. He had heard it over the radio. We thought, well, he doesn't know what he's talking about. And we started to laugh. We put the radio on in the car. And we heard it. And we didn't laugh anymore.[3]

In relating these stories, I have resisted the temptation to paint a glowing picture of Minnesota citizens united in the war effort. It's tempting, for example, to claim that Minnesotans performed their patriotic duties with little complaint or resistance. Certainly the vast majority of Minnesotans understood the grave dangers facing the world during the late 1930s and early 1940s, but they responded to those dangers in various ways. Most draftees reported for induction, but many actively tried to avoid military service. Most civilians put up with the inconveniences of rationing, but many dabbled in the black market. Most business owners strove to maximize wartime production, but many balked at hiring minority workers who might help them meet their production goals. The list goes on. If my research has taught me nothing else, it's that the Minnesotans who lived and died during the World War II years were a complicated bunch capable of great bravery, selfless sacrifice, and a variety of other deeds—many admirable, and many not. And that's what makes them so interesting.

WORLD WAR II TIMELINE, 1939–1942

1939

September 1   Germany invades Poland

September 3   Britain and France declare war on Germany

September 17   Soviet Union invades Poland in accordance with Nazi-Soviet pact

1940

April 9   Germany invades Denmark and Norway

May 10   Germany invades France, Belgium, Luxembourg,
               and the Netherlands

May 26   British forces begin evacuation of Dunkirk

May 28   Belgium capitulates to Germany

June 10   Norway capitulates to Germany

June 22   France capitulates to Germany

July 10   Battle of Britain begins as German planes attack South Wales

September 16   Selective Service Act becomes law in United States

September 27   Germany, Italy, and Japan form tripartite alliance

October 29   First peacetime military draft in U.S. history

1941

March 11   Roosevelt signs Lend-Lease Act

April 17   Yugoslavia capitulates to Germany

April 27   Greece capitulates to Germany

June 22   Germany invades the Soviet Union

June 25   Roosevelt signs Executive Order 8802 prohibiting discrimination
               in hiring

December 6   Soviet Union launches major counteroffensive against Germany

December 7   Japan attacks U.S. naval forces at Pearl Harbor

December 8   United States and Britain declare war on Japan

December 10   Japan invades the Philippines

December 11   Germany declares war on the United States

1942

January 13   German U-boats begin sinking ships off U.S. coast

February 19   Roosevelt signs Executive Order 9066 authorizing the internment of
               Japanese Americans

April 9   U.S. forces in the Philippines surrender to Japan

April 18   U.S. aircraft under the command of Lieutenant Colonel Jimmy Doolittle
               bomb Japan

June 4   United States scores decisive naval victory over Japan during
               Battle of Midway

November 4   British forces defeat German Afrika Korps in Battle of El Alamein

November 8   U.S. and British forces invade North Africa

1943

February 2	German forces at Stalingrad surrender to the Soviets
March 4	Allied naval forces defeat Japanese naval forces in Battle of the Bismark Sea
May 13	German forces in North Africa surrender to the Americans and the British
May 30	U.S. forces complete occupation of Aleutian Islands
July 9	Allied forces invade Sicily
July 25	Italian dictator Benito Mussolini overthrown
September 8	New Italian government announces Italy's surrender
September 9	Allied forces establish beachhead at Salerno, Italy

1944

January 22	Allied forces establish beachhead at Anzio, Italy
January 27	Soviets break 900-day siege of Leningrad
June 5	Allied forces enter Rome
June 6	D-Day: Allied forces land at Normandy
June 20	U.S. naval forces prevail against Japanese in Battle of the Philippine Sea
August 25	Allied forces liberate Paris
October 25	U.S. forces defeat Japanese forces at Leyte Gulf, the Philippines
December 16	German forces launch Battle of the Bulge offensive on the western front

1945

January 9	U.S. forces invade the Philippine island of Luzon
January 16	Battle of the Bulge ends in German defeat
January 17	Soviet forces liberate Warsaw
January 26	Soviet forces liberate Auschwitz concentration camp
February 4	Roosevelt, Stalin, and Churchill meet at Yalta
February 14	Allied incendiary bombs ignite firestorm in Dresden, Germany
February 19	U.S. forces land on Iwo Jima
March 3	U.S. forces liberate Manila in the Philippines
April 1	U.S. forces invade Okinawa
April 12	Roosevelt dies and Harry Truman assumes presidency
May 8	Victory in Europe (VE) Day
August 6	United States drops first atomic bomb on Hiroshima
August 9	United States drops second atomic bomb on Nagasaki
August 15	Victory over Japan (VJ) Day
September 2	Japanese delegation signs formal documents of surrender aboard U.S. battleship *Missouri* in Tokyo Bay

MINNESOTA GOES TO WAR

The drive for the 1941 national championship. Gophers fullback Bill Daley catches a pass during a Saturday game at Memorial Stadium.

Introduction

It was late in the fourth quarter, and the Golden Gophers of the University of Minnesota were manhandling the overmatched Wisconsin Badgers. The score was 34–6. A few more minutes and the Gophers would wrap up their fifth national championship in eight seasons. With the crowd of fifty-three thousand at Memorial Stadium roaring in anticipation, coach Bernie Bierman sent in all his seniors for one last drive down the field. Leading the way was the team's captain, a mesmerizing halfback from Faribault named Bruce Smith. Smith was, in the opinion of former Gopher great Pug Lund, "the most beautiful, deceptive runner" ever to wear the maroon and gold.[1] Although he had struggled with injuries all season, he was still considered a top contender for college football's most coveted individual award, the Heisman Trophy.

A few plays into the drive, Smith crumpled to the ground while attempting an end sweep. Nearly everybody in the stands assumed he had reinjured his leg, but he had actually been knocked silly by a blow to the head. As Smith staggered off the field for the last time, the crowd erupted in what the *Minneapolis Tribune and Star Journal* would call "the noisiest ovation any Minnesota individual ever got in the [school's] long and colorful football history."[2] Late-afternoon shadows crept over the stadium. The clock on the scoreboard counted down the remaining seconds. With Smith on the sidelines, the Gophers scored one more touchdown. Final score: 41–6.

The postgame locker room rang with a cacophony of cheers, laughter, good-natured profanity, and shouts of congratulations, but still an air of finality hung over the celebration. As he took off his Gopher jersey for the last time, Bruce Smith couldn't help but look back on all that he and his teammates had accomplished over the years. "It seems as though it were only yesterday that I was a freshman," he mused.[3]

It was 1941. The Gopher dynasty, and all it had meant to the people of Minnesota, was over.

For the better part of a decade, the Gopher football team had been one of the few things that Minnesotans could cheer about. Bernie Bierman had joined the Gophers in 1932, the year the Great

Hard times. Job seekers line up outside the St. Paul office of the Minnesota State Employment Service in January 1938.

Depression began devouring Minnesota in earnest. At the time the state's farmers were struggling to fight off foreclosures, bankruptcies, and plummeting commodity prices (hogs were fetching three cents a pound and milk was going for two cents a quart).[4] In the cities, the ranks of the unemployed were swelling to crisis proportions (Minneapolis' Union City Mission reported it was serving eighteen hundred homeless men each day).[5] On the Iron Range, the jobless rate was pushing 70 percent. The state's first Farmer-Labor governor, Floyd B. Olson, was running—successfully, as it turned out—for reelection by promising to protect the downtrodden working classes from "the forces of reaction and of special privilege."[6] Minnesotans were starving for a little good news, and it was their good fortune that Bernie Bierman's Gophers decided to peak at just the right time. In 1934, the team went undefeated and earned its first national championship. To *Minneapolis Tribune* sports columnist George Barton, the Gophers were nothing short of a blessing.

Not only did Bernie and his Gophers bring glory galore to Minnesota, but they did much to make everybody forget their cares, business and otherwise. Everybody was so happy over the remarkable deeds the Maroon and Gold athletes performed on the gridiron that their worries were smothered with joy. I cannot recall any other year when everybody was so wrapped up in a football team as Minnesotans were this year. It was a grand and glorious season, believe you me![7]

There were more glorious seasons to come. The team repeated as national champions in 1935, 1936, 1940, and 1941 (with Bruce Smith leading the way) and as Big Ten champs in 1937 and 1938. Only in 1939 did the Gophers stumble, managing just three wins.

Through it all, the team continued to provide Minnesotans with a very welcome diversion from their troubles. Federal New Deal programs such as the Works Progress Administration (wpa) and the Civilian Conservation Corps (ccc) had taken some of the sting out of the economic crisis (between 1933 and 1939 New Deal agencies pumped more than one billion dollars into the state),[8] but many problems remained. Especially telling were statistics showing that, during the bulk of the Gophers' glory years, manufacturers in the state still employed between fifteen thousand and twenty thousand fewer workers than they had in 1929.[9] At the same time, the state's and the nation's continuing economic troubles were accompanied by political upheaval. In 1938, disgruntled voters replaced the gruff and ineffective Farmer-Labor governor, Elmer Benson, with a thirty-one-year-old Republican, Harold Stassen.

Still, as the new decade dawned, things were beginning to look up—at least where the economy was concerned. By the second half of 1941, the federal government was spending more than half a billion dollars in the state through defense contracts, and employment in the state's manufacturing

Governor Floyd B. Olson, a self-described "radical," guided Minnesota through the harshest years of the Great Depression.

Harold E. Stassen was the first of four consecutive progressive Republicans to hold the governor's office between 1939 and 1955.

sector had jumped more than 28 percent.[10] Minnesotans no longer needed the Gophers to cheer them up.

Two weeks after the Gophers wrapped up their fifth national championship with the victory against Wisconsin, Japan attacked Pearl Harbor. Bernie Bierman, a veteran of World War I, reenlisted in the marines. He would return to coach the Gophers after the war but would never again win a national title.

Two days after the Pearl Harbor attack, Bruce Smith appeared at New York's Downtown Athletic Club to accept the Heisman Trophy.

In his acceptance speech, Smith said all the right things. He thanked his teammates and coaches. He acknowledged the other finalists. And then he closed with a few words of appreciation for the game he loved—the game that had helped the people in his home state weather the Depression, and that would, in his opinion, help America win the war. "Those far eastern fellows may think that American boys are soft," he said, "but I have had, and even now have, plenty of evidence in black and blue to show that they are making a big mistake. I think America will owe a great debt to the game of football when we finish this thing off."[11]

Head football coach Bernie Bierman (far right) turned the Gophers into a national powerhouse during the height of the Depression.

Co. A - 194TH TANK BATTALION - BRAINERD, MINN. FEB. 18, 1941

The men of Company A, 194th Tank Battalion, posed for this photograph on
February 18, 1941, two days before leaving Brainerd.

The first onlookers began arriving at Brainerd's Northern Pacific depot at about eleven-thirty P.M.—early enough to stake out a good spot on the platform, but not so early that they'd freeze in place before the night was over. The mercury in the thermometer read twenty below zero, and it was still dropping. It was the kind of night that would freeze your nostrils closed if you weren't careful. As the minutes passed, the sprinkling of people turned into a crowd—a few hundred strong at least. Parents embraced drowsy children in tight hugs. Boots stomped, bringing temporary feeling to numb toes. The first service regiment band, under the direction of Everett Nelson, provided musical diversion and prompted more than one person to wonder how it was possible to play a cornet in such weather without getting your lips stuck to the mouthpiece.

A few minutes before midnight, the men the crowd had come to see marched into view—eighty-two of them, all dressed in khakis, responding on cue to barked commands. The men entered the depot, came to a halt, and then, on their officers' commands, fell out.

It was instant bedlam.

Each man waded into the crowd, searching for the faces he most wanted to see. Wives and sweethearts ran into their lovers' arms. In one corner of the platform, a young man and his mother wept openly on each other's shoulders. Gray-haired men, veterans of the Great War, thought back on similar scenes more than two decades earlier, thankful that the situation was so different this time around. Farewells lengthened, their sweetness and sadness prolonged, as the 12:19 pulled into the station fifteen minutes late.

The conductor called, "All aboard." The band struck up "The Star-Spangled Banner." The men fell in and marched into the passenger cars. As the crowd surged forward, the men inside in the train raced to the windows, squeezing themselves out until it looked as though some would fall out onto the tracks. Hands reached out and grabbed other hands. Final kisses were stolen. The train pulled away, slowly gathering momentum, and disappeared into the night.[1]

Eight-year-old Don Arm was among the many Brainerdites who waited on the platform until the train was out of sight. His stepfather, Russ Swearingen, was on board, and he already missed him. While many adults would claim later that a sense of foreboding hung over the depot that night, young Don Arm was aware only that the man he'd grown to love was being taken away. "You don't have any idea why," he would recall years later, "but that's the way it was. And we stand there and watch them go."[2]

The eighty-two men who left Brainerd during the earliest hour of February 20, 1941, were all National Guardsmen—citizen soldiers of the recently mobilized Company A, 194th Tank Battalion. They were heading out to Fort Lewis, Washington, for training with the two other units that comprised their battalion: Company B from St. Joseph, Missouri, and Company C from Salinas, California. They were to train at Fort Lewis for one year and then head back home. That was the plan.

Company A was a mechanized unit specializing in the still unappreciated and undeveloped techniques of tank warfare. The unit, originally known as the 34th Tank Company, had received its first tanks in early 1937, and since then had trained with the big machines each summer at Camp Ripley, outside Little Falls. During the winter, the men of the company drilled indoors at Brainerd's new armory and took classes in tank maintenance. The "tankers," as the men were known, became fixtures in the town's Memorial Day and Labor Day parades.

The men of Company A were part-time soldiers—farmers, pipe fitters, recently graduated teenagers—most of whom dreamed rarely, if at all, of military glory. Some joined to be with their buddies or to put a few extra dollars in their pockets. Others did so figuring that they would soon be drafted anyway. A few, including twenty-one-year-old Ken Porwoll, signed up mainly to get into the Guard's annual New Year's Eve ball:

> *You had to be dressed in a tux if you weren't a military man. The women wore long formal dresses, and it cost twenty-five bucks a person. This was Depression times, and that's a lot of money. And us young fellows that wanted to be part of that, we says, "Why don't we join the Guard, and then we get new clothes, we get new boots, we get the whole bit, and you go as a shined-up soldier and you get in free?" And there must have been ten, twelve of us that signed up at that time to get in there and go to that New Year's dance.*[3]

When word came down in January of 1941 that the company was being mobilized for federal service, most of the men seemed to take the news in stride. After all, they were being sent off for training—not to war. They would be back in a year. Still, everyone realized that the mobilization carried certain risks. "We were all concerned," recalled Leonard Strobel, brother of Corporal Herbert Strobel. "We knew there were storm clouds in Europe and Japan was starting to prepare."[4] Pernina Burke, wife of Second

Lieutenant Ed Burke, was apprehensive as well. "There was a shaky feeling and a little distrust of Japan," she said, "but nothing was said publicly about that."[5] The company's commander, Captain Ernie Miller, acknowledged that his men faced a somewhat uncertain future, but he urged the people of Brainerd not to worry too much. "You will hear about us in the future," he assured them, "and you will be proud of your [men's] contribution to national defense."[6]

Perry, Pernina, Marionne, and Ed Burke, 1945

For a while after the mobilization, everything went as planned. The men of Company A trained at Fort Lewis with the rest of their battalion. Some were joined out in Washington by their wives and children. The demands of military life became routine. But then, in mid-August, during training maneuvers on the Olympic peninsula, the men received new orders: they were being sent overseas; they were to ship out the first week of September; their destination was secret.

Back in Brainerd, speculation about Company A's ultimate destination was all the buzz. Some guessed Alaska, some guessed Hawaii, others the Philippines, but no one knew for sure. Every little clue was pored over. When word arrived that all the men of Company A had been issued tropical uniforms—no woolens—and that the officers had received waterproof watches, it seemed to confirm suspicions that the company was heading someplace warm and damp. On September 5, the Brainerd men left San Francisco on the ocean liner *President Coolidge* under a heavy veil of secrecy. When, about three weeks later, they arrived at their destination, the Army finally took the lid off the story. The banner headline on the September 29 edition of the *Brainerd Dispatch* read: "Guards Are In Philippines."

Over the next two months, the men of Company A battled nearly constant tropical rains and supply glitches as they and the rest of the battalion struggled to turn their new home, Fort Stotsenburg, about sixty miles north of Manila, into a functioning headquarters for armored operations. During their free time, the Brainerd men wrote letters to their friends and relatives back home, describing the occasional joys and regular tedium of military life in the Philippines. Herbert Strobel wrote to his family that the country was fascinating, but he couldn't get over how "backward" it was.

The SS *President Coolidge carried the men of Company A to the Philippines in September 1941.*

BRAINERD, 1941

Ken Porwoll sent his sister a bolt of white sharkskin cloth that he purchased for a song in Manila. All in all, it seemed to the people of Brainerd that the men were getting by quite well.

Whatever comfort Brainerd residents took in the letters they received was shattered by the news of December 7. Japan had attacked Hawaii. It seemed safe to assume that the Philippines would be next. Russ Swearingen's stepson, Don Arm, was in his family's living room when he heard the news:

> We were listening to this report on the radio. And my mother was in tears. And you're sitting there thinking, "What's going on?" But I remember my sister and I and my mother—she was sitting and we were standing alongside of her. And she was just sobbing. . . I'm sure that the full seriousness of the whole thing went right over my head. [I thought], "Okay, he'll be home tomorrow."[7]

The worst fears of the people of Brainerd were fully realized within hours of the Pearl Harbor attack. Japanese warplanes bombed Fort Stotsenburg in what was assumed to be a prelude to a full-scale invasion of the Philippines. Within days, Japanese forces landed on the island of Luzon. During the last week of December, reports started filtering out that U.S. forces in the Philippines were engaged in a "valiant last-ditch battle for Manila," and that the men of the 194th Tank Battalion were in the thick of it. Details were sketchy. The people of Brainerd kept vigil at the radio and devoured whatever information they could glean from the newspapers. On New Year's Eve, the mother of Sergeant Donald Paine received a telegram signed by her son and two of his friends, Ken Porwoll and Billie Mattson. It had been sent just a day or two earlier. "Are well," the telegram read. "In good spirits. Happy New Year. Love to All."[8] It was the last message that anyone in Brainerd would receive from Company A for quite some time.

1 Call to Arms

At a little after eleven on the morning of Tuesday, October 29, 1940, Milton and Sophia Westberg were manning the family grocery store on South Eighth Street in Brainerd. The radio crackled in the background. Customers shuffled in and out, making small talk with the proprietors as their orders were rung up. On most days, the people who shopped at Westberg's Grocery talked about the same old things—the weather, the kids, business. But this day was different. Just one thing seemed to be on everyone's mind: the lottery.

At that moment in Washington, D.C., several well-dressed and grim-faced men—including President Franklin D. Roosevelt—were gathered on a stage around a huge fishbowl. The bowl was filled with thousands of cobalt-blue capsules. Each capsule contained a number. The stage was set—literally—for the first peacetime military draft lottery in American history.

Roosevelt, visibly exhausted from his ongoing presidential campaign against Republican challenger Wendell Willkie, took his place behind a bank of microphones and, in a solemn voice, addressed the nation.

> *You who will enter this peacetime army will be the inheritors of a proud history and an honorable tradition. You will be members of an army which first came together to achieve independence and to establish certain fundamental rights for all men. Ever since that first muster, our democratic army has existed for one purpose only: the defense of our freedom. It is for that one purpose and that one purpose only that you will be asked to answer the call to training.*[1]

Milton and Sophia Westberg turned their attention to the radio and listened closely as the president spoke. They, like millions of other Americans, had plenty at stake. Milton had registered two weeks earlier with the local draft board. Although his chances of being called to military duty were slim (he was thirty-five years old and the father of two young sons), the possibility that he might be drafted was, nonetheless, extremely unappealing. He and Sophia joked nervously about the chances that his number—158—would be the first one pulled.

In Washington, Secretary of War Henry Stimson—wearing a blindfold fashioned from a strip of cloth cut from a chair used during the signing of the Declaration of Independence—thrust his hand into the fishbowl and pulled out a capsule. He handed it to the president. Roosevelt opened it, waited for the newsreel photographers to signal that they were ready, and then made his announcement. "The first number," he intoned, "is one—five—eight."

Milton and Sophia Westberg looked at each other in disbelief. Nine thousand numbers in the fishbowl, and his was the first drawn? Word spread quickly throughout Brainerd that Milton Westberg was Crow Wing County's first potential draftee. Within minutes of the announcement, a reporter from the *Brainerd Dispatch* arrived at the grocery, spouting nonsense about how Westberg must be "thrilled" to be part of such a select group. "Thrilled—that's no word for it," Westberg responded. "The announcement nearly floored me."[2]

Throughout the country and throughout Minnesota, young men who had been assigned the number 158 by their local draft boards were confronted by the sudden reality that they would likely be among the nation's first peacetime draftees. In Ramsey County, twelve registrants shared the distinction of being 158s, and most seemed to take the news in stride. "Too bad this lottery wasn't a horse race," laughed Leo Hendricks, a thirty-year-old truck driver. Twenty-three-year-old packinghouse worker Thomas Gannon likewise tried to look at the bright side. "I know I'll have to take the training sometime," he said, "and I'd just as soon be in the first batch."[3]

By the time the last of the nine thousand lottery numbers was announced in Washington the following morning, more than sixteen million American men, ages twenty-one through thirty-five, knew the order in which they might be drafted. In the days that followed, those whose numbers were pulled early in the lottery were assigned draft classifications. If they had no dependents and were not employed in "necessary" jobs, they landed in Class I, and were ordered to stand by

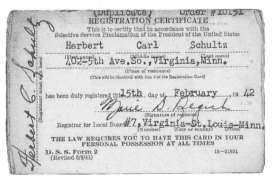

Herbert Schultz's draft registration card

for their call to induction. Those with wives and children—like Milton Westberg—and those working in industries deemed essential by the government received deferments.

The imminent conscription of hundreds of thousands of men was, in many ways, the expression of a collective change of heart. Millions of Americans—many of whom had clung to the hope that the United States would remain aloof to the war in Europe—had concluded that their country was now destined to join the fight. The bill establishing the draft had been introduced—over the objections of anti-interventionists such as Minnesota Senator Henrik Shipstead—two days before France surrendered to Nazi Germany and had been signed into law during the Luftwaffe's bombing raids on London. It was the product of the growing realization that totalitarian aggression was a truly global threat. "The passage of the draft law," wrote historians Garry Clifford and Samuel R. Spencer, Jr., "helped to condition the country, both psychologically and militarily, for the war that lay ahead."[4]

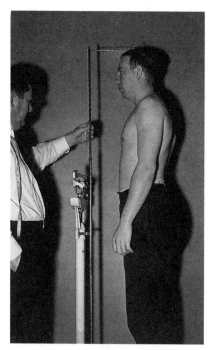

Minneapolis' first post–Pearl Harbor enlistees. Francis James Zywicki gets a physical at the navy recruiting office.

Gung Ho

Army, navy, marine, and coast guard recruiters in Minneapolis were prepared for a busy day, but still, the response was overwhelming. When they opened the doors on the morning of December 8, 1941, their offices immediately filled with men, all eager to join the fight that the Japanese had started the day before at Pearl Harbor. In all, about 150 Hennepin County men applied for enlistment before lunchtime. "The enthusiasm of the men seeking enlistment is just what you would expect in view of developments," one recruiting officer said.[5] Over the next few days, the flood of would-be soldiers, sailors, marines, and coastguardsmen swelled even further. The marine recruiting office at the Metropolitan Life building stayed open twenty-four hours a day to handle all the applications. Army and navy recruiters announced that they, too, would keep working as long as potential recruits kept showing up. Most of the 1,500 men who applied for enlistment in Minneapolis in the first two days after the Pearl Harbor attack were rejected for age and health reasons, although rejection rates fluctuated

John D. Sweet joins the Marines, following in his father's footsteps.

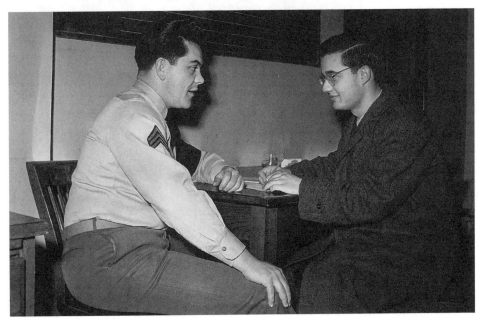

Herbert Irwin Efron signs up for the Army Air Forces.

among the services. The navy, for example, loosened its application requirements considerably in the wake of the attack: married men were now eligible if they could show that their dependents would "be supported adequately"; so were men with police records for offenses that were "not too serious." As a result, the navy accepted about half of its Minneapolis volunteers.[6]

By October 1942, some 125,000 Minnesotans had entered the nation's armed services, either as volunteers or draftees, and many more were getting ready to join up. While the War Department had considerably pared down its original manpower goals, it still aimed to build an armed force of nine million soldiers, sailors, and marines.

Navy enlistees on their way to the train depot.

State officials estimated that if current trends continued, Minnesota would eventually contribute more than 212,000 men to that total—more than a third of its eighteen-year-old to forty-five-year-old male population[7]—but they never really doubted that the state would meet its obligation.

After all, it seemed that everyone wanted to join the fight.

"If I were a man, I would fight them myself," a housewife in Alexandria proclaimed after learning what the Japanese had done.[8] In Fergus Falls, a judge responded to the emergency by suspending the sentences of two convicted felons who said they wanted to enlist.[9] Ninety-five-year-old Civil War veteran James Gillespie of Riverton knew he was too old to fight, but he demonstrated his patriotism by walking thirty-two miles to Brainerd and back, to be on hand as his son joined the navy.[10] Minnesotans from all walks of life were answering the call to arms.

The state's Ojibwe and Dakota were among the most willing recruits. They joined the armed services in proportions far exceeding those of the general population. According to the 1940 census, some 12,000 to 13,000 Ojibwe and Dakota lived in Minnesota during the war, and more than a thousand of them served in the armed forces. Minnesota Chippewa Tribal Secretary Joseph Northrup, for one, was intimately familiar with the contributions that his people were making to the war effort. He had four sons in the army—one in North Africa, one in the Solomon Islands, one in Colorado, and one at Fort Snelling.[11] While some Indians questioned the logic of fighting for a government that historically had mistreated them, many others felt an obligation to serve. "We Indians fought for three hundred years to defend our country," an unnamed Dakota recruit from Prairie Island told the *Red Wing Daily Republican*, "and we are ready to fight again if need be."[12]

Black Minnesotans displayed a similar eagerness to enlist. A few days after the Pearl Harbor attack, the African American newspaper the *Minneapolis Spokesman* interviewed a sampling of local residents and discovered what it called "a universal unity among them for defeat of Japan or any other country which attacks America." The comments of a young man named J. Everett Harris were typical:

As a young Negro of America, I realize our democracy is not perfect, but we are not going to stand idly by and let Japan and other nations destroy the gains we have made. A state of war exists and we are ready to go and protect what others have already gained for our democratic freedom.[13]

The Reverend Clarence T. R. Nelson (right) accepts a military honor roll listing seventeen members of Camphor Memorial Methodist Church in St. Paul.

While many black Minnesotans wanted to enlist, they were not always given the opportunity to do so. On the Tuesday after the attack on Pearl Harbor, army recruiters in Minneapolis turned away five African American men because there was "no Negro quota." "Imagine the feeling of these five patriotic American men who went down to offer up their lives for their country and were turned down as scores of other fellow Americans were accepted," the *Spokesman*'s editor, Cecil Newman, wrote. "There is no reason why an American Negro who wants to join our army or navy . . . should have to stand aside to wait until some general or admiral decides he may join."[14] As the war dragged on, the army did accept thousands of black recruits, but only into segregated units. The navy accepted only a few African American mess hall workers. The marines initially refused to accept any black enlistments whatsoever.[15]

Reike Schwanke of Austin, Minnesota, had made headlines in 1940 when she managed to become the only woman in the nation to successfully register for the draft. (She had persuaded the reluctant local registrar to let her sign up.) When Selective Service officials discovered the mistake and informed Schwanke that women were not eligible for military service, she was clearly annoyed. "There ought to be some place for a woman in the Army," she complained.[16] It didn't take long for the military brass to agree. With America's entry into the war, the nation's women got their first real chance to serve in the military. Between 1942 and 1945, about 140,000 American women enlisted with the army as WACS (Women's Army Corps) or WASPS (Women Airforce Service Pilots). Another 100,000 served as navy WAVES (Women Accepted for Volunteer Emergency Service), and smaller numbers joined the marines, the coast guard, and the army and navy's nurse corps. University of Minnesota sophomore Anne Bosanko was among the hundreds of Minnesota women who volunteered for military service during the war. Like many of her comrades, she enlisted in the WAC out of a sense of duty and a yearning for excitement:

I decided this spring to do it because I felt so useless going to school and being Big Deal On Campus (big sucker on Campus if you ask me,) and I felt that I could do some good in the Army

First Lady Eleanor Roosevelt congratulates new inductees during a WAC *induction ceremony at the Minneapolis Auditorium in 1943.*

and it certainly will do me good. In fact, it's a good deal all around and I'm very enthusiastic about the whole thing. Think of the interesting people I'll meet and the places I'll see. I might even get to go abroad, though I'll be satisfied doing anything they give me.[17]

Women were not sent into combat. Instead, they mostly "typed, filed, telephoned, and chauffeured," thereby making available for combat thousands of men who might otherwise have been stuck in office jobs. Still, many servicemen abhorred the thought of women serving in what had always been an exclusively male bastion, and they actively discouraged their wives, girlfriends, and sisters from joining up. In 1943, enlistments into the women's corps dropped sharply when servicemen began spreading false rumors about women soldiers' sexual promiscuity.[18] In Minnesota, the Women's City Club of St. Paul responded to the drop-off in enlistments by sponsoring a recruitment rally on behalf of the women's corps. The

Anne Bosanko (far left) and friends at William Beaumont General Hospital, Fort Bliss, Texas, in January 1945.

evening culminated with the swearing in of 125 Minnesota women into five services.[19]

Qualms

Most newspaper editors in the state reacted—in print, at least—with resolute stoicism to the news that clattered across the wire machines in the minutes and hours after the bombs started falling on Pearl Harbor. They wrote of the need to unite for victory, to see the fight through to the end. But C. H. Russell of the *Mankato Free Press* was not like most editors. Instead of offering his readers predictable words of patriotic encouragement, he banged out a long column describing the scene in his newsroom when the first flashes came across the wire. The day had "dawned bright and sunny [and had] turned dark and cold about midday with spitting snow and a high wind," Russell wrote. The first bulletin crossed the wire, and a mad scramble ensued. Staff members rushed in from wherever they were spending their Sundays and began toiling on the extra. The newsroom buzzed with terrible excitement. And then, as the chaos began to subside, a young man walked in—a paperboy, ready to deliver the bad news that the people of Mankato were waiting to read. It was at that moment, Russell wrote, that the words "Pearl Harbor—350 known dead" really sank in:

> And [that] carrier boy, summoned to the office remarks, "I'm seventeen—hope it goes another year and I can get in it." Those few words ["Pearl Harbor—350 known dead"] are going to make a difference to hundreds of thousands of teen age school boys—that's the greatest tragedy of all.[20]

Despite all the lines at the recruitment offices, despite all the brave words, most Minnesotans realized, as C. H. Russell did, that there was nothing particularly glamorous about going off to fight for one's country—no matter how righteous the cause. Many men were going to die in this war, and as that sobering realization sank in, more and more Minnesotans overcame their initial urge to enlist. As historian David M. Kennedy noted, "Contrary to much later mythology, the nation's young men did not step forward in unison to answer the trumpet's call, neither before nor after Pearl Harbor."[21] This was the case throughout the country, including Minnesota. While most young men felt duty-bound to join up, few were excited about the proposition.

As the nation built up its armed forces, local draft boards came under intense pressure to grant military exemptions to certain young men in their communities. During a short stint with the draft board in Moorhead, Marie Kirkevold found that she especially dreaded the times when draftees showed up with their entire families in tow. "They'd bring the kids along," she recalled, "and [we would] say, 'Well, no exemption. He has to go.' And it was really sad." Things finally got so bad at the draft board that Kirkevold decided to quit. "I didn't last long because I just could not take it." The draft board, she said, was "the saddest thing that you could ever work for."[22] Most of the hundreds of boards in the state were composed of prominent local residents—many of whom were World War I veterans—and in many places, board members faced accusations of favoritism. William Ernst, whose only son was drafted toward the end of the war, came to believe that the board in his hometown of Alberta, Minnesota, was either biased or bought. "It just wasn't just," he said. "Some of these people had four boys and none of them ever got [drafted]. Another one had one or two and they're both in for three years. Some never came back. So it wasn't just."[23]

St. Paul native William Cummings was among the many Minnesotans who spent the war worrying about the day they would have to report to the local draft board. When the war broke out, Cummings was twenty-four years old—prime drafting age—but as a husband and father of two young children, he was in no rush to go off to war. As time passed, and the rules governing military exemptions tightened, Cummings poured his apprehensions into his faithfully kept diary:

December 11, 1941
Italy and Germany declared war on the United States this morning . . . So many of the young men at work expect to go in the service any time now. If I were single I would enlist in the navy. But having such a lovely family I am anxious to stay out of the war.

January 29, 1942
I got my form to fill out from the Selective Service. This is the draft board. My draft number is 2572 . . . I expect to be classified in IIIa. That is the classification of those who have dependents. If I were not married I would join the Navy. Such is life. How different it would be if I had not married and how glad I am that I did get married. Not from the standpoint of being ex-

empted from the draft but because I have such splendid children
and a swell wife.

June 7, 1942

*I felt down in the dumps for a while when I would think of the
probability of going to war. Then I got over it. I figure this way
now: if I have to go I'll go and make the best
of it. I have always wanted to visit England
and now I will, no doubt. But, oh how I
would miss Betty and the children.*

February 2, 1943

*According to today's edict which is effective
April 1st all men between 18 and 38 if physically and mentally OK and are in non-de-
fense work are to be drafted regardless . . .
For a moment I thought of myself as a soldier seeing those about me being killed and
then myself being blown to bits. That's a hell
of a feeling!*

November 23, 1943

*[I found out today] that I will be placed in
1A in January and that I will actually be
drafted March 15th! Now I know where I
stand at least.*

William Cummings, like many Minnesota
men, was in no rush to go off to war.

December 2, 1943

*I rode gloomily over to the draft board . . . I signed a paper vol-
unteering to enlist in the armed services of the United States. I
am to report for the first physical on Dec. 3rd and at the Fort
[Snelling] on December 20th. Thus ends the long speculation as
to when, if ever, I would be inducted.*

December 22, 1943

*[The officer at Fort Snelling says,] "The doctor and myself feel
that the army life would be too hard for you so we are rejecting
you." And he puts a big red X on the sheet and I took it down
the aisle and handed it in asking if that meant 4F. Yes, you're
rejected. Put on your clothes and go to the induction center. I
could hardly realize that I was actually 4F. It didn't seem
possible.*

December 23, 1943
Betty was [so] happy when I got home that she laughed and
cried. Jimmy was real happy too. Little Ellen did not realize that
anything was amiss.

William Cummings celebrated Christmas of 1943 with his family, happy in the knowledge that he would never have to go to war. The fact that the enlistment officer didn't think he could handle army life did not seem to bother him in the least. He was willing to put up with the snide comments and nasty looks that many 4-FS— even those who *wanted* to join the services—had to endure. And besides, he certainly wasn't alone. About a quarter of the men who passed through Fort Snelling's induction center were rejected because of "physical or mental defects."[24] What mattered most to Cummings was that he would be able to stay with his family. He had his exemption.

Like many draft-wary Minnesotans, Cummings had originally based his hopes for an exemption on the fact that he was a husband and father. Married men had been exempted from the first draft calls—a provision that prompted Selective Service director Lewis B. Hershey to declare in early 1942 that he presumed most recent marriages were conducted "for the purpose of evading the draft." Fathers—especially those with children born before the Pearl Harbor attack—remained nearly immune to conscription throughout much of the war. One popular story of the time told of a man and woman who had named their new son "Weatherstrip" because "he had kept his father out of the draft."[25]

Work exemptions were also common. During the last year of the war, state Selective Service officials reported that about 11,000 Minnesota men, aged eighteen to twenty-nine, had received military deferments because they worked in war industries or performed other nonagricultural jobs deemed necessary to "national health, safety and interest." The number of exemptions granted to farmworkers was even greater. By the fall of 1942, about 23,000 single men in Minnesota had been deferred for "agricultural purposes," and by 1945 the number of farm exemptions in the state topped 34,000.[26] Complaints about the agricultural exemptions were a common refrain on newspaper editorial pages. One reader, for example, claimed in a letter to the *Minneapolis Tribune* that farmers were exaggerating the farm labor shortage that supposedly made the exemptions necessary. "I do know several farmers," he wrote, "who have retired, moved to town, got their sons married, and put them on the farm. Why? To keep them out of the army, of course."[27]

Some who wanted to avoid military service simply ignored their draft notices. FBI Director J. Edgar Hoover reported in the fall of 1943 that, during the course of the war, more than 6,000 Americans had been convicted of violating the nation's draft laws.[28] Minnesota, like every other state, had its share of draft evaders (or, as they were often identified in the newspapers, "slackers"). In one typical case, a Minneapolis man named Raymond Baker drew a four-year prison sentence after admitting in court that he threw away his draft papers as "quick as he got them." Showing a distinct lack of judicial restraint, Judge Matthew Joyce told Baker that, after serving his sentence, he should "go back to Germany from where your father and mother came."[29] In another less typical case, Leslie Otto of Hutchinson sent a letter to several newspapers declaring his refusal to report for induction. His reason: he believed that the war was the product of a global Jewish conspiracy. "The Jews are seeking to destroy [our] way of life," he claimed. "I do not intend to help in that destruction."

Passing Muster

Still, those who actively avoided the draft were in the minority. Most Minnesotans answered the call to duty when it came, and nowhere was their willingness to do so more evident than at Fort Snelling. Perched on the bluffs overlooking the confluence of the Mississippi and Minnesota rivers, Fort Snelling was the state's oldest active military post, and it had served many functions over the years. During the first half of the nineteenth century it was an imposing symbol of westward expansion. During the Civil War, it served as a training post for recruits. Thousands of new soldiers passed through the fort during World War I, and in the years that followed, the Third United States Infantry—the oldest regiment in the Army—made its home there. With the coming of World War II, the army once again turned Fort Snelling into a mustering point—a recruiting and induction center—for hundreds of thousands of young men who had either volunteered for or been drafted into the nation's armed services. The first large contingent of raw recruits—353 volunteers from all parts of the state—began arriving at the fort on November 21, 1940. Draftees started reporting for possible duty the following January. These new soldiers formed the vanguard of a seemingly endless stream of men who would pass through Fort Snelling during the coming months and years.

Herbert Schultz was one of those men—and he was one of the oldest. Born in 1903, Schultz was thirty-seven when the first draft lottery was held in 1940—too old even to register. But then came Pearl Harbor. By early 1942, the nation was at war, and all men between the ages of twenty and forty-five were required to sign up for possible military service. Suddenly Herbert Schultz didn't seem so old. Now thirty-eight and graying at the temples, Schultz dutifully registered with the draft board in his hometown of Virginia, Minnesota. A few weeks later he moved to St. Cloud to take a new job with the highway department, joined the Civil Air Patrol for a taste of military-style regimentation, and settled in to wait for the call that he assumed would come soon. As it turned out, the call didn't come until October. His orders instructed him to report to Fort Snelling. After the war, Schultz joked that the people at the draft board had postponed calling such an ancient selectee for as long as possible. "It wasn't easy," he wrote, "but they finally said, 'We'll take a chance.'" On the morning of October 16, 1942, Herbert Schultz and a couple dozen other draftees from the St. Cloud area marched up St. Germain Street—in their civilian clothes—and boarded a bus for Fort Snelling.[30]

Leland Rowberg was on the other end of the army's age scale—twenty years old, to be exact—when he was drafted in March of 1943. Rowberg had grown up in Northfield and was attending his hometown college, St. Olaf, when his number came up. His parents, Andrew and Marie Rowberg, were prominent members of the Northfield community (his father was the longtime editor of the *Northfield Independent* newspaper), and they sent him off to war with strict instructions to write home—often. Rowberg obeyed his parents' directive, chronicling his arrival at Fort Snelling in a series of letters—most of which ended with the admonition "Don't worry."[31]

The Fort Snelling Reception Center had been operating for more than two years by the time Herbert Schultz arrived for induction, and for about two and a half years by the time Leland Rowberg got there. It was an efficient operation, designed to process up to eight hundred men a day. To maintain this impressive pace, all selectees—whatever their age or background—were herded through the same highly regimented induction and classification process.

After arriving at the fort by bus or by train, the men got their first taste of an unavoidable fact of military life: standing in line. One by one, they walked through all the steps in the induction process—checking their suitcases, filling out paperwork, opening their mouths for dental checkups, stripping down to their shorts for physical exams. Those who failed their medical tests were classified 4-F and told to go home. Those who passed were fingerprinted and sworn in. The newly minted soldiers were ushered to the mess hall for their first army meal. ("Not bad at all," Leland Rowberg wrote. "We had fish [very good], soup, bread, butter, corn, potatoes, coffee and peaches for dessert.")[32] Then they were assigned to wood-and-tarpaper barracks known disparagingly as "dog houses." For many, including Herbert Schultz, the first night in the dog house was the final night in civilian clothes. "I brought along a pair of pajamas for the usual overnight attire," Schultz recalled. "That was the end of pajamas. From [t]here on [all soldiers] in the Army slept in their underwear."[33]

The next step after induction was classification—a process designed to improve on assignment practices during World War I,

Fort Snelling, October 31, 1942. "Our first chow line," wrote Herbert Schultz, "and many more to come."

when the army had tried "to jam round pegs into square holes." ("If such mistakes can be avoided," the *St. Paul Pioneer Press* reported, "the present emergency will produce no crop of jokes about men who were made into cavalry stable sergeants because they were skilled fry-cooks in civil life.")[34] Each recruit endured a series of examinations, including an intelligence test, an aptitude test, and an interview to determine his skills and interests. Along the way, he received his shots (typhoid, tetanus, and smallpox), signed up for life insurance (average policy: more than eight thousand dollars), watched a double feature of army movies ("Articles of War" and "Sex Hygiene"), and exchanged his civvies for a new uniform. Leland Rowberg, for one, was dumbfounded by the tall stack of personal effects that the army dropped into his outstretched arms.

We have a heck of a lot of clothes. I have two fatigue suits, one blouse, two O.D. [olive drab] shirts, two O.D. pants, two pairs of shoes, two pairs of long winter underwear, three pairs of summer underwear, two overseas caps, one knitted cap, one fatigue hat, two summer shirts, two summer pants, four pairs of socks for my uniform, and three pairs for general wear. One overcoat, one field jacket (very nice), one mess kit, one canteen, shaving brush, razor, blades, one large bath towel and two face towels, two ties, two barracks bags and one helmet, leggings and some other stuff I can't remember.[35]

A newly outfitted soldier awaits the next step in his processing at Fort Snelling.

Before they knew it, the men had received a short list of possible assignments—sometimes a maddeningly eclectic mix. Rowberg, for example, was told he would make a good shop clerk, typist, or "ski troops" soldier. Still, at that point, nothing was certain. Most inductees had to wait at least several days before learning exactly what their assignments would be and where they would report for basic training. Once their assignments were official, the men usually were granted a short furlough. After a few nights on the town or a last visit with their families, the new soldiers reported back to the fort and shipped out. A

Soldiers, most likely from the 99th Infantry Battalion, train for winter warfare at Fort Snelling.

little more than a third of the recruits who passed through Fort Snelling went directly to Replacement Training Centers (RTCs), such as Camp Wolters in Texas (where Rowberg was sent) and Camp Crowder in Missouri (Herbert Schultz's first stop). The RTCs trained new soldiers to become reinforcements—individual replacements for troops lost on the battlefield. A slightly smaller percentage of the Fort Snelling inductees were sent to other camps around the country to train with specific army units. Most of the rest were assigned to the Army Air Forces. Fort Snelling's percentage of inductees sent to the air forces (32 percent in 1943) was considerably higher than that of most other reception centers around the country—a distinction explained by Fort Snelling's higher rate of inductees receiving top scores on their classification tests.[36]

The Fort Snelling Reception Center inducted more than a quarter of a million men from 1941 to 1945 (43,000 into the Navy, the rest into the Army). Perhaps even more astounding, the medical staff at the fort performed more than six hundred thousand physical examinations.[37] The overwhelming majority of Fort Snelling's inductees were, like Leland Rowberg, very young. In 1943, for example, 64 percent of the fort's inductees were eighteen to twenty-three years old. Fewer than 10 percent were, like Herbert Schultz, in the "old man" range—thirty-four and older. Some Fort Snelling recruits came from surrounding states, but the majority were "Minnesota

Members of the St. Paul Semper Fidelis Club's "Kiss the Boys Goodbye" committee give new recruits "a good send-off."

boys." For most of the soldiers who called Minnesota home, Fort Snelling was the place where the war began.

While processing troops was a massive undertaking, it was not Fort Snelling's only function during the war. At various times from 1941 to 1945, the fort served as a training ground for specialized army units. Military police organized there to provide security at airports and government installations. Soldiers with the Military Railway Service learned the techniques of railroad operation—everything from laying track to dispatching trains—and went on to serve in North Africa and France. Students at the Military Intelligence Service Language School (MISLS)—mostly Nisei, or second-generation Japanese Americans—studied Japanese military tactics, produced propaganda, and translated documents.[38] And in the fall of 1942, a unique unit called the 99th Infantry Battalion transferred for a few months to Fort Snelling from Camp Ripley, near Little Falls. The men of the 99th—or, as they liked to call themselves, the Viking Battalion—formed an elite group. Every one of them could speak and understand Norwegian. Nearly half were Norwegian-born. Most of the rest were Americans of Norwegian extraction—many from Minnesota and surrounding states. (According to one report, there were ten Hans Hansens in the battalion's Company B alone.)[39] While stationed at Fort Snelling, the men of the Viking Battalion trained to fight on skis and snowshoes, hoping for an eventual opportunity to help liberate Norway from the Nazis. The 99th never did fight in Norway, but it did see battle, including the Normandy invasion.

With thousands of soldiers moving through Fort Snelling each month, the man in uniform became an increasingly common sight in the Twin Cities area. ("It seemed like everybody was looking at me," Leland Rowberg noted after his first night on the town.)[40] At first, many of the soldiers who left the fort in search of off-duty fun were left to their own devices. City officials lamented that "young men in uniform [were] walking the streets, frequenting places of entertainment—all with no central gathering place they could call their own."[41] But by the summer of 1942, citizens' groups in both St. Paul and Minneapolis had opened servicemen's clubs to keep the men entertained—and out of trouble. Operated by United Service Organizations (USO), the clubs provided a range of activities including floor shows, holiday dinners, and—most popular of all—dances. On Thursday evenings, hundreds of soldiers hit the dance floor at the Minneapolis servicemen's center on Hennepin Avenue and jitterbugged with their "hostess" dates to the sounds of a live orchestra. On other nights they had to settle for a phonograph. In addition, the clubs served as dance-partner clearinghouses for dozens of private soirées held around the cities. The matrons who organized such dances were notoriously picky, detailing their requirements in their invitations.

> *Please send two soldiers for Saturday night. They must be tall, good dancers, between 25 and 30. Would prefer college men who can talk well and are at least sergeants . . . but anyway, tall and good dancers.*[42]

The USO volunteers also provided a host of other services for soldiers, many of whom weren't particularly light on their feet. Among the most popular were the gift-buying and gift-wrapping services

Dancing topped the list of the most popular activities at the Minneapolis servicemen's club. Billiards came in second. "Heavy reading" ranked third.

that many soldiers and sailors depended on to keep their long-distance romances alive. While the letters and cards received by the usos indicated that most of the servicemen who visited the centers were pleased with their treatment, a few of them left unimpressed. "In the three years I have served in this country and overseas, I have never had poorer hospitality than in Mpls.," wrote Sergeant John Nelson from Fort Bragg, North Carolina. "The girls I [met there] have only icy stares and frigid hearts for the service men. With the few exceptions that will go out, they want money lavishly spent on them."[43] The facts, however, suggest that not all hearts at the Twin Cities usos were as frigid as Sergeant Nelson suggested. After only a few months in operation, the center in Minneapolis was reporting that more than a dozen of its hostesses had already "got hitched" to visiting servicemen.[44]

As the war wound down, Fort Snelling took on a new mission: turning soldiers back into civilians. In September 1944, the War Department designated Fort Snelling as a personnel center where each returning serviceman would receive a physical exam, back pay, and a new uniform. Those who had earned enough "points" (determined by date of induction and time overseas) were discharged and sent home. Those who still had time to serve were given furloughs and then reassigned.

Herbert Schultz, who had entered the army at Fort Snelling during the fall of 1942, was among the thousands of troops routed through the fort on their way home from war. Schultz had spent much of the war overseas, in England and France, but had never seen combat. When the war in Europe was over, he boarded a ship at Le Havre and headed for home by way of New York. Years later, on the back of a photograph, he wrote a few words that summed up his relationship with the old fort on the bluffs. "By train back to Fort Snelling where it all started," he wrote. "At 42 years of age I am sure that Schultz will be a resident of St. Paul in due order." Indeed, Herbert Schultz settled in St. Paul and lived there the rest of his life.

Leland Rowberg, who had mustered into the army at Fort Snelling a few months after Schultz, never returned. He was killed on October 24, 1944, during a battle in northern France.

Leland Rowberg arrived in France with the 317th Infantry Regiment on August 3, 1944. The 317th was one of the units trying to drive the Germans out of France under the command of General George Patton. Rowberg continued to write his parents as the regiment moved through France, but with the hardships of combat his letters became more sporadic. As he had in his first letters from Fort Snelling, Rowberg continued to reassure his parents with the words "Don't worry."

August 12, 1944

You probably heard over the radio some of the action in which I have participated. However, don't worry as things look pretty

good from where I am . . . I don't believe, in fact I know, that I don't look quite as sharp as in former years. Shaving every other day as I usually do is quite impossible . . . Please don't worry as I am feeling fine and am optimistic about future.

August 22, 1944

There isn't much I can say about what I am doing. Have run into some Germans. They are everything that you have read about them. Some are fanatical in their devotion to the Nazi cause while others seem quite reticent about sacrificing their lives for the Fuhrer.

September 10, 1944

Well, I am 22 today and it was some birthday. I wanted to go to church today but was too busy. The day was perfect, warm

Leland Rowberg

and sunny but still it was France. Received the vitamin tablets yesterday, thanks a lot. Please send food of any shape if you can. Candy bars, cookies, etc. We get very tired of rations and there is nothing else. Have seen quite a few instances of Nazi efficiency that they have favored the French with. It seems impossible to believe that people can be so vicious in this day and age. The war news is certainly excellent. It seems like the war should end within another month or so.

September 27, 1944
War news continues to be good and I am quite optimistic about its end. However, the Germans we have been meeting are quite fanatical and are fighting hard.

September 30, 1944
I had an opportunity to take a shower today and you can't imagine how good it felt. I don't believe I ever was as dirty as I was until that shower.

October 2, 1944
I am sorry I can't write you oftener but circumstances prevent me from doing so. We have been so busy that we seldom have time even to think about writing . . . There isn't much more to say except that I am feeling fine and am anxiously awaiting the packages you have been sending.[1]

One week after writing that last letter, on October 9, 1944, Leland Rowberg was killed in action while trying, with his platoon, to retake the village of Sivry from the Germans. A comrade said later that Rowberg knew even before his squad made its advance "that the attack would be a suicidal affair."[2]

Andrew and Marie Rowberg continued to write to their son, not knowing that he was dead. As the weeks passed with no word from Leland, they began to fear the worst. In her last letter to her son, Marie Rowberg could hardly disguise her panic. "We are afraid you are back 'on the line' again," she wrote. "I know this must sound terribly absurd . . . the trouble is we do know something of what is going on and we feel so helpless."[3] The next day, a telegram arrived informing the Rowbergs that their son was missing. It was another week before they learned he was dead.

2   The Home Front

Minnesota's political and business leaders responded to the news of the Pearl Harbor attack with a mixture of calm reassurance and imaginative fearmongering. Governor Harold Stassen was among the more levelheaded. He had been on his way to Washington when the attack occurred. After hearing the news, he turned around in Chicago, rushed back to St. Paul, and issued a short public statement calling on the people of the state to go about their daily lives in a "manner that will best add to the total united strength of America."[1] Ten days later, in a statewide radio address, he made a loftier appeal—one calculated to inspire in his fellow Minnesotans a sense of common purpose in defense of the home front.

> *Let us not forget . . . that war as waged by our totalitarian enemies does not involve armies and navies and air forces alone. Frequently and suddenly the civilian population find themselves in the front lines. For there is being waged against us total war—war that arises from the perverted concepts in the minds of dictatorial groups, that brute force and decrees and slavery should take the place of a system of justice, of laws, and of liberties. Consequently, it is war against free people as a whole and all they cherish. Thus it is clear that it is our duty to be prepared at home.*[2]

Contrasting sharply with Stassen's measured response were the deliberately provocative statements of Fourth District Congressman Melvin Maas. Like most of Minnesota's congressional delegates, Maas had opposed U.S. intervention in the war. But after the Japanese attack, he made an about-face and tried to rouse Minnesota out of what he considered a state of complacency. In a speech to a group of Ramsey County Republicans, Maas claimed that St. Paul and Minneapolis were likely bombing targets of the Axis powers. "Imagine the lift it would give to the Germans, the Italians and the Japanese to be told this great railroad and ammunition center—right in the heart of America—had been bombed, maybe destroyed," he said.[3] Diarist Alice Brill pasted the article about Maas' comments into her scrapbook, noting that the congressman claimed it was "necessary to be extreme to wake people up."[4] Some Minnesotans objected to Maas' statements. "Let us gag irresponsible politicians," wrote one *Minneapolis Star Journal* reader. "The farfetched statements made by Mr. Maas, undoubtedly with good intentions, can do little but provoke undue panic and alarm." But to others, the warning served as a jolt. The owner of an underground garage in St. Paul, for example, felt compelled by the congressman's assessment to announce that his parking spaces would thereafter be available for public shelter in the event of an air raid.[5]

Although the possibility of an Axis attack on Minnesota was remote, the idea that German and Japanese war planners might be poring over maps of the Twin Cities, St. Cloud, and Luverne remained a powerful—and in some ways thrilling—incentive to community vigilance. (In this respect, Minnesota was no different from many other states where it was fashionable to claim inclusion on a hypothetical "enemy's list.")[6] In a series of effective advertisements, the Twin Cities weapons maker Northern Pump Company used world maps to demonstrate how easily Japanese and German bombers could reach Minnesota. The first ad in the series was titled "So You Think Minnesota Can't Be Bombed?" and urged readers to "look twice at this startling map . . . [and] see how enemy planes might drop in by America's back door!"

> *"It can't happen to me. I'm in the safest spot in the world. I live in Minnesota."*
>
> *If that's what you think you'd better learn this little geography lesson.* And learn it quick.
>
> *Look at the map again. Follow the arrows from Norway. They make it clear that a Berlin bomber, using Greenland as a stepping stone,* could drop its load on Duluth as easily as on New York.
>
> *And military experts say that is just the course an enemy air attack would probably follow. For while the Atlantic coast is fairly well protected by an arc of newly acquired bases, America has a wide open back door through the wilderness of Canada.*
>
> That door leads straight to Minnesota's iron mines . . . mines that feed raw material for half the world's supply of steel.
>
> *Yes . . . and your home is but an hour away.*[7]

A similar Northern Pump ad pointed out that Minneapolis and San Francisco were "almost exactly the same distance from Tokyo," while another featured a shadowy, monocled German officer standing menacingly in front of a map of Minneapolis. "See those circles on the air chart of Minneapolis shown in this picture?" the ad asked. "Those circles mark Minneapolis hospitals, schools, churches and homes—all of which would be considered perfectly legitimate military objectives by Nazi strategists."[8] After reading one of the ads, a writer for the business periodical *Commercial West* claimed that he "went right down into the basement and began to plan how a place in it could be fixed up against a bomb crash."[9]

Minneapolis Daily Times, *February 1, 1942*

Clearly many Minnesotans were spurred into action either by fear of attack or by a sense of civic responsibility. By early 1943, surveys showed that more than 250,000 Minnesota civilians were taking "advantage of this democratic opportunity to share in the defense of their state, and the ultimate goal of winning this war."[10] Many dove into their new wartime responsibilities with an almost giddy, patriotic relish. Many others did their part, although with noticeably less enthusiasm. Still others grumbled and groused about the deprivations of wartime life and performed their wartime duties only grudgingly. In short, the civilians on Minnesota's World War II home front responded to the war emergency in predictably human fashion. They were selfless and selfish, lazy and tireless, and, above all, adaptable. They sacrificed, whether they liked it or not. And while their sacrifices were minor compared to those made by members of the armed forces, they were nonetheless a crucial element of Minnesota's war effort.

Civilian Defenders

The four B-25 bombers took off from Wold Chamberlain Field, south of downtown Minneapolis, at about four-fifteen on the afternoon of July 5, 1943. Conditions were less than ideal. Severe storms were approaching, and the pilots seriously doubted whether they could complete their mission, but they forged ahead anyway. The planes headed south, following the path of the Mississippi River. About fifteen minutes later, they reached their target. Flying at an altitude of 500 feet, the bombers dropped their payloads on the unsuspecting populace of Red Wing.

On the ground, confusion reigned. Sirens and whistles wailed, but most Red Wing residents had no idea what was going on. Neighbors telephoned neighbors, fishing for information. People jumped into their cars and raced through the streets, looking for the reason for the alarms. Air raid wardens fanned out across the city and did their best to control traffic. But as far as anyone could tell, there were no fires, no explosions—just the disconcerting hum of what could only be several large planes flying overhead. Eyes turned to the overcast sky. The unthinkable came to mind. Was it possible? Had Red Wing just been bombed?

The answer, as it turned out, was yes. Sort of.

For several weeks, officials with the state Office of Civilian Defense (OCD) had been hatching a plan designed to shake the people of Red Wing—and several other Minnesota communities—out of what the officials feared was a collective state of wartime complacency. The plan was to send four bombers from the Royal Netherlands Flying Corps—the Dutch aviators were making a goodwill stop in the Twin Cities—on a triangular flight down to Winona, across to Mankato, and back to Minneapolis. On the way, the bombers would drop hundreds of sand-filled paper sacks on the communities of Red Wing, Lake City, Kellogg, Wabasha, Waseca, Minnieska, Owatonna, Mankato, and St. Peter. The sacks would be tagged with blue, yellow, and red tickets signifying types of bombs: red for incendiary, blue for high-explosive, and yellow for gas. The simulated bombings would come as a complete surprise to all but a few top-ranking officials and would give each community the chance to test its emergency response plans under the most realistic conditions possible.[11]

Civilian defense volunteer ribbon

Bad weather on the designated day cut the mission short. Only Red Wing got the bombs it had ordered. The rest of the mission was aborted—perhaps luckily, given the resulting havoc.

The "bombing" demonstrated "how terribly unprepared we are for actual air raids," Red Wing Mayor William Mossberg declared. Not only had most Red Wing residents been utterly confused by what happened, but even many of the city's air raid wardens and auxiliary police officers had failed to report for duty when the sirens sounded. Of the one hundred or so "bombs" dropped, not one was ever found.[12] In a follow-up letter to state officials, the secretary-manager of the Red Wing Civilian Defense Council, Leo Koll, tried to put the best face on an admittedly disappointing performance. "The general idea was to make this a complete surprise at the most inopportune time possible [the July Fourth holiday weekend] to see just how badly we could fool our defense force," Koll wrote. "We were pleasantly surprised to see many units on the job as they should be."[13]

Red Wing was the only Minnesota town "bombed" during World War II—no other communities wanted to set themselves up for similar embarrassment—but its citizens' response on that stormy day dramatized the many difficulties that faced civil defense authorities throughout the state. Public confusion, ignorance, and apathy often combined to undermine the best efforts of the state's sizeable civil defense apparatus. But that didn't stop thousands of

Minnesotans from volunteering to defend their state against a possible attack.

Before the war, Minnesota's civil defense program was a mishmash of state and local efforts that largely ran independently of each other, but that all changed after the Pearl Harbor attack. On December 10, 1941, Governor Stassen issued an executive order establishing the Minnesota Office of Civilian Defense (OCD)—later known as the Civilian Defense Division. OCD coordinated all civilian defense activities in the state. It supervised local defense councils and oversaw most state-level defense functions. (Minnesota's adjutant general handled strictly military matters.) Its responsibilities included supervising auxiliary police and firefighting units, organizing a forest fire fighting corps and a statewide program for

Downtown Minneapolis during its first civil defense blackout, July 1942

women volunteers called Victory Aides, and overseeing various social welfare programs. But by far its biggest job was preparing the state for a possible attack. To that end, OCD staff devoted much time and effort to planning practice blackouts and recruiting air raid wardens. "There is little question that the program of Air Raid Wardens is going to steal the show in this program of Civilian Defense," wrote OCD's first chief of staff, C. A. Zwiener. "It will ultimately be the one venture upon which all things will be judged, because it covers all communities in the state and therefore will have its repercussions in all communities."[14] By the summer of 1942, OCD was ready to try out its program with a series of test blackouts in communities around the state.

The iron range town of Virginia was the first community put to the test. On July 15, 1942, a siren sounded at ten forty-five P.M., sending more than fifteen hundred volunteers scurrying through the darkened city to perform their assigned tasks. Wardens pulled switches on streetlights. Victory Aides stood guard over fireboxes to prevent false alarms. Ambulance crews rushed to the scenes of imaginary bomb explosions and treated the imaginary wounds of mock victims. "No one tried to cross the streets; wardens were on the job, and there wasn't a gleam of light from the residences," Adjutant General Ellard Walsh said later. "One of the most amazing things was that I didn't see a single person smoking a cigarette."[15]

Over the next several months, Minnesota communities big and small proved that they, too, could go dark at a moment's notice. During St. Paul's first blackout, a mythologically inclined reporter mused: "It was almost as though Mars himself, in one fell swoop, had fanned out a million flickering candles with his mighty wings of war."[16] A Hennepin County civil defense official, viewing Minneapolis' second blackout from a plane, marveled that "despite the heavily star-studded sky, there were practically no reflections visible from the air and we couldn't even determine locations of the different lakes within the city."[17] After Ely's third blackout, in December of 1942, town authorities announced that the people of their city were "ready for anything that the Axis may send in our direction."[18] In Detroit Lakes, newly married Hildred Long passed the time during her first blackout by writing a letter to her husband Frank, a soldier stationed in Colorado.

Shoot, I didn't get as much done as I expected to do before the blackout which should start any minute now. The whistle just blew and I turned out my lights so if I misspell a few words you will know why. I never realized until now how much I depend on my eyes because it is so dark I can't see anything in my room but the face of my clock. Outside it is a trifle lighter. I can understand now how nerve-racking [it would be] to go through an actual alarm, and without you it would be terrible, beyond description.[19]

Despite misgivings, it seemed that many Minnesotans were exemplary in their commitment to public vigilance. But in fact, the state's civil defense efforts often did not go off as smoothly as advertised.

While it seemed that most Minnesotans were committed to public vigilance, behind the scenes the OCD was struggling daily to cope with questions and gripes from local civilian defense councils. Complaints about government red tape were among the most common. In Duluth and Little Falls, for example, the problem was streetlights. Because of their wiring, most streetlights in those cities had to be turned off one by one during test blackouts. In Little Falls, workers had to manually unscrew the bulbs—a practice that would be dangerously slow in the event of a real emergency. Officials in both cities wanted to purchase new switches that would allow the local power company to shut off all streetlights from a central location. But the federal War Production Board (WPB) denied their repeated requests to make such a purchase: the materials used to produce the switches were needed to make weapons. After trying, without success, to get the WPB to reconsider, the OCD's new chief of staff, Allan Briggs, expressed his frustration in a letter to a federal civil defense official. "While I realize it is not in your power to compel the WPB to pay some attention to our needs," he wrote, "it might not hurt to tell them how much we are crying out at the policy of one division of government telling us we are in a critical area and another denying it."[20] Briggs encountered similar resistance from the WPB when he tried to help the southwestern Minnesota village of Taunton procure a new siren: the bell on the town's fire truck wasn't loud enough. "The Regional Office of Civilian Defense advises us that the WPB does not consider communities in this region to be critically in need of sirens," he wrote to Taunton's civil defense chief. "It is obviously going to be necessary for you to use your ingenuity to get along with what you have."[21]

The biggest problems emerged on August 24, 1943, when Minnesota experienced its first statewide "surprise" blackout. Up until that time, most communities in the state had received advance warning that a blackout was scheduled. This time it was different. Local authorities were told only that the blackout would occur sometime during the week of August 22 and that their civilian defense organizations should be ready to snap into action on a moment's notice. As it turned out, many communities were caught almost completely off guard. The experience in Eveleth was typical.

> Street lights which were left aglow throughout the blackout period in Eveleth, Tuesday from 10:30 pm to 11 pm, clearly outlined the entire city to any enemy bombers which might have been overhead if this raid had been real rather than a practice. Eveleth's important mines, the city proper, locations, and surrounding territories could have been virtually "wiped off the map." Citizens of Eveleth either didn't hear the siren or did not heed the warning and left lights on throughout the practice raid.[22]

In their reports to the state OCD, many local civilian defense officials were forced to admit that their hometowns were simply not ready for a surprise attack—simulated or otherwise. "It seems that the party operating the main switch was very much out of line, as he would pull the switch or throw it whenever there was a whistle sounded," recounted a blackout observer in St. James. "In all ways it was a flop. Hoping to be able to send you a better report next time."[23] The news from the air warden in Sturgeon was no better. "I am sorry to say that the Blackout of August 24th, as far as the Town of Sturgeon (St. Louis County) is concerned, was a total failure," he reported. "This failure was due to the fact that we were not notified."[24] Minneapolis Mayor Marvin Kline, aware of numerous blackout violations, managed only lukewarm praise for his city's performance. It was "a good effort," he said.[25]

The failures of the August 24 blackout raised a difficult question: what to do with blackout violators? Harvey Kelly, editor of the *Faribault Journal*, drew the wrath of several civilian defense officials when he suggested in an editorial that most first-time violators deserved leniency. "It made me quite warm under the collar," wrote Rice County's chief air raid warden, Irwin Smith, after reading Kelly's piece. "The tone of such editorials is of no benefit, to say the least, to the morale of local Air Raid Wardens."[26] Ortonville's chief warden, Gus Kleinschmidt, was similarly incensed after reading an account of seemingly lax enforcement in Minneapolis.

*In Ortonville we don't monkey around with those who think
they are the privileged sons and daughters of some one important. We hauled up before the judge three of our most prominent
merchants, one who particularly told me the night of the Blackout that in as much as his light was very tiny that he didn't have
to blot it out. He found out differently the next morning. I'll bet
you that if ever the next Blackout comes along, test or otherwise,
that we will have a one hundred percent Blackout, what do you
think?[27]*

Hundreds of Minnesotans were ultimately arrested for violating blackout restrictions during the war. In one typical case, a
St. Paul druggist was fined twenty-five dollars for leaving the lights

J. B. McGrath and G. E. Brissman cover their ears during a test of the air raid
siren atop the St. Paul courthouse.

on his shop during a "semi-surprise" blackout.[28] But as the war progressed and the threat of attack receded to the vanishing point, Minnesotans were less and less inclined to take civil defense seriously. Harvey Kelly, the *Faribault Journal* editor, spoke for many when he wrote that he had always wondered whether the state's civil defense efforts were really necessary—at least in his region. "What Nazi or [Italian] would pass up the docks at Duluth or Minneapolis and St. Paul to bomb our Holstein cows down in this section?" he asked.[29] Still, in the end, it turned out that the threat to Minnesota wasn't quite as far-fetched as Kelly had supposed. In late March of 1945, a Japanese incendiary balloon bomb landed in northern Minnesota. No one was hurt and no damage was done. It was apparently the only enemy attack ever recorded on Minnesota soil.[30]

Consuming for Victory

As the first anniversary of the Pearl Harbor attack came and went, Minnesotans braced for what promised to be one of the biggest shocks yet to the home front system. A rumor was flying: the federal government's Office of Price Administration (OPA) was planning to ration meat—canned and fresh—within the next few months. Serious shortages were already cropping up in several parts of the country due both to an increased demand by the armed forces and to a pinched supply: farmers were holding back their stock in anticipation of higher prices. Minnesotans were still trying to get used to life with rationed tires, rationed sugar, and rationed coffee. Somehow the prospect of meat shortages and meat rationing seemed especially egregious. "Housekeepers will be hard put to use ingenuity to find vitamins and food values in things not used before," diarist Alice Brill wrote.[31]

By February of 1943, beef was vanishing from the state's butcher shops and Minnesotans were looking for alternatives—at least that's what they seemed to be doing in St. Paul.

> *Sale of ground, frozen horse meat in St. Paul has increased materially in the past month, William Campbell, manager of Booth Fisheries, Inc., the jobbing outlet for the Northwest reported today.*
>
> *"I would not be able to say definitely if the meat is being used for human consumption," Campbell said, "but it is my belief that a great deal is"…*

The meat comes in 12½, 25 and 50-pound packages. No roasts or steaks are obtainable here now.

Persons who have eaten horse meat report that it has a sweet and a likeable taste.[32]

For those who couldn't stomach the thought of Swedish equine-balls, the Minnesota Division of the Izaak Walton League had another suggestion: eat more carp. It launched a "Carp for Victory" campaign, encouraging Minnesotans to make "the unjustly maligned carp" a dinnertime staple. "The carp contains all of the health-giving food values of its more respected finny brethren,"

Worth the wait. Queuing up for a cut of beef or pork at People's Meats on St. Paul's Wabasha Avenue.

wrote C. F. Culler of the U.S. Fish and Wildlife Service, "and, properly prepared, is excellent eating."[33]

We may never know how much carp and horse meat Minnesotans actually ate during the war, but certainly many spent an inordinate amount of time trying to cope with wartime shortages and government price controls. Most learned to get by quite well, but that didn't mean they had to like it. "The prices are so high due to the war," diarist William Cummings wrote, expressing an almost universal lament. "We really should get another raise."[34]

Perhaps Minnesota consumers' favorite target for complaints about shortages and prices was the federal government's Office of Price Administration. The OPA was charged with regulating the nation's wartime economy, and it did so by vigorously enforcing a combination of rationing and price controls. As the war progressed, nearly everything U.S. citizens "ate, wore, used, or lived in" was regulated in some way by the OPA. "It was," wrote historian Richard Lingeman, "the most concerted attack on wartime inflation and scarcity in the nation's history, and by and large it worked."[35]

Minnesotans got their first taste of rationing in early 1942 when the OPA slapped restrictions on rubber—or, more to the point, tires. Japan's conquest of Malaya and the Dutch East Indies had cut off the nation's main supply of natural rubber, and stockpiles were dangerously low. The OPA responded to the emergency by restricting sales of new tires, and then by extending those restrictions to retreads. Officials hoped that, by rationing tires, the nation could get by on its dwindling rubber reserves until new synthetic rubber plants could be built and Brazil's dormant rubber plantations could start producing again. But the plan didn't work. It soon became apparent that American drivers were continuing to burn rubber at a furious pace, despite tire rationing. More drastic measures were needed.

In late 1942, President Roosevelt ordered new restrictions aimed at cutting tire consumption even further. They included a ban on pleasure driving (rarely enforced), a 35-mile-an-hour highway speed limit, and—most noticeably—nationwide gasoline rationing. Under the rationing system, all drivers received *A*, *B*, or *C* stickers for their windshields. Those with *A* stickers had the lowest priority and were eligible to buy just four (later, three) gallons of gasoline a week. *B* sticker holders—servicemen and war workers, mostly—got ten gallons. Doctors, mail carriers, and other workers deemed "essential" by the OPA received *C* stickers, which allowed them to buy as much gas as they needed. The definition of "essential" was quite flexible, and many drivers pulled multiple strings to move up in the gas rationing

James C. Ferguson of St. Paul received these coupons in August 1945, the month gasoline rationing ended.

pecking order. According to one OPA estimate, almost half of all American drivers were considered "essential" enough to qualify for the coveted *B* or *C* stickers.[36]

Foiling the OPA's gasoline restrictions became something of a pastime for many Minnesotans. William Cummings tried his hand at the black market after learning that he could buy gasoline for use in certain makes of stoves—if he pumped the fuel directly into a red can. "I [took] a two gallon can and painted it [red]," he wrote. "Got some gas then and put it in the car when I got home."[37] Harold Eastland, a school textbook salesman from Glenwood, took advantage of the fact that many school superintendents served on their local rationing boards.

In many schools that I called on, where the superintendents were friends of mine, [they] would say, "Harold, are you running short of gas?" Well, one is always running short of gas and one recognizes the question right away. He would call the filling station and tell them who he was and say, "I'm sending a fellow down there, give him ten gallons of gas, will you?" So quite often we got gas . . . It was done because the superintendent felt that salesmen were an important part of his work. It helped him to run the school and do it the right way, the way he wanted to. Therefore he was willing to help the salesmen to the extent of six gallons of gas or ten gallons of gas.[38]

In Albert Lea, a shoe-store owner tried—apparently unsuccessfully—to obtain a *B* or *C* sticker by claiming that he was doing "military intelligence" work for the local Civil Air Patrol. The allegedly confidential nature of his supposed duties made it difficult for the skeptical Albert Lea rationing board to verify his claim.[39]

Despite the best efforts of many Minnesotans to get around the OPA's restrictions, gasoline rationing did what it was supposed to do—it cut down on driving and removed vehicles (and their precious tires) from the roads. In St. Paul, the Emporium department store adapted to gas and tire rationing by abandoning its in-house delivery service and joining with other downtown merchants to launch an independent delivery company.[40] Newspapers and company newsletters printed columns of classified ads for carpoolers. And while many Minnesotans remained determined to take their annual summer vacations at the lake up north, most had to settle for destinations a little closer to home. Resorts that fell north of gas-rationed driving range from the Twin Cities suffered. Those that were closer—like Howard and Lela Welty's Wigwam Inn Resort on Lake Mille Lacs—did remarkably well. Vacationers "could not go all the way up to Bemidji or all the way up to the north shore of Lake Superior," recalled the Weltys' daughter, Neva Williams. "There was just not enough gas stamps to go that far . . . so they came this far. And we were so busy, we couldn't hire enough people, and we didn't have enough space to house more. We worked very hard and it was very profitable."[41]

The gasoline and tire restrictions may have been frustrating, but at least they were relatively easy to understand. The same could not be said for food rationing. Many Minnesotans spent the war years trying to unravel the mysteries of the ration book and its unfamiliar language.

Sugar was the first food item to hit the ration list. Shortages had begun to develop in early 1942, after the Japanese cut off imports from the Philippines. In April the OPA announced its plans to ration sugar, launching a wave of hoarding. Many hoarders were ashamed of their actions, but William Cummings was not among them. A week before rationing was to begin, Cummings purchased twenty pounds of sugar and then fretted in his diary that he hadn't bought enough. "I could have boughten a couple hundred pounds tonight," he lamented.[42] In early May, Cummings and thousands of other Minnesotans filed into their local schools to sign up for War Ration Book One. Cummings' fellow diarist, Alice Brill, called it "a very tedious proceeding."

*Took me 1½ hours! That was nothing compared to many. Some
took 4 hours, many 2. Husbands frantically telephoning for
wives and maids. Many didn't get home until 7 o'clock. Women
had left little children etc. Crowd very quiet and well behaved.
No one acted upset. Only 2 persons tried to get in ahead of their
turn.*[43]

Each citizen was eligible for one ration book, each book contained four stamps, and each stamp was good for one pound of
sugar every two weeks. All families were required to declare how
much sugar they already had stocked, and if they declared any,
stamps were removed from their books accordingly. In that respect,
sugar rationing operated on an honor system. Many Minnesotans
submitted gladly to what they considered an early opportunity to
make a wartime sacrifice (about 10 percent of all Minnesota registrants admitted having excess sugar stocks),[44] while others conveniently forgot to mention the bag or two in their cupboard. Still,
peer pressure proved a powerful incentive for following the rules. In
a letter to her husband, Frank, Hildred Long scolded herself for buying more sugar than she needed. "If I don't begin using it," she
wrote, "I will have all my containers full and people will begin ac-
cusing me of hoarding."[45]

During the following months, the OPA added more and more
food items to the ration list: coffee in November of 1942; canned
meat and fish the following February; canned fruits and vegetables,
fresh meat, and cheese in March. With each added item, the rationing system itself grew more complex. War Ration Book Two had
rows of red and blue stamps marked with different letters. Red
stamps were for meats, cheeses, and fats. Blue stamps were for
processed foods. And just to make matters more confusing, the
number of stamps it took to purchase certain items often fluctuated
from day to day. For many Minnesotans, like Hildred Long, it
seemed one needed to be an accountant to make sense of it all.

*We're to have only 48 points for our canned food rationing with
a No. 2 can peas counting 16 or 18 points—other foods accordingly—fruits more and soups and baby foods less. It will
amount to about a can a week per person.*[46]

Fresh fruits and vegetables were among the only foodstuffs that
remained unrationed throughout the war, and their relative abundance was enhanced by the most popular of all the civilian war

Pupils at Tilden School in St. Paul show off their victory garden bounty.

efforts: the Victory Garden program. Some victory gardens—like the ones managed by war plants to help feed their employees—spanned several hundred acres, while many others were small plots tended carefully by novice gardeners. At the program's peak in 1943, an estimated twenty million victory gardeners across the country were producing about 40 percent of the nation's vegetable crop. In Minnesota, surveys showed that participation reached nearly 100 percent on farms and in rural villages, although in the big cities it never topped 33 percent.[47] The program cultivated Minnesotans' desire to contribute to the war effort, and those who did participate enjoyed seeing the fruits (or, in this case, vegetables) of their labors. If anything, the program may have been too successful. Jerome Burns never forgot the embarrassment of riches from his victory garden in western Minnesota. "One summer we had so many tomatoes that we could not give away or sell many bushels," he recalled, "so we dumped them in the local dump. My mother canned over one hundred quarts that year and it still sticks in my mind of the waste."[48]

Not all consumer items were rationed, but shortages were ubiquitous. New typewriters and bicycles were almost impossible to find. A shortage of alarm clocks produced a rash of war workers late to the job. Even the most mundane items were in short supply. Diarist Alice Brill vented her frustration after trying unsuccessfully to purchase a new mop head. "The war again," she grumbled. "So we will continue to use the old one—'and like it.'"[49] A shortage of whiskey in Twin Cities liquor stores produced a holiday season run on neckties. (The *St. Paul Dispatch* speculated that husbands and fathers who normally received a bottle of their favorite hooch for Christmas were getting ties instead.) Newspapers regularly reported on shortages that interfered with traditional concepts of feminine beauty. "Women seem to want bobby pins and hair pins as much as they want anything of which there is now a shortage," the *St. Paul Pioneer Press* reported.[50] In an article about the shortage of nylon

These young students of St. Paul's Groveland School were part of a nationwide "knit for victory" campaign.

and silk stockings, the *Dispatch* observed that "a girl can get around 390 pairs of stockings out of a gallon of liquid leg makeup" (this according to a study by the *Dispatch*'s "scientific and happy-hour department").[51] To be fair, the newspapers' coverage of wartime fashion was not completely unfounded. The stocking shortage was, in fact, a hot topic of conversation among many Minnesota women. In a letter to her husband Frank, Hildred Long described her feelings after finding a run in a pair of nylon hose. The discovery was, she wrote, the "climax to a very nerve wracking day and a tragedy in a woman's world."[52]

As shortages intensified, the underground economy known as the black market grew. A postwar study found that one in fifteen

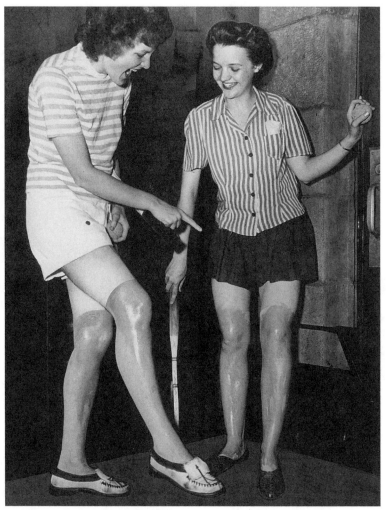

Wartime fashion faux pas. Two young women forget to remove their leg makeup before suiting up for tennis.

American businesses was charged with making illicit transactions during the war, and that many more were told to stop violating OPA rules.[53] In Minnesota, price ceiling violations were among the most common. In the spring of 1942, the OPA ordered merchants to freeze the prices of most food items at their March 1942 levels. The General Maximum Price Regulation (better known as "General Max") went into effect in May, and almost immediately reports of violations began pouring into local ration boards. A month later, a survey found that three-fourths of the retailers in St. Paul had failed to post their frozen prices as required by the regulation.[54] Many shop owners claimed that they simply didn't understand General Max's confusing rules, but many others openly defied the OPA. Marie Kirkevold, an inspector with the Moorhead ration board, remembered a particularly obstinate grocer in Dilworth who raised his prices as soon as the inspectors left. "They'd fine him," she said, "but that didn't seem to help. I think we went back there half a dozen times and he'd have that price [back] up."[55]

Waste Not

A sign of the times from the September 22, 1942, edition of the *Minneapolis Star Journal*:

> *Anybody got a cannon—a real cannon?*
>
> *The plan was to have a field piece or two for the opening of the Minneapolis Symphony orchestra season Oct. 24—but cannon are getting scarce. The government has asked that all old field pieces be turned in to be melted down so they can be recast into modern weapons to fight the Jap and the Nazi.*
>
> *So it begins to look as if the great Tschaikowsky [sic] "Overture 1812" which will be one of the features of the special opening concert dedicated to the United Nations, will go without benefit of cannon—unless . . .*
>
> *Caught in similar situations in years past, Arthur J. Gaines, manager of the Minneapolis orchestra, has filled in at the spot where booming guns and clanging bells bring the music to a climax by firing a pistol into an empty wooden barrel.*[56]

Few Minnesotans would have listed the Minneapolis Symphony's cannonless *1812 Overture* among the war's great tragedies, but the scarcity of cannon illustrated just how salvage-conscious the state—and the nation—had become. The War Production Board

(WPB) had begun issuing dire warnings about impending shortages of raw materials—especially steel, aluminum, and tin—within days after the Pearl Harbor attack, and it followed up those warnings with a massive campaign to convince Americans to fight their throw-it-away impulses and conserve. Suddenly it seemed that all Minnesotans were scouring their homes and neighborhoods for any kind of scrap metal that might be turned into weaponry. They were taking part in the biggest scavenger hunt of their lives. Children carefully peeled leaves of tinfoil from gum wrappers and cigarette packages, rolled them into balls, and turned them in at collection sites. The people of Hanley Falls, in Yellow Medicine County, handed over an old school bell weighing 485 pounds, hoping that their scrap drive would "ring in the ears of the Nazis."[57] In St. Peter, the townsfolk donated several old Civil War cannons that had been on display in the city for years. (The cannons were not capable of accompanying an orchestra during the *1812 Overture*, but they were genuine historical artifacts that, in hindsight, should have been spared.)[58]

Salvage drives made real contributions to the nation's war effort (St. Peter's, for example, yielded more than 250 tons of scrap), but more than that, they built morale and community spirit during a time when the war was not going well for the United States. Nowhere was the attraction of scrap drives more evident than in the Twin Cities, where the people of Minneapolis and St. Paul turned their drives into an expression of their sibling rivalry.

It started, as these things often do, with a silly wager.

In the fall of 1942, Minneapolis Mayor Marvin Kline bet St. Paul Mayor John McDonough a barrel of Mill City flour that Minneapolis would collect more scrap per capita than St. Paul would during the cities' upcoming scrap drives. McDonough accepted the wager, offering a dressed fifty-pound lamb from the St. Paul stockyards in return. "If there were any possibility of St. Paul's losing this wager," McDonough announced with bravado, "you may be assured we would not risk a harmless lamb, the symbol of innocence, being tossed to the werewolves of Minneapolis." As the headline in the *Minneapolis Star Journal* joyously declared, "The Battle of Scrap Is On!"[59]

The manufactured rivalry, stoked for all it was worth by the newspapers in both cities, helped tap many Twin Cities residents' latent willingness to contribute to the war effort. "All we were doing in fact was to offer them an outlet for their dammed-up patriotic desire," wrote St. Paul organizer T. Glenn Harrison. "To me it was *the* motivating factor. For ten months the American people, on the home front, had seethed with frustrated desires to DO SOMETHING."[60]

Minneapolis launched its drive first. Residents around the city hauled junk of all kinds—pianos, old safes, pots and pans, ancient jalopies—to curbs for pickup. On the morning of Sunday, October 11, fleets of trucks rumbled through the neighborhoods, stopping every few yards so that volunteers could add more pounds of junk to their ever-expanding loads. At one stop on Lyndale Avenue, a homeowner asked a volunteer crew to wait a moment while he finished mowing his lawn; when he was done, he tossed the lawn-mower into the back of the truck. Elsewhere the collection crews themselves got a little overzealous. In one case, a young mother chased down a collection truck after crews made off with her daughter's wagon and scooter. The trucks delivered their loads to collection points around the city. The largest pile, at Logan School, weighed in at an estimated seven hundred tons. Initial calculations put the city's total haul at about seventy-five hundred tons—about

Scrap drive reminders seemed to pop up everywhere during the fall of 1942.

thirty pounds per person—and that didn't include heavy industrial scrap to be added later in the month. "It made me proud just to be a citizen of Minneapolis, let alone its chief executive," Mayor Kline said.[61]

St. Paul took its scrap drive—held the following weekend—to another level. Organizers, led by T. Glenn Harrison at the *St. Paul Pioneer Press*, played up the patriotic aspects of the drive by recruiting hundreds of Boy Scouts to plant miniature American flags in the yards of all participating households. ("This was later declared to be the largest single order for American flags ever placed by an individual," Harrison claimed.)[62] The response, wrote diarist Alice Brill, was "thrilling."

> We stood outdoors and watched the other houses, as it was interesting. Clank, clank, clank—as things landed high up, or jostled on down between this and that to find a place near the bottom of the truck. Little girls down the street waited all that time to see theirs go in and [were] finally rewarded—waving their flags and the men responding waving as they rode up the street. We were amazed at the amount of space our piles took up in the block.[63]

Boy Scouts add to a mountain of aluminum pots and pans during a scrap drive at St. Paul's Franklin School.

In the end, each city claimed that it "outscrapped" the other, but by the time final estimates were published, few people seemed to care who the victor really was. In November, the Minnesota Editorial Association published the results, calculated by county—not city—and Ramsey County came out on top with a per capita total of 109 pounds of scrap versus Hennepin County's 98. Still, Hennepin and Ramsey both ranked far behind the state's top scrap-collecting region, Big Stone County, where residents amassed more than 324 pounds per person.[64]

Schools throughout the state organized regular salvage campaigns to channel the patriotic impulses of "grade school commandos."

Minnesotans did not confine their recycling activities to the collection of scrap metal. The WPB and other government agencies urged citizens—specifically "housewives"—to save a variety of household leftovers for use in the production of weapons and other war-related items. Tin extracted from salvaged cans was used to line food containers for the troops and to produce tin oxides for blood purification and plasma units. Scrap paper was recycled into pack-

Minnesota housewives were told that one pound of kitchen fat would produce enough glycerin to manufacture half a pound of dynamite.

aging for all sorts of military supplies. Old silk and nylon stockings were turned into gunpowder bags. Thousands of Minnesota housewives also collected meat drippings and greases as part of a nationwide "fat salvage" campaign. Kitchen fats were a source of glycerin, and glycerin was an essential ingredient in some high-powered explosives. "It is possible," claimed organizers in New Ulm, "that the pound of fats you save and turn in may be just the LITTLE EXTRA which will keep our boys—even our New Ulm boys—in ammunition and power to win."[65]

Minnesotans contributed in other ways as well. Red Cross chapters in Minnesota collected thousands of pints of blood—more than 160,000 pints in 1945 alone.[66] Hunters throughout the state donated deer hides for use in aviator gloves and duck feathers for stuffing sleeping bags.[67] Children collected milkweed pods and sold them—for a nickel a pound—to processors who extracted the floss for use in navy life jackets.[68] In Warren County in the Red River valley, residents old and young fanned out into the frozen-over Mud Lake National Wildlife Refuge to harvest cattail fluff, which, like milkweed floss, made good life-jacket stuffing. (A local entrepreneur, hoping to cash in on the county's abundance, opened a cattail fluff processing plant in the town of Holt in 1944.)[69] And several hundred Minnesota pet owners pitched in by volunteering their dogs for military duty.[70] Many of the animals completed basic training successfully and went on to perform with distinction in the Army Canine Corps. A few, however, washed out. In 1943, the McKewin family of St. Paul sent their four-year-old black Labrador to the army, figuring he would be a good fit. (He was known around the neighborhood as a vicious animal with a taste for Scotties.) Four months later, the dog reappeared—in a crate—on the McKewins' doorstep. A telegram informed the family that the animal had been released with an honorable discharge because he was "not aggressive enough for a war dog." The army's assessment was, however, of little consolation to the McKewins or their neighbors. The dog had gained forty pounds at Fort Robinson and no longer obeyed anyone who wasn't wearing a uniform.[71]

Red Cross canteen workers in training. Herbert Lewis, Timmy Ritchie, Jack Hanstein, Blaire Klein, and Phyllis Margolis serve up paper sandwiches and donuts at Irvine School in St. Paul.

But of all the contributions Minnesotans made to the war effort, none was as widely shared as their purchase of war bonds. Throughout the war, the Roosevelt administration conducted a series of bond campaigns designed to boost the treasury, to fight inflation by sopping up excess civilian purchasing power, and—perhaps most importantly—to sell the war to the general public.[72] (Children were encouraged to save their pennies for small-denomination war stamps.) Local organizers worked tirelessly to make sure their communities reached or exceeded their bond quotas. In one creative campaign, thousands of bond purchasers in the Twin Cities signed their names on scrolls called the "War Bond Roll Call." The scrolls were then placed inside many of the B-24 bombers being modified for combat at St. Paul's Holman Field, "so that men on the fighting fronts could see the people of this area were backing them by buying war bonds." (In a related program, several of the Holman Field B-24s were named after organizations that bought enough bonds to pay for a bomber. This resulted in several unlikely names, including "Beauticians of Oklahoma" and "Infants and Childrens' Wear.")[73] Minnesota's final war bond tally: more than $2.8 billion—168 percent of the quota assigned to the state.[74]

A father and son purchase war bonds in Minneapolis.

Leonard Strobel was working the two-to-ten shift at Brainerd's B&L Diner when his brother, Bob, walked in and took a seat at the counter. Bob didn't seem himself that evening of January 12, 1942. He was quieter than usual. When Leonard asked him if anything was wrong, he just shook his head and stared off into the distance. Leonard shrugged off his brother's strange behavior and returned to the kitchen to finish cleaning up for the night. As he was washing the bowl he'd used to mix the donut batter for the next day's breakfast, Bob came back to join him. He was ready to talk now. Bob told Leonard that their older brother, Herbert—a tank commander with Company A of the 194th Tank Battalion in the Philippines—was dead. That was about all Bob could say. Herbert was dead and he wasn't coming back. Fighting back tears, Leonard closed up the diner, slipped into his car, and drove home to the family farm on Star Route, a few miles east of town. He walked into the house, not knowing what to expect. Scanning the rooms, he saw no friends, no relatives, gathered to lend support—just his parents, speaking in hushed tones. In the years to come, Leonard would have trouble remembering exactly what happened after that. "We just went to bed and just cried, I guess," he said. "Nobody slept in the Strobel house all that night."[1]

Herbert Strobel's high school graduation photo

The telegram that carried the news of Brainerd's first World War II fatality contained few details. It said only that Herbert had died on December 26 in action against Japanese forces in the Philippines. In fact, Herbert had been killed in a mortar shell explosion during combat near the Agno River. The battalion's commander, Major Ernie Miller, had pulled Herbert from his tank after the explosion and could tell that the young soldier was mortally wounded. "He was from Brainerd, Minnesota, my home town," Miller later wrote. "He had a milk route before the war, and the thought kept repeating itself in my mind, 'Herb won't deliver milk anymore.'"[2]

Until that point, the war had seemed—at least to some people in Brainerd—an abstraction. Now it was real. "If Brainerd is more conscious of the war, and more determined to see it through to success than most other Minnesota communities, it's because of the stalwarts in Co. A, 194th tank battalion," the *Brainerd Dispatch* observed. "With such a splendid example to guide them, Brainerdites cannot do enough to make certain that the guardsmen's work will not be in vain."[3]

Over the next several weeks, the people of Brainerd followed the daily dispatches from the Philippines with mounting concern. By this time, U.S. forces on the Philippine island of Luzon—including the 194th Tank Battalion—had withdrawn into the Bataan peninsula and were trying to hold off further Japanese advances despite dwindling supplies of weapons, ammunition, and food. In mid-February, the Japanese landed a second invasion force on Luzon in a final push to overwhelm the exhausted Americans. On April 3 they launched their all-out attack. Six days later, on April 9, the besieged Americans on Bataan finally surrendered.

Neighbors gather in Nick Wasnies' Brainerd grocery store to read the bad news about the fall of Bataan.

News of the Bataan surrender hit Brainerd like a blow to the gut. With more than sixty men in the 194th Tank Battalion, Brainerd was "probably harder hit by the fall of Bataan than any other city of its size in the United States." Family and friends of the Brainerd guardsmen gathered in small groups to console each other and listen for news on the radio. Some cried. Others spoke bravely of their men's valiant stand against the Japanese. "We wouldn't have it any other way than to have our boys give their all for this country," boasted Oscar Root, father of Lieutenant Arthur Root. Ken Porwoll's girlfriend, Rene Anderson, while worried, couldn't help but admire what the Brainerd men had done. "Didn't they put up a great fight, though?" she asked.[4] All over town, men downed beers at their local taverns, cursing President Roosevelt and General MacArthur for failing to send reinforcements when "only a little help at the right time would have brought glorious victory." "The war is very close to Brainerd homes today," wrote the editor of the *Brainerd Dispatch*, "and Brainerd men and women . . . have picked up the torch and will carry on."[5]

About the only thing that the people of Brainerd could do now was hope and pray that their men were all right. With the fall of Bataan, communication lines out of the Philippines were severed, and there was no way of knowing whether Brainerd's guardsmen were alive, dead, or captured. In mid-May, U.S. Army Chief of Staff General George Marshall notified Minnesota Governor Harold Stassen that he was "forced to conclude" that the men of Company A were now prisoners of the Japanese. To many men and women in Brainerd, Marshall's words were a relief. "There was a time when we felt there would be nothing worse than to have our husbands and boys fall into the hands of the Japanese, but that's changed," said Ernie Miller's wife, Ann. "It's good news to know that, in all probability, they are alive, even though in the hands of the Japanese. It's much better than getting a death notice."[6]

As spring turned to summer, friends and relatives of the Brainerd men waited impatiently for any news about the fate of their loved ones. In August, several families received letters from their guardsmen indicating that all was well. But on closer inspection it turned out that the letters all had been written before the fall of Bataan. (According to the War Department, the letters came from a mail pouch found floating in the ocean after the ship carrying it was sunk.)[7] On the first anniversary of Company A's departure from San Francisco, Pernina Burke wrote a tribute to her husband and his missing comrades.

Come what may, I will never allow myself to have regrets for having let him go. That isn't because I don't love him, and I'm sure anyone who has ever known us will testify to the fact that we were as close as any two people could ever be. But if he knew in his heart that he was right—then must it not have been right? If he, as the one who had to do the fighting, dared to go, could I be any less brave about letting him go?... Now—well, all we can do is hope, and I'm sure we all do that. And somehow, in the end it has to be worth it—else the world is not fit to live in anyway.[8]

Brainerd residents kept telling themselves that no news was good news, but clichés provided little comfort. For eight-year-old Don Samuelson, the days passed very slowly. His father, Sergeant Walter Samuelson, was among the missing, and the long wait for information was excruciating. "Everybody was just scared stiff, not knowing, not having any idea what was going on," he recalled years later. "Suspense is tough."[9]

Finally, in December, the suspense—or at least some of it—lifted. On December 7, Ann Miller received a telegram confirming that her husband, Ernie, was alive. "Information received indicates your husband, Lieutenant Colonel Ernest B. Miller, infantry, is now a prisoner of war of the Japanese government in the Philippine Islands," the telegram read. It was the first official word that anyone from Company A had survived the Bataan fighting. "It is not entirely good news, but it is wonderful to know that he is alive," Ann Miller said. "This message has done more than anything to relieve the tension under which I have lived since the fall of Bataan."[10] One week later, Pernina Burke received a similar telegram, informing her that her husband, Ed, was also a war prisoner.[11] She had tried to prepare herself for the news, but the telegram left her stunned. "First I had this feeling—Oh, the poor man!—because I didn't imagine he was being treated very well," she later recalled. "And then the next instant I thought, well, at least the kids still have a dad."[12]

As the year came to a close, the news about Ernie Miller and Ed Burke raised hopes throughout Brainerd that the fates of the other guardsmen would soon be known. Few would have guessed that the information they craved would be as elusive as it ultimately proved to be.

3 Help Wanted

Of all the wartime privations Minnesotans endured, few were as disruptive as the shortage of young, able-bodied men. The war siphoned tens of thousands of workers from the state's labor pool—ninety thousand in 1942 alone—and the great majority of them were male. There were two main reasons for the shrinking workforce: thousands of workers were joining the armed forces, and thousands of others were migrating to "construction projects, shipyards and war plants" in other states—especially on the West Coast.[1] Editorial writers fretted about the "manpower problem" and wondered how the state would manage its affairs with so many young men leaving its borders.

In the months after the Pearl Harbor attack, the problems caused by the rapidly shrinking workforce became increasingly acute. Schools across the state braced for the loss of one-third of their male teachers.[2] Minneapolis restaurants—already short about fifteen hundred workers—found it "impossible to compete against the lure of fat pay envelopes offered in defense industries after having . . . lost many cooks and waiters to the armed services."[3] A shortage of pinsetters forced seventeen St. Paul bowling alleys to close their lanes.[4] Trained mechanics were almost impossible to find, as were pallbearers.[5] Ice companies scrambled to find enough strong backs for their annual ice harvests.[6] And most ominously, the state's farms were in trouble. Hired hands who had always showed up in early March for the beginning of the growing season now were informing their former employers that they had landed better-paying jobs in the big shipyards and aircraft assembly plants on the West Coast. Many others were leaving to join the armed services. A survey conducted in early 1943 found that 45 percent of the farms in Sibley County had lost regular workers the previous year.[7] A similar survey showed that only a quarter of all the farmers in Lyon County had managed to hire the help they needed for the 1943 season.[8] "We recognize," said the head of the state's Agricultural Extension Service, Paul Miller, "that tremendous problems lie ahead and that all our resources will be taxed to the utmost, if a serious shortage of farm hands is to be avoided."[9]

The state obviously needed workers. The question was where to find them.

Paul Miller, for one, thought the answer was obvious. "We know that we will have to 'scrape the bottom of the barrel,'" he said, referring specifically to "young people, old people, and womenfolk."[10] Others, including President Roosevelt, cast a wider net—and, thankfully, chose their words more carefully. In June of 1941, Roosevelt issued an executive order designed to ensure "full participation" of all Americans in the war effort. (He signed the order, in large part, to head off a massive civil rights protest organized by A. Philip Randolph of the Brotherhood of Sleeping Car Porters. Randolph had threatened to go ahead with the march unless Roosevelt acted to ensure equal rights in employment.) Under Executive Order 8802, government and defense industries were prohibited from discriminating against workers on the basis of "race, creed, color, or national origin." The nation was now committed—on paper, at least—to "the firm belief that the democratic way of life within the nation can be defended successfully only with the help and support of all groups within its borders." The fact that the president had to issue such an order was, in itself, an acknowledgment that some groups were going to have to fight for the opportunity to participate fully in the war effort.

Prejudice and discrimination were among the most serious obstacles blocking efforts to utilize the talents and skills of all citizens. (Assertions by the Minnesota Division of Employment and Security that the state had "no minority group problems of any significance" were, even for the time, remarkably Panglossian.)[11] Governor Harold Stassen sought to combat bigotry by forming the Minnesota State Committee on Tolerance, Unity, and Loyalty. In a brochure titled "An Appeal to the Citizens of Minnesota," the committee asserted—despite its own conspicuous blindness to the contributions of Minnesotans whose ancestors were not European—that its main goal was to "prevent misunderstanding and animosity."

> *During a war we lose some of our freedom of action, but we should try to preserve as many liberties as possible; and if we wish to keep our own, we should accord the same right to our neighbor. We are privileged to live in a great State—made so by the sweat and blood of sturdy pioneers who found a wilderness and created a garden. Those fine men and women came from*

France, Ireland, Norway, Sweden, Germany, and other Euro-
pean countries, but none looked down upon the other—they all
joined hands and made Minnesota the great commonwealth it
is today. Let us live up to their example and exercise that toler-
ance upon which not only our State but our entire nation is
founded. Neither race nor creed nor nationality should raise a
barrier between one citizen and another. Be their name Schulz
or McCarthy or Olson or Cohen or Martinelli—let none be
ashamed of his ancestors and let none think he is better than
others—we have room for them all.[12]

Efforts to combat bigotry and promote greater tolerance took a
variety of forms. In Minneapolis, officials tried to prove that their
city did not deserve its long-established reputation as a hotbed of
anti-Semitism. In 1939, as details of Hitler's terror campaign against
the Jews became more widely known, prosecutors won a disorderly
conduct conviction against a Minneapolis man who had circulated
bogus pamphlets containing false and inflammatory "evidence" of
a worldwide Jewish conspiracy. During the war, Mayor Marvin
Kline ordered an investigation of several city residents who sponsored an appearance and speech by the notorious anti-Semite, Gerald L. K. Smith.[13] (These and other efforts to dispel Minneapolis'
reputation for anti-Semitism were only partially successful, however. Author Selden Cowles Menefee reported in 1943 that he found
militant anti-Semitism "to be almost entirely lacking in the Middle
West . . . except for Minneapolis.")[14] Likewise, the Minnesota Division of Civilian Defense tried to counter prejudice against Indians
by highlighting the wartime contributions of the state's Dakota and
Ojibwe. "Approximately 650 young [Minnesota Ojibwe] men and
women are in the Armed Forces, and many others are working in
some phase of war industry," it reported. "The [division] is grateful
to the Indians for their participation and earnest work in behalf of
the many home front and war service programs."[15]

The government's determination to utilize every available pair
of hands in the war effort also resulted in an influx of new people.
In one of the most improbable consequences of the war, thousands
of Japanese Americans came to Minnesota in a migration that
helped change the complexion of the state's population. At the same
time, manpower shortages in the state's agricultural regions led to
the importation of labor from several very unlikely locales.

In the end, just about every Minnesotan who could help the
United States achieve victory *did* help. The war created opportuni-

ties for thousands of people who might otherwise have been denied them. Jews, Indians, women, African Americans, Japanese Americans—even a few German and Italian prisoners of war—were encouraged (or in the case of the POWs, compelled) to join in the fight for the simple reason that the nation needed all the help it could get.

Womanpower

Twenty-one-year-old Margaret McGillis (everybody called her "Muggs") forced herself out of bed as the sun rose across the bay over Superior, Wisconsin. As was her routine, she donned her white coveralls, stuffed her hair under a bandanna, grabbed a quick breakfast, and headed off to work. It was a long walk from her parents' house on Minnesota Point to the Duluth docks, but she didn't have much choice. There was no one to catch a ride with most mornings. The country was at war. You got to work however you could. After crossing the canal bridge, McGillis headed over to Superior Street, cut down the bank to the railroad yard, and wove her way among the rail cars, hoping that none of them would move unexpectedly. It was a potentially dangerous shortcut, but McGillis found it invigorating. "[Kept] you on your toes bright and early,"[16] she would recall with a laugh years later. After negotiating the maze of trains, it was a simple matter to reach the gate of the Zenith Dredge Company.

McGillis worked inside the unfinished Coast Guard cutters that Zenith was building for the government under a wartime contract. She was employed by a subcontractor—a local insulation company—and her job was to glue tape over the seams of the fiberglass insulation that covered much of the ships' interiors. It was hard work: ten hours a day with a half-hour break for lunch. The Dolphinite glue fumes "could get you a bit giddy," and during the summer, the heat could be oppressive. McGillis especially hated the days when men came down into her work area to straighten a twisted bulkhead with a big blowtorch and sledgehammers. "I tell you, it was like a sauna," she said.[17]

Muggs McGillis didn't think much about the fact that she was one of the first women to break into the shipbuilding business in Duluth. Work came naturally to her. In her previous job, she had delivered stacks of periodicals to the customers of a local magazine distributor. Before that, she had lugged five-gallon tins of ice cream for the concession stand operator at the neighborhood beach. She was used to physical labor. And besides, the country was at war. "We were there for the [war] effort," she said of herself and her female co-workers. "We were there because we were needed."[18] Still, not everyone reacted to the new workplace reality with the nonchalance of Muggs McGillis. To many people in Duluth, the presence of women in shipyards signaled a radical break with the past.

Zenith had triggered the local revolution in early 1943, when it announced a change in hiring policy.

> *Inasmuch as the War Manpower Commission, together with the Selective Service Board, will have more and more regulations and restrictions affecting the male personnel in our shipyard, it is necessary for us to take steps immediately to introduce women workers in so far as humanly possible in the various activities of the shipyard . . .*
>
> *The Management feels certain that the whole-hearted cooperation of the shipyard workers will follow once they understand that this move is made solely in the interest of our country's war effort to obtain the maximum production results from all citizens of our country—both male and female.[19]*

By 1944, women welders, or "welderettes," were a common sight at the shipyards in Duluth and Superior.

On April 1, 1943, Zenith hired its first women shipbuilders—six welders and one burner.[20] During the next few months, it hired about a dozen more and referred several other women—including Muggs McGillis—to its subcontractors. By 1944, most of the major shipyards in Duluth and Superior were doing the same.

At first, many men had trouble adapting to working side by side with women. Doris Bovee recalled going to work as a welder (she and female colleagues were known as "welderettes") at Globe Shipbuilding Company in Superior, where her father, Ernie, was a long-time employee: "The old-timers said, 'Ernie, if someone had told you in the First World War that you'd have a daughter working with you in the shipyard, what would you say?' And he says, 'I'd say they were crazy.'"[21] Still, it didn't take long for most of the women shipbuilders to earn the respect of their male co-workers. A 1944 edition of the Walter Butler Shipbuilding newsletter (Butler had yards in Duluth and Superior) acknowledged that, as strange as it might seem, women did, in fact, "fit into a man's shipyard."

> *They are in the yard and on the job. There seems to be quite a lot of them. There are pipefitters, welders, burners, scalers, carpenters, yard helpers, sheetmetal workers, machinists and outfitters. They are doing a man's job and doing it well. They are serious about it, very serious. They are in the yard to build ships. There is no foolishness, coyness, coquetry. They mean business . . .*
>
> *As old-time shipbuilders we respect them. As men we are proud of them. Their work isn't easy, none of it is. It's all done the only way it can be done—the hard way, and these women are doing it that way. They're building ships.*[22]

While the women in the shipyards were, for the most part, treated with respect by the men they worked with, they were rarely treated as equals. Some men seemed genuinely confused about how to act around their female co-workers. The Zenith Dredge newsletter, for example, described the case of an employee named John Kolander ("always the perfect gentleman") who couldn't come up with a proper way to inform a woman welder "that her trousers had caught fire."[23] Other men reacted to the new shipyard reality by customizing common workplace pranks for a new batch of female victims. Muggs McGillis liked to tell the story of one woman who was instructed to track someone down in the ship's "afterbirth." "She went all over the ship asking where the afterbirth was," McGillis laughed.[24]

In all, an estimated thirty-five hundred women worked at the Twin Ports shipyards during the war—about a quarter of the entire workforce. For some women, like Muggs McGillis, the jobs in the shipyards were just jobs—important wartime jobs, to be sure, but mere jobs nonetheless. But for many others, the work was a revelation. "A lot of women, that was their first job," McGillis recalled. "Their husbands were gone. They had kids. It was the first freedom they had."[25]

Throughout the state, women from practically every background imaginable were going to work. The trend became especially noticeable during the second half of 1942. Surveys of major Twin Cities–area defense contractors showed that in the five months between July and November of that year, the number of women workers rose dramatically—indeed, during that short period, their share of the job market increased from 20 to 28 percent. By January of 1943, about four of every ten war production trainees were women, and the pressure was on to further boost that ratio.[26] "If necessary, we will ring every doorbell in the Twin Cities and get women enlisted into jobs," declared War Manpower Commission regional director Frank Rarig. "Women are badly needed and we hope they will realize that this war is their fight as well as that of the men."[27] Companies such as Minneapolis-Moline responded to the changing workplace by publishing special manuals to help acclimate their new female employees.

Working in a plant is a new adventure for most of you. It is an opportunity to gain experience and acquire knowledge that will help you all the rest of your lives whether you continue in industry or do something else. We have been warned that many of our problems would be multiplied if women went to work in our shops. Among these problems were increased accidents, lowered production, frequent tardiness and unwarranted absenteeism. We don't believe it. In our opinion these are imaginary difficulties, based on old prejudices and tradition. Certainly they need not be true in your case. We have enough confidence in you to believe that, with certain regulations and provisions that have been worked out for your convenience and protection, you will maintain a record as good as, if not better than, male workers in these respects.[28]

At the Twin Cities Ordnance Plant (TCOP) in New Brighton, early projections that women would account for 40 percent of the facility's total workforce turned out to be surprisingly conservative. In the end, figures showed that more than 60 percent of TCOP's wartime employees were women.[29]

As the war dragged on, Minnesota women took on a variety of jobs that previously had been reserved exclusively for men. In the summer of 1943, the shortage of male workers forced the Twin Cities Rapid Transit Company to put female conductors on its streetcars.[30] The city of St. Paul began hiring "girl lifeguards."[31] Dozens of women—mostly recent high school graduates—packed Western Union's Minneapolis headquarters to learn how to send "the telegrams upon which the government, army, navy and the war industries depend to direct and coordinate their activities."[32]

Nowhere, however, did Minnesota women make a greater contribution than on the farm. Minnesota farmers, under intense pressure to increase production for the war effort, desperately needed to replace all the hired hands who were leaving to join the armed forces and the war industries. Surveys indicated "that much of the

Packing cartridge belts at the Twin Cities Ordnance Plant. More than 60 percent of TCOP's wartime employees were women.

Women streetcar conductors began working on Twin Cities trolleys for the first time in the summer of 1943.

Women from Walker and Cass Lake stop in Minneapolis on their way to de-tassel corn in southern Minnesota in July 1943.

replacement" was coming "from the labor of farm wives and older daughters."[33] In many cases, the man of the family was himself called to military duty, leaving the wife (or mother) to assume all responsibility for the operation of the farm. Ruthe Rosten's experience was typical. Rosten was a widow, and when her two oldest sons went off to war, she was left to farm more than one hundred acres outside Glenwood with only her twelve-year-old son, Knut, for help.

> He'd harness up the horses in the morning before he went to school, and I knew how to hitch them to the wagon, and I'd go out there in the fall and pick corn until noon. Then I'd tie them up. Then I'd go in and eat and untie them and go and pick in the afternoon until he came home about at two-thirty or three. The principal wouldn't let him come to help on the farm. And then we'd go out and pick until evening, and we'd shovel off the load together, and then we'd be ready for the next morning again.[34]

But despite the hardships, most Minnesota farm women fared quite well while the men were away. Male farmers told state investigators that wives and daughters learned "to use [farm] machines quickly and well," and provided much "greater help on the farm than hired women or inexperienced men."[35] *Minneapolis Tribune* reporter Ed Shave marveled that the state's farm women were "performing a sturdy—yes, a heroic war service." "I have seen enough women at work in the fields," he wrote, "to know that the total number is a large one, and that the tasks they are performing are invaluable."[36]

Still, not everyone was convinced that women belonged in the fields and the factories. At Cargill Incorporated's shipbuilding operation on the Minnesota River, managers proudly said that they "never succumbed to having members on 'the distaff side' in our production department."[37] Many Minnesotans—men and women alike—believed that women should "be home tending their families,"[38] and in fact, most of the hand-wringing was over working mothers and the welfare of their children.

In a directive issued in 1942, Paul McNutt, chairman of the War Manpower Commission, declared, "No women responsible for the care of young children should be encouraged or compelled to seek employment which deprives their children of essential care until all other sources of supply are exhausted."[39] But as McNutt implied in his directive, the nation's labor supply was not limitless. By 1943, child welfare officials in Duluth were warning that "unattached women and a great majority of the married women without children are already working."[40] The situation was similar elsewhere in the state. In Minneapolis, authorities noted that the dwindling "roster of employable unattached women" would almost certainly result in "an increasing number of mothers of young children [seeking] gainful employment."[41]

State and local leaders worried publicly about what seemed to be an impending child care crisis. "We do not want to wake up here some day, which we are likely to, and find hundreds of women going to work at defense plants with no place to leave their children," warned Spencer Brader, an administrator with the state's Division of Civilian Defense. At first, the child care problem did not seem especially severe. Many working mothers were able to leave their young daughters and sons with relatives and friends. At the Twin Cities Ordnance Plant, for example, about half of all female employees with children under twelve relied on their mothers or mothers-in-law to look after the kids, freeing them to perform their jobs "without a care."[42] Many other women, however, were not as fortunate. Without friends or family members to watch the children, they often were forced to rely on acquaintances and strangers. Hilda Rachuy, a single working mother living in St. Paul, shuttled her two children through a series of unsatisfactory child care arrangements. In one case, she pulled the children out of an elderly couple's home after she noticed her son's back was blistered from sunburn.[43]

Larger communities such as the Twin Cities and Duluth responded to the perceived child care problem by opening federally subsidized "nursery schools," but the schools enjoyed only limited success. In St. Paul, for example, enrollment at the city's three child care centers peaked at just 110.[44] Indeed, nationwide only about 130 thousand children were served by subsidized day care.[45] Like their counterparts elsewhere, most young mothers in Minnesota either stayed at home or—if they went to work—found other arrangements for their children. Those who did take advantage of child care programs were often looked down upon by both men and women. Diarist Alice Brill was among the many Minnesotans who wondered why the government seemed to be encouraging young mothers to work outside the home. "I usually believe in women doing things," she wrote, but "why should [the] community foot [the] bills while women get extra pay and neglect children?"[46]

Minnesota women, like those in other states, were being asked to balance conflicting expectations. On the one hand, the government was telling them that it was their patriotic duty to go to work outside the home. On the other hand, much of the rest of society seemed to expect them to continue in their traditional roles as wives and mothers. As the war progressed, it became clear that traditional ideas about femininity remained firmly rooted, despite wartime demands. In one typical article, the *Minneapolis Tribune* applauded women for going to work, while simultaneously extolling the virtues of a new hairstyle called the "factory bob." "Operators of war plants have already discovered their best women are those who are well groomed," the article claimed. "Women actually turn out more shells and drive more rivets when they know they are tidy and attractive."[47] In a similar vein, *Ladies' Home Journal* downplayed the go-to-work trend, claiming that American women—and one Minnesota woman in particular—were itching to have babies: lots of babies.

> *When young Mrs. Betty Conrad, of Minneapolis, comes out enthusiastically for big families—and proves it by having seven*

Eulalia Collins poses at a mock vanity to help the Minneapolis Tribune *make a dubious point about wartime morale. The headline that accompanied this 1941 photo read "Powdered Noses Paying for Defense."*

*children, with ten as her goal—she may not realize it, but she's a
harbinger of a new American trend. Our population experts and
authorities foresee a growing popularity for larger families, not
only because a war-ravaged world will want more children, but
because increasing numbers of women, disillusioned with their
present roles or with what the workaday world can offer, will
turn toward motherhood as the happiest road to fulfillment.*

*Contributing enormously to this trend will be these wartime
influences: Vast numbers of young American women have embarked on childbearing much earlier than usual, and have
found motherhood to their liking; millions of women in war
jobs are now convinced they'll be happier as homemakers when
their duty is done; and returning servicemen will be hungry for
family life.*[48]

As the war drew to a close, women began leaving the workforce
in droves. Many were laid off to make way for the men returning
from war, but many others quit voluntarily. Surveys conducted
toward the end of the war suggested that many working women in
Minnesota—and the rest of the country—were ready "to swap their
factory overalls for a kitchen apron." (A few surveys suggested
otherwise, including one that showed three-quarters of employed
women in Duluth hoped to keep working after the war, but these
surveys were apparently aberrations.) "I will be glad to get back into
the apron," said one female munitions worker at the Twin Cities
Ordnance Plant, echoing the sentiments of many of her co-workers.
"I didn't go into war work with the idea of working all my life. It
was just to help out during the war."[49] Postwar statistics reflected
this apparent preference for domesticity. Nationwide, the rate of
women's participation in the workforce, which stood at 26 percent
in 1940, spiked to 36 percent in 1944, and then fell back to 28 percent in 1947.

Still, the image of the confident and conscientious working
woman of the war years endured. As historian David M. Kennedy
observed, the "Rosie the Riveter" mystique "helped inspire a later
generation of women to challenge sexual stereotypes and to demand what Rosie never had: economic freedom as well as family security, a child and a paycheck, a place of work and a place to call
home, too, not one or the other."[50]

Race Factor

Like many of his friends, Harry Davis had hoped to go to college—probably the University of Minnesota—after he graduated from Minneapolis' North High School in January of 1942, but the attack on Pearl Harbor altered his plans beyond recognition. Within weeks after the attack, some of his closest friends received their draft notices. Davis figured he was next. After graduating, he took a series of odd jobs, knowing that his number could come up at any moment. When his notice finally did come in early July of 1942, it was almost a relief. Now he could get on with his life, even if it was the life of a soldier. Davis reported to Fort Snelling for induction, but doctors there classified him 4-F—physically unfit for military duty. (His legs were of slightly different lengths, the result of a childhood bout with polio.) In some respects, the rejection was disappointing. "I wanted to do my part," he recalled years later. But Davis was also relieved. His relationship with his girlfriend, Charlotte NaPue, was getting serious, and he could hardly bear the thought of being away from her. If the army didn't want him, he'd just have to find another way to contribute to the war effort. He'd stay in the Twin Cities, remain close to Charlotte, and get a job at a defense plant.[51]

There was just one potential problem: Harry Davis was African American.

In the months leading up to the war, and in the first months after the Pearl Harbor attack, black Minnesotans had little reason to believe that their own opportunities to contribute to the war effort would match those of white Minnesotans. Racial discrimination was a long-entrenched feature of the state's workplaces—a fact acknowledged during the postwar years by a special state commission. "Prior to the war," the commission reported, "a considerable number of employers [in the state] denied employment to Negroes." About the only reliable line of work available to African Americans in Minnesota, the commissioners said, was "janitorial service."[52] Even black college graduates could rarely do much better than a job in the post office.

Well aware of the state's sorry record in the area of equal employment, several African American organizations, led by the Minneapolis and St. Paul chapters of the Urban League, launched a campaign to secure jobs for black workers in local defense plants. At first, hopes were high that the war would bring immediate change. After a meeting in the spring of 1941 with Urban League officials, the state's industrial coordinator, E. L. Olrich, urged all defense contractors in Minnesota "to not show any discrimination in the employment of workers." A couple of months later, President Roosevelt issued Executive Order 8802. The African American *Minneapolis Spokesman* newspaper hailed what it called a "very favorable" employment outlook, noting that two black men had recently landed jobs at a local foundry and that "calls for car washers and other unskilled jobs show a slight increase."[53]

But predictions that Minnesota's employers would suddenly throw open their doors to black workers were premature. In October of 1941, a regional director with the National Youth Administration charged that several large defense contractors in the Twin Cities were "stubbornly [refusing] to hire Negro labor on the ground they don't get along with other workers, a theory which has been widely

Harry Davis, Charlotte Davis, Betty Strawder, and Jack Strawder celebrate the Onan Company's "E" Award (for excellence in war production) from the U.S. Navy.

disproved."[54] African American graduates of local technical schools such as Dunwoody Institute were "giving up the idea of ever trying to become skilled in trades which they never will be given a chance to practice."[55] By the summer of 1942, when Harry Davis set out to find a defense industry job, black leaders were claiming that 95 percent of the war plants in Minnesota still discriminated against black workers.[56] Among the largest offenders were the Northern Pump Company (which engaged "in the virtual barring of Negroes"), Minneapolis-Honeywell (which employed only two African Americans), and Munsingwear (which employed none). "The Negro worker stood on the outside looking in," wrote Cecil Newman, the *Minneapolis Spokesman*'s editor. "He bought defense bonds, saw his sons drafted and sent to Southern army camps; but he himself, his wife or daughter could not get past the guarded gates of the defense plants which were advertising frantically for workers."[57] The War Manpower Commission, hearing the steady stream of complaints, sent a representative to the Twin Cities to investigate.[58]

But even as black Minnesotans struggled to knock down the hiring barriers erected by many of the state's largest employers, a few defense contractors were altering the employment landscape. Chief among them was the Federal Cartridge Corporation—operator of the new Twin Cities Ordnance Plant (TCOP) in New Brighton. Federal Cartridge's president, Charles Horn, was well known among black leaders in the Twin Cities as an enlightened employer who believed racial discrimination was both morally repugnant and bad for business. Albert Allen, Jr., who would later serve as president of the Minneapolis chapter of the NAACP, recalled listening to Horn declare his hiring philosophy during a meeting of business and political leaders in 1941.

> He finished his statement by saying, "I've listened to the speeches of the others, about hiring and so on. I want everybody here to know (and you, too, Governor) that when this plant opens up I don't give a—[pause]what color the person is. It's gonna be open to employment for all. I've [heard] some of you say here that you would hire Negroes but the whites don't want to work with them. Well, I'm telling you this: when I open up this place, if the whites don't wanna work with them then the whites don't have to come out there."[59]

During construction of the plant, subcontractors hired—with Horn's prodding—more than five hundred local black workers. At its peak of production, TCOP employed about one thousand African Americans in eleven departments and thirty-two job classifications. The numbers encouraged black Minnesotans and fostered hope that other employers would follow Horn's lead. "When it is recognized that there are only about 10,000 Negroes in St. Paul and Minneapolis," Cecil Newman wrote, "it can readily be understood how the employment of [so many] members of that group would heighten morale."[60] Officials in Washington called TCOP "the model plant of the country in its integration and treatment of Negro labor."[61]

Harry Davis considered working for TCOP after receiving his 4-F classification, but in the end, he took a job with another defense contractor, D. W. Onan and Sons. While not as aggressive as TCOP in minority hiring, it was nonetheless known as a progressive employer. Onan manufactured electric generators for the military. Davis was familiar with the company because he had grown up near Onan's original plant in North Minneapolis and because his older brother already worked there as a spray painter. When Davis went to work at Onan's plant on Stinson Avenue in Minneapolis, only a handful of other African Americans worked there, but as the company landed more government contracts, it hired more black workers. Eventually, more than one hundred African Americans worked there.

Some of Onan's white employees chafed at the presence of black workers on the production lines, but usually they kept their objections to themselves. "There were people there who you could tell didn't like you, but you didn't have to come in contact with them," Davis recalled. "If there were any troublemakers, [the managers] didn't care what color you were, they got you out of there." One day after work, Davis learned just how much attitudes had changed at Onan when he and a black friend joined some white co-workers, including plant manager Gene Bursch, at a neighborhood bar called the Streamline.

> *Bursch, he says, "Hey . . . why don't you guys come over and we'll buy you a beer." I says, "Okay." And so we sat down at the table, and . . . the waitress came over there—I think there were five of us—and they say, "Bring us five beers." And so when she came back she only had three. So Gene says to her, "Why three?" She says, "Well, my boss says we don't serve Negroes." So Gene says, "Well, you will serve us or you'll lose our business." [Gene] says, "Where's the owner?" The owner comes out to talk with Gene, and they talked. We didn't get the beer.[62]*

As Davis watched in amazement, Gene Bursch stood up and instructed all the Onan employees in the bar—about fifteen total—to walk out in protest. Later, the company filed a complaint against the Streamline, prompting the bar's owners to make a formal apology and cash settlement to Davis and his friend. "I will never forget that apology and how good it made me feel," Davis recalled.[63]

As Davis' experience at the Streamline demonstrated, the slow progress toward integration in some war plants was not always easy to replicate outside the workplace. Housing was still largely segregated by race in the Twin Cities, and a Minnesota poll conducted shortly after the war showed that 60 percent of the state's white population believed African Americans should *remain* segregated.[64] The Minneapolis chapter of the American Red Cross found itself at the center of a controversy when officials there admitted that they kept the blood of black donors separate from that of white donors.[65] Governor Harold Stassen incurred the wrath of many black leaders when he refused to let African Americans serve alongside white Minnesotans in the state's Home Defense Force, a quasi-military organization designed to assume some duties of the activated National Guard. Looking back on the defense force episode as a missed opportunity, the *Minneapolis Spokesman* claimed that "the governor could have done much for the strengthening of real freedom and democracy in Minnesota by repudiating the Army policy of discrimination and segregation, and issuing an order to permit the enlistment of Negroes . . . without segregating them into separate companies."[66]

Still, black Minnesotans' employment gains during the war were real. In a postwar survey of Minnesota employers, about 20 percent of the respondents said they employed African Americans, while another 53 percent said they were willing to do so. While the actual percentages were no doubt considerably smaller than the survey indicated (only 601 of the 2,231 employers contacted actually responded), the Governor's Interracial Commission reported that "the total number of employers hiring Negroes [continued] to increase."[67] In addition, those companies that did hire African Americans during the war almost always continued to do so once the fighting was over. Harry Davis lost his job at D. W. Onan and Sons after the war but was rehired three years later as a junior foreman—a job that set him on a path to "rise out of the dirty-coverall, menial tasks [he] had been doing and become a manager in a shirt and tie."[68] In 1965, Davis was promoted into Onan's personnel department, making him the first black employee to earn a white-collar position at the company. As Davis saw it, his rise into the management ranks was the culmination of a slow process that began in 1941. "Because of the war, those jobs were open," he said. "The war opened the doors."[69]

Relocated

Within hours of the attack on Pearl Harbor, federal agents began moving in on the handful of Japanese nationals who lived in Minnesota. They ordered Jiro Akamatsu to close his gift shop on East Sixth Street in St. Paul. They shut down Ed Yamakazi's café in Minneapolis and Ken Nakamura's West Hotel in Crookston. They told Kano Ikeda, a prominent pathologist at St. Paul's Miller Hospital, to put his practice on hold. All Japanese living in Minnesota were ordered to stay in their homes while treasury officials studied their financial records. They all were presumed to be potential enemy agents until the evidence proved otherwise.[70]

But many Minnesotans resented the federal government's reaction, and they were in no rush to make scapegoats out of the three or four dozen people of Japanese ancestry who lived in the state. Two hundred local physicians signed a petition demanding that Kano Ikeda be released from house detention. He was freed a week later. Jiro Akamatsu and his family were allowed to leave their home after members of their church, Central Park Methodist in St. Paul, interceded on their behalf. Newspapers took up the cause, pointing out that many Japanese who wanted to become American citizens were prevented from doing so by U.S. immigration laws. In its article about the Akamatsu family, the *St. Paul Dispatch* reminded readers that the Akamatsus were "in no way to blame for the actions of the Japanese" and that their loyalties were "with this community and the United States."[71] The St. Paul Resettlement Committee was organized after St. Paul's public safety commissioner tried to institute new rules barring Japanese from entering the city. In a postwar summary of its activities, the committee asserted that Minnesotans were appalled at the federal government's heavy-handed treatment of their Japanese neighbors.

> *Bitter as the sudden and unjust detention had been for these . . . Americans of Japanese birth, it served to arouse the people of St. Paul to the dangers of war hysteria. The fact that unjust restraint could come to Japanese-Americans who had won the trust and esteem of their fellow townspeople . . . swiftly won*

sympathy for the tragic plight of citizens whose birth placed them at the mercy of officialdom. On this sympathy, so dramatically aroused at the very beginning of the war, it was possible later to build a program of action which had city-wide support.[72]

The restraint that many Minnesotans showed in the days following Pearl Harbor stood in stark contrast to the growing anti-Japanese sentiment surging through other parts of the country—especially the West Coast. In late January the federal government released a report alleging—without proof—that some Japanese Americans had betrayed their country by providing information to Tokyo prior to the Pearl Harbor attack. In February, President Roosevelt signed Executive Order 9066, authorizing the army to designate "military areas" from which "any and all persons may be excluded." (While the order did not identify any particular group to be excluded, it was clearly aimed at Japanese Americans on the West Coast.) Several weeks later, General John DeWitt, chief of the army's Western Defense Command, ordered all Japanese in California, Oregon, and Washington to leave their homes in preparation for evacuation to locations farther inland. Evacuated Japanese reported first to "assembly centers"—temporary holding places at fairgrounds and horse racetracks. From there, they were sent to "relocation centers"—barbed wire–ringed concentration camps in some of the most desolate areas of the Western interior.

Many Minnesotans, seeing what was happening on the West Coast, fancied their state an oasis of racial harmony. And while that perception didn't always mesh with reality (Japanese were, for example, consistently denied membership in private organizations such as the Minneapolis Athletic Club and the Automobile Club of Minneapolis),[73] Minnesotans' apparent distaste for scapegoating helped earn the state a reputation for tolerance that many other parts of the country did not enjoy. This perception, in turn, helped initiate a chain of events that led to an unprecedented increase in Minnesota's Japanese population.

It all began in the spring of 1942, when Colonel Kai Rassmussen of the U.S. Army came to Minnesota on official business. Rassmussen was the commandant of the army's Military Intelligence Service Language School, or MISLS, which trained Nisei (second-generation Japanese Americans) to become Japanese language specialists—and he was in Minnesota to find a new home for his school. The MISLS had originally operated out of the Presidio in San

Francisco, but in the wake of the Pearl Harbor attack and the anti-Japanese backlash that followed, the army temporarily shut down the school and ordered Rassmussen to relocate it far from the West Coast. After studying the pros and cons of about a dozen Midwestern cities, Rassmussen concluded that the Minneapolis–St. Paul area was the best fit.

The exact site that Rassmussen chose for his school was an old Civilian Conservation Corps (ccc) camp in the town of Savage. Camp Savage, as it was known, sat on 132 wooded acres, about a half-mile from the Minnesota River and had last been used as a home for indigent elderly men. The site had everything Rassmussen was looking for: adequate facilities; a location convenient to a major military installation (Fort Snelling); and, most of all, a local population that displayed little anti-Japanese prejudice. Early on, Rassmussen had decided to seek a community that "would accept oriental-faced Americans for their true worth." As far as he could tell, Minnesota fit the bill. The Twin Cities area "not only had room physically," he said, "but also had room in the people's hearts."[74]

Toshio (Tosh) Abe of San Diego, California, was among the first two hundred MISLS students to arrive at Camp Savage in May of 1942, and it didn't take long for him to discover that Minnesota was nothing like the West Coast. Abe had been at home on a three-day pass when the Japanese attacked Pearl Harbor, and he had immediately felt the sting of racial hatred. "I was in uniform and a neighbor said to me, 'What army do you think you're in?'" he recalled.[75] Now, as Abe got to know his new, albeit temporary, home, he was pleasantly surprised at Minnesotans' responses to him and his fellow students. "They didn't look at us as if we were sub-humans like they [did] on the West Coast," Abe said. Since few Nisei women lived in the Twin Cities area at the time, many of the men began dating local women of German, Irish, and Scandinavian extraction—something that would have been considered taboo in California. They danced with their dates to the sounds of the Spike Jones Orchestra at the St. Paul Ballroom. They walked hand in hand down Minneapolis' Hennepin Avenue. "God, we couldn't believe what we were seeing here," Abe said.[76]

Many of the students at Camp Savage had friends and relatives living in the relocation centers out West, and they soon began arranging to have their loved ones join them in Minnesota. In April of 1943, Tosh Abe received permission to move his mother and brother from the huge concentration camp in Posten, Arizona. The Abe

Tosh Abe at Camp Savage. Abe later spent more than a year and a half in the Pacific theater, including eight months in miserable jungle combat in Burma.

family's reunion was among the first in a wave of Nisei resettlements in Minnesota. Some families, like the Abes, worked out the arrangements on their own, but many others depended on intermediaries. Two local resettlement agencies—one each in Minneapolis and St. Paul—combined forces with the War Relocation Authority's district office in Minneapolis to pave the way for the influx of new arrivals from the detention camps. Agency workers kept files on every Nisei who expressed an interest in moving to Minnesota and spent the bulk of their time trying to place applicants in jobs with Twin Cities employers. By the end of 1943, more than four hundred Japanese Americans had resettled in the Twin Cities area. A year later the number of relocated Nisei in the state had risen to nearly fourteen hundred.[77]

Most of the new arrivals were, like Tosh Abe, gratified by their welcome in Minnesota. In a series of interviews with relocation officials in Minneapolis, resettled Nisei residents repeatedly compared Minnesota's warm reception with the harsh treatment they encountered out West.

We have found Minneapolis a refreshing experience as compared with what other Nisei have found in the communities they have chosen to enter. Here the atmosphere is so much freer. The people express no feelings of animosity. We've wondered why this is so. Is it that you are more simple, natural, and religious?

But there has been something in the air in Minneapolis. People are so kind and friendly. We have been permitted equal entry into the schools, the shops, the places of amusement. It has not been that way before, nor is it that way in other places. Like many other Japanese we will live here forever.

People have really been wonderful to us. I am no longer afraid of walking down the street any more. If people stare at me it is

*only because they have normal curiosity for strange features.
No one seems to be afraid or antagonistic. I think that I should
be paid by your Chamber of Commerce because I laud your
city so much. It is so beautiful, and the people are so kind and
considerate.*[78]

Still, Minnesota was not the wonderland of racial bliss that many
imagined it to be. As more and more Nisei arrived in the state, relocation authorities began receiving troubling reports of discrimination. Housing discrimination was a particularly insidious problem, as the comments of one Nisei women indicated.

*Many Japanese internees included photographs of themselves when
they applied to come to Minnesota. Arthur Takemoto and his family were
confined in the camp in Poston, Arizona, when they sent their application.*

If we have met with any anti-Japanese feeling here it has been with housing. At first we thought we had trouble because there was a housing shortage. Later I "caught on." It was because of the pigment of my skin that I couldn't get into a decent home. I'd call a prospect by phone and everything seemed agreeable, but when they saw either myself or husband the rooms would be rented, or they would suggest that we call at another time.[79]

Sara Tanigawa was being held at the Tule Lake camp in California when she applied to come to Minnesota. "My fiancé is a soldier in the United States Army stationed at Camp Savage Minnesota," she wrote. "I am anxious to join him so that we may be married."

Discrimination showed up in other places as well. While many employers in the Twin Cities welcomed Nisei workers (all but two of the major war plants in the area had Japanese Americans on their payrolls by the end of the war), some of them did not. In one case, a Nisei worker stood for hours in long lines at thirteen employment offices, only to learn in each instance that the position he sought had been filled. In Red Wing, labor leaders publicly discouraged a Nisei nursing student from entering a training program at St. John's Hospital, claiming that since "Indians and Negroes were not favorably received in Red Wing . . . Japanese would fare no better." Between the summer of 1942 and the summer of 1944, the University of Minnesota refused to admit Nisei students on the grounds that the federal government had failed to set a quota for Japanese admissions. (Other Minnesota schools including Macalester College, Hamline University, and St. Thomas College welcomed Nisei students.)[80] None of these problems, however, stemmed the wartime flow of Japanese Americans into the state.

As the number of resettled Nisei civilians grew, so too did the number of MISLS graduates. In August 1944, the school, which had outgrown the facilities at Camp Savage, moved to its new home at Fort Snelling. By the time it held its final commencement in June of 1946, it had trained about six thousand students (including fifty-one female linguists with the Women's Army Corps, or WAC). About 85 percent of the graduates were Nisei.[81]

MISLS graduates went on to serve with distinction throughout the Pacific theater. They did most of their work behind the scenes, performing a wide range of duties that included translating captured Japanese documents and interrogating Japanese prisoners. In 1944, MISLS graduates made an essential contribution to the defeat of the Japanese navy in the Philippines when they translated a set of captured Japanese battle plans.

When the war was over, Tosh Abe had a decision to make. He had to decide where to live. Minnesota was the obvious choice. His mother and brother still lived in Minneapolis. He could join them there. But then he remembered the winter he had spent at Camp Savage. He recalled how, when the temperature hit thirty-five below, he had raised his southern California hands to the heavens and declared, "I'll never spend another winter here."[82] But what other choice did he have? San Diego was out of the question. His mother had been forced to sell the family home. As far as he was concerned there was nothing left there for him. Minnesota was the only home he had left. After receiving his discharge in November of 1945, Abe returned to Minneapolis, moved in with his mother and brother, and contributed to a startling postwar statistic. By 1950, the census would show that more than one thousand people of Japanese ancestry lived in Minnesota—more than ten times the prewar number. Abe, like hundreds of other Nisei, had decided he felt more comfortable in Minnesota than any place else—even during the winter. "There was no question I would come back here," he insisted years later. "There was no place else to go."[83]

The Military Intelligence Service Language School (MISLS) at Fort Snelling continued to train language specialists like these, shown in October 1945, for about a year after the war ended.

Such Nice Fellows

In June 1943, newspapers throughout Minnesota carried a story that
put a smile on the face of many an overworked and overwrought
farmer. Paul E. Miller, chairman of Minnesota's Farm Help Coordi-
nating Committee, announced that the War Department had
agreed to make German and Italian prisoners of war available to
work on Minnesota farms. (In addition, Miller revealed that the
state had received permission to bring in 350 "Jamaican nationals"
to work in the vegetable canneries near Fairmont.)[84] For many Minnesota farmers, this was welcome news. The state was facing a serious farm labor shortage brought on by the exodus of rural men into
military service and defense industry jobs. Miller had promised earlier in the year that the state would utilize "all farm help sources,
some of which heretofore have not been considered at all."[85] Now it
appeared that he was living up to that pledge.

Among the thousands of Minnesotans who read the news about
the soon-to-be-available POW workers was a pair of vegetable farmers from Moorhead: Hank Peterson and Paul Horn. The Peterson
and Horn truck farms were among the largest in the Moorhead
area, together spanning more than six thousand acres. They grew a
variety of crops, including beets, potatoes, cabbages, and tomatoes.
With harvest fast approaching and the war draining the pool of
available farm workers, Peterson and Horn were starting to wonder
how they would get their crops out of the fields. To them, POWs
sounded like the perfect solution. "We needed some help," Horn recalled, "so we took a trip."[86]

Horn and Peterson traveled to Omaha, Nebraska, headquarters
of the Army's Seventh Service Command, to put in a formal request
for POW workers. A few weeks later they made another trip—this
time to a large prisoner of war camp outside Algona, Iowa—to make
further arrangements. The process was slow. No prisoners were
available for the 1943 harvest. But in the spring of 1944, Peterson and
Horn signed contracts to bring 150 German prisoners to Moorhead.
If everything went according to plan, they would arrive in late May.

The imminent arrival of the German POWs was the talk of the
town. The people of Moorhead didn't know quite what to make of
the whole idea. Were the prisoners dangerous? Were they really
needed? Horn tried to make his case without being confrontational.
"There's no doubt that bringing in of prisoners would relieve considerably the indicated labor shortage in this area," he said. "But if
public sentiment is against the move it will probably be aban-

doned." At one point it appeared that Peterson and Horn's plan was in serious jeopardy when a group of Moorhead residents complained that the site chosen for the prisoners' barracks was too close to their homes and businesses. When the two farmers found another site—a warehouse on the east side of town—the opposition dwindled.[87]

The first forty POWs arrived in Moorhead on May 28, 1944, and spent the night in tents on Horn's farm. Three days later, a train pulled into town carrying about 120 more captured Germans. The prisoners came from the camp in Algona and were guarded by a contingent of nearly four dozen soldiers. As the people of Moorhead looked on, the POWs marched through the streets to their new

German prisoners of war at Algona Branch Camp Number One in Moorhead

When they weren't laboring in the fields, the POWs often did basic maintenance work, such as roof repair, for Peterson and Horn.

warehouse home, now known officially as Algona Branch Camp Number One.[88]

Over the next six months, the prisoners in Moorhead did whatever work they were told to do. Their main job was to tend and harvest beets and potatoes, but they did other work as well. They installed plumbing in the warehouse. They painted barns and repaired roofs on the Peterson farm. "We found them a little reluctant to work," Horn recalled, "but under the circumstances, I think they did quite well." Horn estimated that the German prisoners—most of whom had no prior experience in the fields—were only about two-thirds as productive as the Mexican and Mexican American migrants who came to the Red River valley for the harvest.

Some prisoners were more reluctant to work than others. Those who had been captured in North Africa, before the war began to turn in the Allies' favor, were among the hardest cases. Peterson's bookkeeper, Florence Drury, remembered three "Nazi types" who liked to "strut around with their chests out like [they were] goose stepping." In one exceptional case, fourteen rebellious prisoners spent a night in jail after breaking a pump with a sledgehammer.[89]

Horn and Peterson paid the army forty cents an hour—the prevailing local wage—for each POW s labor. The army, in turn, paid each prisoner ten cents an hour in coupons that could be redeemed at the camp's canteen. When the harvest was over in November, the prisoners went back to Algona. A new contingent arrived the following summer.

Moorhead was one of twenty-one Minnesota communities to accommodate prisoner of war camps between 1943 and 1945. What the prisoners did while in Minnesota depended largely on where they were assigned. POWs in Moorhead and the other Red River valley communities worked almost exclusively on farms. Those in the southern part of the state were brought in mainly to provide much-needed labor in the region's pea and corn canneries, although many of them also worked for other companies such as nurseries, milk processors, and ice manufacturers. In north-central Minnesota, prisoners lived in converted Civilian Conservation Corps (CCC) camps, and were assigned to work at various logging operations.

The exact number of prisoners who worked in Minnesota is unknown, but one conservative estimate places it between 3,000 and 4,500. While not insignificant, the state's share of the war prisoner population was just a small fraction of the more than 400,000 German, Italian, and Japanese POWs interned in the United States during the war. It was also considerably smaller than the contingent of workers from Mexico, Jamaica, and Barbados who were brought into the state to provide wartime labor (these totaled some 2,800 in 1944 alone).[90] Most of the prisoners assigned to Minnesota were German, but a few hundred Italians worked out of camps in Princeton and Olivia—Minnesota's first POW camps, both of which opened in the fall of 1943.[91]

Security at the camps was haphazard at best. The camp in Moorhead, for example, was supposed to have a guard tower, but somehow it never got built. A few prisoners there tried to escape by crawling underneath a fence, but, as Paul Horn recalled it, "they didn't get very far."[92] The attempted escape in Moorhead was typical. Only a handful of the prisoners in Minnesota ever tried to "leave confinement without permission," and those who did were caught almost immediately.

Except in one case.

On the night of October 28, 1944, at the POW camp near Bena, two German prisoners—Heinz Schymalla and Walter Mai—stole away to nearby Lake Winnibigoshish and jumped into a rickety homemade boat that they had hidden in the rushes along the shore. The vessel was called the *Lili Marlene #10*, and it was the key to a naïve and wonderfully grandiose plan. Schymalla and Mai, working without even a basic knowledge of North American geography, had hatched a plot to paddle the *Lili Marlene #10* down the Mississippi River to New Orleans, where they would catch a ship to some neutral country. Five and a half days after their breakout, Schymalla and Mai were captured near Jay Gould Lake—about fourteen hundred miles north of New Orleans.[93]

News of the Bena escape reinforced some Minnesotans' misgivings about the POWs in their midst. Unions representing lumberjacks in the north and cannery workers in the south had always objected to POW labor, arguing that employers used the prisoners to keep wages artificially low. (According to historian Edward Pluth, there was "no evidence, at least in Minnesota, that prisoners of war displaced civilian labor.")[94] In the summer of 1944, a brief furor erupted when newspapers reported that the state had granted fishing licenses to some prisoners.[95] And for many Minnesotans, the mere sight of them was disconcerting. "One day I was walking down Main Street with my mother and she pushed me against a store front because there were two trucks of POWs coming towards us," recalled Jerome Burns, a native of western Minnesota. "Of course there were armed guards with them, but my mother was deathly afraid of any German."[96] In New Ulm, the prisoner camp at nearby Flandreau State Park was a constant source of controversy. Joyce Aufderheide—whose husband, Jack, had been taken prisoner in Europe—thought the Nazi POWs who occasionally worked at her family's brickyard were downright spooky.

> *They were the most arrogant bunch of soldiers that I have ever seen. There was one that was called Joe. And he had to be the meanest looking thing I have ever seen. I'd hate to meet him in the dark at night. Then there was a tall blond. He'd have made a good one for the movies. Blond, steely cold blue eyes, and just a grim-set mouth. I was really afraid of him. And if he was around I didn't linger.*[97]

Still, to most Minnesotans, the prisoners were merely exotic curiosities, best viewed from a distance. In Moorhead, the camp's commanding officer begged the city council to temporarily close an adjacent street because so many residents were driving by, hoping to glimpse a POW.[98] Those few Minnesotans who did encounter them often discovered that they were nothing like the Nazi monsters they had come to imagine. Faith Evers Sprung was pleasantly surprised when she and her husband hired prisoners from the Moorhead camp to work on their Clay County farm. "They were such nice fellows," she recalled. "One of them picked up my little boy—he was about three. He picked him up and he loved him and he said he thought he had a little boy about that age. He didn't know for sure. He hadn't heard. But he figured his little boy was about that age."[99]

For their part, many of the POWs grew fond of the people they met in Minnesota—and of the state itself. According to one camp inspector, those at the camp in Remer liked northern Minnesota "because it was 'shust like Germany.'"[100] The prisoners in Moorhead

Prisoners of war on a logging operation near Deer River, March 1945

were especially fond of Hank Peterson, who made a habit of bending military rules on fraternization. Peterson frequently bought beer for the POWs who worked for him, and on at least one occasion accompanied prisoners to a popular tavern called the Magic Aquarium.[101] After the war, Peterson received letters from several of the prisoners who had worked on his farm. One claimed that his time in Moorhead was the "best of my life."[102] "You may be sure," wrote another in broken English, "everyone who has been working with you remembers with pleasure that time of POW camp Moorhead."[103]

Al Hafner loved his wife, Milly, but he wasn't sure she had the makings of a successful businesswoman. The Hafners owned and operated Hafner's Ice Cream Shop on South Broadway in Rochester. Al handled the business end. Milly dealt with the customers. Both were comfortable with the arrangement, and they managed to do quite well for themselves, even after the war broke out. Then, in October of 1943, Al was drafted into the army and Milly was left to run the shop on her own. Over the next two years—during his postings at Fort Leonard Wood, Missouri, and Fort Lewis, Washington, and during non-combat assignments in France and the Philippines—Al wrote Milly dozens of letters, many revealing his skepticism about her management skills. To his astonishment, Milly proved to be a savvy businesswoman who turned the shop into a much bigger moneymaker than it ever had been when he was in charge.

Al Hafner with his dog, Pal, at home in Rochester.

November 15, 1943
(Fort Leonard Wood)

Don't work or worry [too] much about the store . . . I don't give a darn whether we have it after the war or not. We can get along without it so at the first sign that you can't handle it sell what you can and close it. All I want is to be sure to have you after the war like I left you.

November 18, 1943 (Fort Leonard Wood)

About the business don't worry about it and don't work too hard. As I told you in a previous letter what I want when this is over is you, just as pretty as you were when I left, and that is tops as far as I'm concerned.

November 22, 1943 (Fort Leonard Wood)

Gee, I wish I was there to help you out. It must be tough to be alone there when you don't know about stuff . . . And as I said in previous letters if the place crumbles around you jump out of the debris and let it lay. I want you in your old sweet self the way I left you and the H— with the store. We'll get along without it if it has to be.

December 9, 1943 (Fort Leonard Wood)

Sunday's receipts were certainly swell Honey. I guess [you're] going O.K. if you aren't killing yourself.

December 12, 1943 (Fort Leonard Wood)

The store must be going awfully good if the bank account is still around $3000.00 cus this time of year it usually starts slipping down.

December 28, 1943 (Fort Leonard Wood)

I just hope you get some help for the store. I can't imagine how lonesome it must feel to go down there alone without any girls coming to help you out. I feel so sorry for you and there isn't anything I can do to help you out except to write often and try to cheer you up. That don't help out physically tho, does it?

January 4, 1944 (Fort Leonard Wood)

You certainly are taking in a lot of money for being almost alone. I'll bet you are busy. Sometimes I can just see you "swishing" around.

January 12, 1944 (Fort Leonard Wood)

You surely are doing a stroke of business for [January]. That [Sunday] must have been a dilly with only three girls. You did as much business over the weekend as we did in a week the first year in Jan. So don't worry anymore about the customers forgetting us.

January 19, 1944 (Fort Leonard Wood)

How's the girl situation? I don't see how you can take in so much money with so little help. You must be working like a slave your self.

February 24, 1944 (Fort Leonard Wood)

I'm sorry you had to work so hard on [Sunday]. You're sure taking in a lot of money tho. Of course that's not much good when you have enough but it does mean you're doing an excellent job of something that's [too] big for one person to do. I hope you don't work [too] hard tho.

February 28, 1944 (Fort Leonard Wood)

Here it is [Sunday] afternoon and I'm wondering what you're doing now. I keep hoping you locked up but I don't suppose you did. I'm sitting here doing nothing and I wish I could help you out. If you have a chance to get rid of the store I think you'd better cus the help situation is terrific and it doesn't seem to be getting any better.

March 2, 1944 (Fort Leonard Wood)

Say, dear, those customers you'd like to "sock in the puss" go ahead and do it. You've got [too] many customers anyway. A few "socks" and you could handle them easier.

March 5, 1944 (Fort Leonard Wood)

We certainly made "hay" in that store last year didn't we? My gosh that's a lot of money (profit) in one year and I wasn't there hardly at all.

May 15, 1944 (Fort Leonard Wood)

I'm so sorry to hear that you lost two more girls. It just seems as tho we just couldn't make it go anymore. I've been thinking all morning about what to do. This is the conclusion I've come to. If you can get $13,000.00 for it lets sell it . . . I can always do something after the war and with that much money we could pay up the house and have some left to last thru the war. It just doesn't seem to be worth the effort to try to keep it running if you can't get any help.

June 8, 1944 (Fort Leonard Wood)
Gee Honey I'm being overwhelmed with $25.00 checks here. Not that I don't like them but I thought one was awful good and lo & behold today I get another. Thank you so much Darling. I'm going to call you in the morning and see if you struck "gold or oil" up there. I think its just cus you love me tho. I love you too but I don't hardly ever get fifty dollars to send you. You always have to make your own money.

September 25, 1944 (Fort Lewis)
Honey if you can spare it I could use some money again . . . I sure hate to write for money all the time. I should have enough so I could live within my income but I guess I'm a spendthrift.

October 4, 1944 (Fort Lewis)
Honey I've been wondering what your [sic] going to tell that popcorn [company] when you send back that popcorn with the rat turds in it? I suppose you could tell them that it had a lot of black kernels that don't want to pop . . . Too bad you can't use it when its so hard to get.

October 11, 1944 (Fort Lewis)
That checkbook certainly is doing O.K. by gosh. I can't see but what I'll have to come home and spend some . . . I'm so lucky— and I know it too—to be able to write for money when I need it.

October 18, 1944 (Fort Lewis)
You certainly are coining money in the store lately. That [Sunday] figure of $245.00 is really a record for [October] . . . You're certainly doing a swell job tho [despite] the help situation. It just boils down to the fact that you're doing all yourself.

October 22, 1944 (Fort Lewis)
Honey you can buy all the dresses you want. You're making the money [and are] keeping me supplied so you can spend some for clothes I hope.

December 14, 1944 (Fort Lewis)
That popcorn is surely doing a bang up job isn't it? Fifty dollars used to be a week's receipts instead of a day.

March 7, 1945 (Fort Lewis)
You surely didn't need to worry about money at the store this winter. Here it is March and you have almost $5,000.00 and besides you were gone a month.

May 1, 1945 (France)
I see what used to be a record breaking day at the store is now considered a light day. I wish I could be there as it would be fun when business is that good. Did I say fun?

June 5, 1945 (France)
Don't hesitate to close part or all of [the store] when the going gets rough and I hope you can get power of attorney soon so you can sell it if you want to. I slipped up horribly on that.

August 11, 1945 (Philippines)
Congratulations on your nerve in firing Ferd. I don't know your reason but you didn't need anymore than you already had so regardless of what it was this time its good riddance. Just how you can get along now is beyond me cus it sounds as tho you were working pretty hard yourself. Just don't forget that you have the key and no matter what happens its O.K. with me. I'm proud of you honey.[1]

4 Arsenals of Democracy

The 1943 Minnesota State Fair was a hodgepodge of patriotic spectacle and end-of-summer frivolity. The "On to Victory" grandstand show was a "sparkling, fast-moving patriotic revue" with fireworks and a simulated tank battle. The 710th Military Police Battalion mounted a "War Show" featuring marching troops, staged military maneuvers, and four-legged representatives of the Army's canine corps. The horses ran as usual at the Grandstand, with Highlawn K setting a record in the two-twenty pace. Crowds flocked to the carnival—which had been moved to Machinery Hill—and to the Fine Arts, Women's Activities, 4-H Club, Agriculture, Horticulture, Conservation, Dairy, and States exhibitions. It was, in short, just about as good a state fair as one could hope for in the middle of a global conflagration. Still, something was missing: the livestock. There were no horses, cattle, sheep, swine, poultry, or goats. The animals had been evicted for the duration, and the war was to blame.[1]

Seven of the fair's most popular destinations—the Cattle Barn, the Horse Barn, the Swine and Sheep Barn, the Poultry, Commissary, and Arcade buildings, and the Hippodrome—were now off-limits to fairgoers. The Army Corps of Engineers had taken them over two months earlier and was in the process of changing them almost beyond recognition. The facing ends of the Cattle Barn and the Hippodrome had been ripped off to make way for a covered walkway. Dirt floors were being replaced by thick slabs of concrete. An eighty-foot smokestack rose near the Horse Barn. Concrete blocks sealed up the windows of the Arcade Building. The fair's entire livestock area looked like a cross between a military installation and a manufacturing facility.[2]

And in fact that's exactly what it was.

The southwest corner of the fairgrounds was now home to the army's newest aircraft propeller plant. The facility was operated by the A. O. Smith Company, a Milwaukee blacksmithing and metalworking firm. By the summer of 1944, the plant employed several hundred people and produced about five thousand propeller blades a month. (The finished propellers were made for warplanes such as the P-47 Thunderbolt and its navy counterpart, the SB2C-1 Helldiver.) The plant had a curious distinction: it was the nation's only war production facility housed in "buildings erected in peace time expressly for farm exhibits, horse shows and recreation."[3]

During the previous five years, the state's political and business leaders had lobbied heavily for what they considered Minnesota's fair share of the billions of dollars being spent on the nation's military buildup. The State Fair propeller plant was a direct result of those efforts, but it was certainly not the only one. Hundreds of Minnesota firms converted to war production during the late 1930s

Aerial view of the Minnesota State Fairgrounds, circa 1945

and early 1940s, and the contracts they secured helped revive an economy that had been devastated by the Great Depression.

The big push to bring national defense work to Minnesota had begun during the second half of 1940. In August of that year, Governor Harold Stassen joined a group of Midwest leaders in demanding that their states receive a "proper share" of government outlays. "This is not a cry for pork," the group declared in a resolution sent to the White House. "It is the voice of the middle west asking for justice." In a letter to the state's U.S. senators, Henrik Shipstead and Joseph Ball, Stassen complained that Minnesota was still "not securing her full share of national defense contracts." But by late 1940, the situation was beginning to change. In November, the National Defense Advisory Commission (later known as the Office of Production Management, or OPM) opened a field office in Minneapolis to coordinate the distribution of defense contracts in the Midwest. A few months later, Stassen appointed a full-time lobbyist to press Minnesota's case in Washington. By June 1941, the amount spent on prime defense contracts in Minnesota had risen to about $43 million—up from just half a million in mid-1940. Minnesota still ranked thirty-first among the states in prime contract spending, but state officials were encouraged by the increase.[4]

The bulk of the money spent on defense work in Minnesota went to a handful of major contractors, including Northern Pump Company (naval anti-aircraft guns), Oliver Mining Company (iron ore), Federal Cartridge Corporation (small arms ammunition), American Steel & Wire Company (barbed wire), Minneapolis-Honeywell (precision instruments such as telescopic sights and periscopes), Minneapolis-Moline Power Implement Company (artillery shells), and International Harvester (machine guns). But most contracts awarded to Minnesota companies were much smaller—some were as tiny as nineteen dollars apiece. Crown Iron Works Company landed several contracts to make portable bridges. D. W. Onan & Sons made generators and battery chargers. Faribault Woolen Mills and North Star Woolen Mills both produced blankets for the army. Munsingwear, Inc. made wool undershirts. Two Winona firms—J. R. Watkins and McConnon & Company—packaged tins of DDT powder (GIs sprinkled the powder in their underwear to kill body lice). Diamond Match Company of Cloquet produced propaganda-carrying matchbooks that were dropped from planes behind enemy lines (the matchbook messages described how to sabotage railways and supply depots).[5] American Gas Machine of Albert Lea made lanterns and portable stoves for

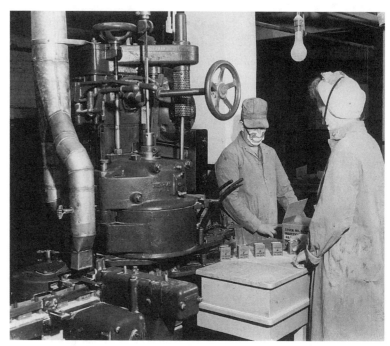

The J. R. Watkins Company in Winona produced 10 million two-ounce tins of DDT in 1945 alone. The company continued to make DDT-based insecticides after the war.

military use. Plants in fourteen southern Minnesota communities, including Jackson, Mapleton, and Blooming Prairie, contracted with the federal government to process locally grown hemp, which was used in the manufacture of heavy rope for the army and navy.[6] While some companies contracted to make products similar to the ones they manufactured during peacetime, many others took on much more radical conversions. An artificial limb company in Minneapolis switched to making parachute folding tools. A hearing aid firm made airplane signaling devices. A refrigerator company stamped out doors for navy ships.[7]

In a report to the governor and the legislature, Herbert L. Miller, Minnesota's official lobbyist in Washington, predicted that the state would continue to land important defense contracts—if only because it was now demanding its fair share. "Official Washington is now quite cognizant of the dissatisfaction which exists in this State so far as its portion of defense business secured to date is concerned," he wrote. "In view of the attitude now held in Washington that work must be spread around, those who wish prime contracts will find in many quarters a very pronounced desire on the part of officials to award more prime contracts in our region."[8] In the end, the state was more successful in securing war-related contracts than most Minnesotans—including Herbert Miller—could have expected. Its eventual $1.6 billion in war supply contracts ranked eighteenth among the forty-eight states.[9]

The Pirate

Many of the stories told around the Twin Cities about Northern Pump Company president John Blackstock Hawley, Jr., were undoubtedly apocryphal, but one tale in particular seemed to sum up the man. As the story went, Hawley once threw an elaborate banquet and invited some of the area's most prominent business leaders to be his guests. He wined them. He dined them. And then he stood up to make what many of the guests assumed would be an obligatory toast. But Hawley had other ideas. "You guys have probably been wondering for hours why I invited you here," he said to the assembled crowd. "You hate my guts. I hate yours. Well, I'll tell you why I asked you—just to tell you all to go plumb to hell."[10]

John B. Hawley, Jr., liked to tell people to go to hell, and he did it often. He was a Texas-born transplant who didn't seem to care what

The Northern Pump Company fitted several of its gun mounts with dummy barrels in this wartime publicity photo.

other people thought. And while his brashness didn't always go over well with the more subdued Minnesotans he did business with, it did help him turn Northern Pump into the nation's largest naval gun-maker.

Hawley had joined Northern Pump in 1924 after graduating from Cornell University with a degree in civil engineering. He was a tinkerer and an inventor, and in 1928 he sold an invention to Northern Pump in exchange for a controlling interest in the firm. He became president, and in the 1930s began transforming the company into something closer to his grand dreams. Before Hawley took control, Northern Pump had been an unassuming firm with some fifty employees, most making pumps for fire engines. But in the mid-1930s, Hawley landed a contract to manufacture submersible pumps and other hydraulic equipment for the U.S. Navy. Northern Pump's payroll jumped to about two hundred, and its plant on Central Avenue in Minneapolis suddenly seemed very cramped.[11]

In 1940, with war raging in Europe and the United States engaged in a massive rearmament, Hawley went after a much bigger prize—a contract to build anti-aircraft guns for the navy. His sales pitch was typically grandiose. "I'm the only man who can defend America," he said. And while his boast was hyperbolic, it did carry a touch of truth. The fact was that, unlike many other cities across the country, the Minneapolis–St. Paul area still had plenty of highly skilled machinists available for war work. Hawley assured the navy that he could assemble a labor force capable of the precision work demanded of an arms manufacturer. He begged the navy to give him a chance and, eventually, the navy agreed. It awarded Northern Pump $50 million in contracts, the biggest of which called for one hundred five-inch .38-caliber gun mounts (each mount was essentially a self-contained weapon system, minus the barrel).

With the signing of the contracts, Northern Pump's Central Avenue plant was officially obsolete. The company acquired a 350-acre site in Fridley, just north of Minneapolis, and construction of a new $5 million production facility began in October 1940. By the fall of 1941, Northern Pump's workforce had swelled to around four thousand, and the Fridley plant was churning out "ack-acks" at a rate of one a day. (In British signalman's letter code, "ack" stood for "A"; "ack-ack" thus meant "AA," which was short for anti-aircraft.) Visitors, like the *Minneapolis Star Journal*'s Cedric Adams, marveled at the vastness of the facility and the sight of workers toiling around the clock.[12]

It's an amazing experience. You gasp at the production. You thrill to the spirit. You're bewildered by the complexity. But through it all you see a Victory purpose in the complete co-ordination of the personnel . . . The plant has the only moving gun mount assembly in the world. There are 30,000 separate pieces being made out there. One of the best lathe men is a one-armed fellow. Oldest man on the assembly line is 80. There are 55 men with at least three fingers off. Nine men have artificial legs.[13]

The navy was ecstatic about Northern Pump's performance (by the spring of 1942, production at the plant was already two years ahead of schedule), but many other manufacturers in the Twin Cities area were resentful. They accused Hawley of "scamping"— siphoning skilled machinists from a finite labor pool, using "fabulous wages"[14] as an incentive. In fact, Northern Pump paid its machinists only about five cents an hour more than the Twin Cities average. The incentives to work there lay elsewhere. Chief among the company's attractions was its overtime policy. Hawley paid his workers time and a half after logging forty hours, and Northern Pump machinists routinely worked twelve hours a day six or seven days a week. Workers joked that the company offered "silk-shirt wages with no time to wear the shirt."[15] When the wife of one Northern Pump employee wrote to a newspaper columnist protesting her husband's work schedule, Hawley responded with a letter of his own.

You might also advise this wife that we have a waiting list of 15,000 men all over the United States, who are bending every effort to get a job in this plant because we have the reputation of letting every man serve his country to the utmost.

We are adequately supplied with every known form of labor saving machinery and 80 per cent of the men do a minimum of physical work. There are no piece work or incentive systems and if a man does not feel well, he does not have to come to work. If this place is not the worker's paradise for fine parking lot, clean washrooms, good food, excellent hospital, good lighting, etc., then it is the fault of John B. Hawley, Jr., president, because the navy gave him 100 per cent free hand to provide the finest machine shop in the world.[16]

Hawley boasted that he hired only the most experienced and skilled machinists, but his selectiveness yielded a workforce that was overwhelmingly male and white—much more so than most defense contractors at the time. Women were relegated to support roles ("good-looking girls, called 'servettes,' move through the shop selling cigarettes and soft drinks," the *Saturday Evening Post* observed),[17] and minorities were virtually nonexistent. In April of 1942, under steady pressure from the Minneapolis Urban League, Northern Pump finally hired three African American construction workers, but a year later a survey found that those three employees were still the only African Americans working at the plant. A representative from the federal War Manpower Commission visited the plant after the agency received complaints about the company's hiring practices, but his visit had no discernible effect. The African American

Minneapolis Spokesman, *August 29, 1941*

newspaper the *Minneapolis Spokesman* lamented Northern Pump's hiring record, pointing out that three African Americans out of a total workforce of about seventy-five hundred was not a ratio that any company should be proud of.[18] Charles Washington, executive director of the Minneapolis Urban League, wrote that "it seems fairly obvious that the plan is to exclude Negroes from all avenues of employment by this company."[19] Hawley refused to comment publicly about the dearth of African American workers at his plant, but many of his critics believed he revealed his true colors when he twice used the word "nigger" in a speech broadcast by KSTP radio.[20]

Hawley solidified his reputation as a wartime maverick when he took on the federal government in an effort to increase his company's profits. Under the 1942 Renegotiation Act, the War, Navy, and Treasury Departments had the power to recoup "excessive" profits from defense contractors, and Hawley was one of the first contractors to run afoul of the new law. In June of 1943, after months of negotiations, Hawley agreed to refund the navy $16 million of his profits for 1941 and 1942, but he wasn't happy about it. In testimony before the House Naval Committee, Hawley claimed that he'd been subjected to "Nazi justice" by the navy's price adjustment board and that his profit for the previous two years had been slashed to 2 percent—not nearly enough to ensure Northern Pump's survival during postwar reconversion. Hawley had hoped his testimony would spark a movement to repeal renegotiation, but his efforts backfired. Under the committee's questioning, Hawley revealed that his salary had jumped from $21,000 in 1937 to $448,000 in 1941 (he later volunteered to retroactively reduce that amount to $25,000).[21]

To many people, Hawley suddenly looked more like a war profiteer than a production miracle man. The rumor spread that he owned a yacht named "Navy Gravy." Hawley couldn't understand why people didn't appreciate his position. "This profiteering stuff is just a lot of numbers," he said. "Today I've got an inventory of ten or fifteen million dollars. What happens if the war ends tomorrow?"[22]

The war dragged on for two more years after the navy got its refund, and Hawley seemed to manage quite well. He created a new subsidiary, Northern Ordnance, Inc., to continue the company's gun-making business, and then used his wartime profits to turn Northern Pump into "the biggest driller of wildcat oil wells in the U.S." Hawley admitted he didn't know much about the oil business, but the man who described himself as "the world's greatest hydraulic engineer" seemed as supremely confident as ever. "Oilmen are a bunch of fuddy-duddies," he said. "I'm a pirate."[23]

Shipshape

To those unacquainted with the shipbuilding business, Minnesota must have seemed a strange place to build oceangoing vessels for the war effort. Why would anyone want to build warships in a place so far removed from salt water? (The Atlantic, the Pacific, and the Gulf of Mexico are all more than one thousand miles away.) And even if ships were built in Minnesota, how would they be launched during the winter when the lakes and rivers were frozen? Under normal circumstances, Minnesota's location and climate probably would have kept its shipbuilding activity to a minimum. But these were not normal times. In a speech to Congress one month after the Pearl Harbor attack, President Roosevelt declared that the Allies' superiority in munitions and ships must be "overwhelming— so overwhelming that the Axis nations can never hope to catch up with it." His goal for the nation's shipyards: eighteen million dead-weight tons of merchant ships over the next two years. (In 1941, U.S. shipbuilders had produced just over one million tons.)[24] Coastal shipyards would assume the great bulk of that burden, but there was no way they could achieve Roosevelt's staggering production goals on their own. They would need help from shipbuilders in "inland" states such as Minnesota.

When it came to building ships, Duluth was about the only place in Minnesota that came immediately to mind. It and its twin port, Superior, Wisconsin, had a long, albeit sporadic, shipbuilding tradition. At one point during the late 1800s and early 1900s, Duluth-Superior was widely considered "the key ship producing area in the country"—with the possible exception of Newport News, Virginia.[25] During World War I, the Twin Ports yards maintained their shipbuilding reputation by building more than one hundred vessels, mostly freighters.[26] But that reputation soon faded. During the 1920s and 1930s, ship construction at the Head of the Lakes virtually stopped. The industry there seemed to be on the verge of extinction. It might have vanished altogether if war hadn't broken out.

In the months before the Pearl Harbor attack, Duluth's oldest shipyard, Marine Iron & Shipbuilding Co., landed the Twin Ports' first World War II–era military contract—an order for two 180-foot coast guard cutters. It was a sign of things to come. In the months that followed, five other shipyards at the Head of the Lakes—two more in Duluth and three in Superior—went to work building ships at a furious pace for the U.S. Navy and Coast Guard. Marine Iron and its neighbor, Zenith Dredge, split a contract and spent most of

the war constructing coast guard cutters similar to the ones that
Marine Iron built under its initial order. The other Duluth shipyard,
Barnes-Duluth Shipbuilding Company (later known as Walter Butler–Duluth), secured a series of contracts to produce much larger
ships—tankers and cargo carriers that were too large for the St.
Lawrence Waterway; instead they had to snake their way to sea by
way of the Illinois and Mississippi Rivers.

The three Duluth shipyards and the three across the bay recruited workers from all over the region. Labor shortages were
chronic and the competition for workers was fierce—so fierce that
the Walter Butler and Globe shipyards in Superior sent buses as far
as Hinckley and Aitkin, Minnesota, to pick up workers.[27] Most of
the employees had never seen a shipyard before, but they learned
fast. They had to. "What I was amazed at was how people could
adapt," one Globe foreman recalled. "I had housepainters on my
crew and farmers, mostly farmers I would say, and people from all
walks of life that came and all of a sudden they were a mechanic or
a welder or a burner or whatever."[28] They worked as much as twelve
hours a day, sometimes seven days a week. Many went to their regular jobs during the day and worked on the ships at night.

The pace of work at the shipyards was frenetic. "I thought I'd
kicked off the top of an ant hill, there were so many people running
around," one Globe employee recalled.[29] Shipyards clamored to set
production records. At Walter Butler, where the SS *Frank Dale* was
launched in a record twenty-three days after its keel was laid, the
unofficial slogan was "speed and more speed."[30]

The hectic pace and the inexperience of the workforce combined
to create occasional problems on the shipyards. "It was really bad,"
recalled labor leader Edwin Drill. "People did so much in such a
short while that there wasn't time to train these people or to get organized with the machinery to operate it right, and yet they were
still putting out stuff."[31] One welder at the Globe yard remembered
looking up at an unfinished ship and seeing a crack in the hull running from top to bottom. "There may have been two hundred
welders working on it, all over the place," she said. "Nobody was
thinking about any sequence of welding or planning for any sequence of welding."[32] Sometimes the pace grew so hectic that workers welded themselves into small spaces so that they could relax on
the job without being bothered.[33]

Still, the shipyards' performance was a source of pride—for the
workers, and for the cities of Duluth and Superior. A writer for
Skillings' Mining Review observed that the launchings in particular

remained awesome spectacles, even though they had, by the summer of 1942, become "somewhat routine."

> *The people at the Head of the Lakes are as keen today to witness a launching as when the shipbuilding companies began consigning new boats to their natural element a year ago. Shipbuilding is in the blood of the people of Duluth-Superior. Shipbuilding is linked with the early days of both Duluth and Superior. It is being conducted now, in support of the war effort, on a larger scale than ever before, and there are more units engaged in the industry here than ever before.*[34]

Most of the 191 ships produced at the Duluth-Superior yards between 1941 and 1945 were launched sideways—a method that required a minimum of real estate. Workers waxed and greased the huge twenty-four-by-eighteen-inch timbers—called sliding ways—that lay between the blocks on which the keel was laid. At the as-

The launching of the coastal cargo ship David R. LeCraw *at Barnes-Duluth Shipbuilding in 1944*

signed moment, dozens of men armed with sledgehammers began driving wedges under the sliding ways until they lifted the keel off its blocks. The men then knocked the blocks away and ran from beneath the vessel as fast as they could. At that point, the ship was being held in place only by a hawser. On the signal, the ship's sponsor cracked a bottle of champagne (or, in the case of the Globe Shipyards, a bottle of locally produced beer) on the bow, and the launch master pressed a button that dropped a guillotine on the hawser. The ship, now free of all restraints, slid down the ways and crashed into the water. "We always felt that they might not bounce back, [that they would fall] straight over on their sides," recalled one longtime Superior resident. "But something powerful made them bounce back. They always did."[35]

While Duluth could rightfully claim to be Minnesota's shipbuilding epicenter, it was not the only community in the state to construct ships during the war. Minnesota had one other major shipyard, and it was in a most unlikely location.

The Minnesota grain trading firm of Cargill Incorporated had entered the shipbuilding business in 1937 when it started constructing its own grain-hauling barges at a yard in Albany, New York. The barges were state of the art, capable of carrying twice as much grain at half the cost of similar vessels. They were the envy of the industry. Encouraged by its success with the barges (and with the successful launch of a huge oceangoing grain carrier in 1941), Cargill executives decided to pursue wartime shipbuilding contracts with the U.S. government. In March of 1942, the efforts paid off, landing a contract to build six 300-foot auxiliary oil and gasoline tankers (AOGS) for the navy. While the contract was a coup for Cargill, its most noteworthy detail was the project's location. Cargill had decided to abandon its shipyard in Albany for a new one in the small Minnesota River town of Savage.

Savage was a strange location for a shipyard. *Time* magazine described the decision to build ships there as a typical Cargill move.

Farmers in the grain-growing north know Cargill, Inc. as one of the world's biggest, most audacious grain companies with a hankering as big as its elevators for taking on unconventional jobs, rushing them through by unconventional tricks. But when Cargill began buying farm and meadowland along the tree-shaded Minnesota River near Savage, Minn . . . even Cargill-wise farmers hooted at the fantastic reason: Cargill was going to set up a shipyard to build ocean-going vessels. They had some excuse for hooting. Savage is 14 water miles from the Mississippi. For most of those 14 winding miles, the Minnesota was barely 3½ ft. deep.[36]

Cargill planned to overcome the problems posed by the shallow waters of the Minnesota River by dredging a nine-foot channel from the shipyard in Savage to the confluence of the Minnesota and the Mississippi. The Army Corps of Engineers would do the work. Cargill would cover most of the cost. Still, many Minnesotans couldn't believe that Cargill was proposing what appeared to be a

The Agawam *passes through the Lyndale Avenue drawbridge on its maiden voyage down the Minnesota River, November 5, 1943.*

colossal folly. "It is hard for me to understand why vessels of any description whatsoever should be launched on a small muddy stream such as the Minnesota river," wrote one *St. Paul Dispatch* reader. "It is equally hard to understand why the government should have even considered placing a shipyard at a point where heavy dredging must be undertaken before the ships can be moved."[37]

Despite the public's misgivings, Cargill went ahead with its plans. It broke ground on the new shipyard in April of 1942 and laid keels for all six of its contracted AOGs the following September. By May of 1943, it was ready to launch its first tanker. As the company band played and the assembled crowd cheered, the *Agawam* slid smoothly into the dredged-out Minnesota, sending a "miniature tidal wave"[38] onto the opposite shore. The *Agawam*, which at that point was not much more than an empty hull, was then moved into an adjacent slip for several months of additional fitting. Port Cargill, as it was now known, buzzed with activity as workers swarmed over six tankers in various states of completion. Finally, in early November, the *Agawam* was ready for delivery to the navy.

Now came the tricky part. Could the 300-foot *Agawam* squeeze through the fourteen miles of twists and turns that constituted the Minnesota River between Savage and the Mississippi? If Cargill officials knew the answer, they kept it to themselves. "The first trip is the one on which you learn how it should be done," said one.[39]

The *Agawam* was, by this time, "complete down to its guns." The only things missing were its masts. (They had been laid on deck to help the ship fit under all the bridges it would encounter on its long journey to New Orleans.) On the morning of November 5, 1943, the towboat *Demopolis* began pushing the *Agawam* down the serpentine Minnesota, a small fleet of tugs providing escort. At several crucial points along the way, crews armed with trucks and cables stood by, ready to pull the tanker out of trouble should it run aground. But their help was never needed. The *Agawam* arrived in St. Paul that afternoon, following just one brief delay at the Cedar Avenue Bridge. The *St. Paul Pioneer Press*, which from the beginning had questioned the viability of the Savage enterprise, hailed the event. "A sleek gray ship, whose cavernous insides may carry fuel for planes to blast Germany or Japan, arrived in St. Paul," it reported. "Fears that the vessel would be grounded on the turns of the Minnesota river . . . proved baseless."[40]

Over the next two years, Port Cargill turned out eighteen AOGs and four towboats for the government. At peak production, the shipyard employed about thirty-five hundred people.

Financially speaking, Port Cargill was a failure (the company reported a $230,000 loss on the shipyard during its four years of operation), but Cargill apparently never expected to make money on its shipbuilding enterprise. In 1943, John Cargill, Jr., told a group of employees that the company had taken up shipbuilding out of a sense of patriotic duty. "The reward which we obtain for this effort lies solely in the feeling of pride we have in making sacrifices for the war effort," he said.[41] Still, in the end, Port Cargill turned out to be more than just a patriotic lark. Half a century later, the company was still using the old shipyard—and the channel that the Army Corps of Engineers had dredged during the war—to move grain and other products from the heart of Minnesota to destinations worldwide.

Either Ore

Many optimistic Americans felt confident that their country would eventually prevail in the war, in part by simply outproducing its enemies. Neither Germany nor Japan, the feeling went, could keep up with the United States when it came to manufacturing bullets, guns, tanks, and warships. America possessed the industrial might to outlast the Axis powers. It also had the raw material to keep its war industries humming—a seemingly limitless supply of iron ore, most of which came from Minnesota's Mesabi Iron Range. "Mr. Hitler is wasting his time," wrote one particularly giddy iron range booster. "The marvelous little Mesabi makes it impossible for him to win."[42]

There was just one problem with the optimists' argument: the easy-to-mine, high-grade ore, for which the Mesabi was so famous, was running out. Few people in or out of government knew this uncomfortable fact when the war began. It took a single-minded professor—a "masculine Cassandra of the Minnesota iron ore business"[43]—to bring the problem to light.

People who knew Edward W. "Bud" Davis often described him as quiet, unassuming, and modest. But the adjective they used most consistently was stubborn. In 1913, while teaching at the University of Minnesota School of Mines, Davis was handed "a sack of rough greenish-gray rock" and told to figure out whether it had any practical use. The sack was filled with taconite—an extremely hard rock from the area between Mesaba and Birch Lake on the eastern Mesabi Range. A few people believed that the future of Minnesota's iron ore industry now lay in taconite, not in the high-grade ore. But first, someone had to invent an efficient way to extract the small amount of iron that was embedded in the taconite.[44]

For the better part of a quarter-century, Davis learned every-thing there was to know about taconite. Early on he and his colleagues at the Mines Experiment Station realized that they would have to crush the rock into fine powder before they could separate the iron from it. After solving that problem, they had to come up with a way to concentrate the extracted ore into a commercially viable form. By 1922 Davis' team had devised a concentration process, and a company called Mesabi Iron was churning out ore at a taconite processing plant in Babbitt. The process, however, turned out to be too expensive, and the plant closed a year later. After that, Minnesota's taconite industry was "very dead for a long time."[45]

During the rest of the 1920s and most of the 1930s, Davis kept experimenting with taconite, convinced he could improve its cost-efficiency. Over time, he developed a new process in which the extracted iron was formed into golf ball–sized pellets. All the while he kept preaching the wonders of taconite to anyone who would listen. But he didn't make much progress. It wasn't until 1941 that he hit upon an argument that resonated with people from the iron ranges of Minnesota to the halls of government in Washington: Taconite was a key to economic survival and national security.

Davis launched his new public relations campaign on behalf of taconite with a series of talks in January of 1941. For a scientist steeped in geological and engineering minutiae, he kept his arguments admirably simple. The Mesabi's high-grade ores "were rapidly being

E. W. ("Bud") Davis, circa 1940

exhausted," he said, due in large part to the country's growing defense needs.[46] But there was good news, too, he told his audiences. The Mesabi still had an essentially limitless supply of low-grade ore—taconite. If mining companies could be convinced to take a chance on taconite, the nation would never again run out of iron, and the communities on Minnesota's iron ranges would enjoy economic stability for years to come. The question was how to get companies to take that chance.

Davis' first recommendation was an overhaul of the state's tax laws. At the time, companies that owned Minnesota iron ore deposits had to pay the state an ad valorem tax for every ton of ore that remained in the ground. High-grade ore was taxed at a higher rate than low-grade ore, and as a result, companies usually mined the best ores first (thus removing them from tax rolls), while leaving poorer ones behind. This tax, Davis argued, did more than anything else to discourage mining companies from taking the leap into taconite processing. Davis urged residents on the iron ranges to take the initiative and push for repeal of the ad valorem tax on iron ore, even though iron ore taxes were what he called "the very lifeblood of the range communities."[47] "It is time you were made acquainted with your predicament so that you can do something about it," he said. Mining companies would stay away from taconite, he insisted, "until you change your ways."[48] His arguments struck a chord. Iron range leaders threw their support behind new legislation to revise the state's mineral leasing program and repeal the ad valorem tax on unmined iron ore. A few months later, Governor Harold Stassen signed the legislation into law.

Now Davis turned his attention to the federal government. With the nation at war, Davis knew that his next argument had real urgency, and he made the most of the opportunity.

On April 15, 1942, Davis appeared before a committee of the War Production Board (WPB) and made a sobering prediction: at the current rate of wartime production, the Mesabi Range's supply of high-grade iron ore would begin drying up by the end of the decade. "It is shocking to realize," Davis said, "that in a comparatively few years, the great steel industry dependent on Lake [Superior] shipments will find itself short of the necessary ore to meet emergency steel requirements."[49] The solution, Davis said, was for the government to throw its weight behind a new push to turn taconite into a viable source of iron ore. He asked the WPB to approve a plan to let the newly formed Reserve Mining Company begin testing taconite concentration methods at the old processing plant in Babbitt.[50] The WPB eventually denied the request, saying that the country needed to invest in technologies that would pay immediate dividends. But Davis had accomplished his larger goal. The nation now realized that it was facing an impending shortage of iron ore.

Suddenly Davis was something of a celebrity. His bespectacled visage appeared often in Minnesota newspapers. National magazines such as *Business Week* and the *Saturday Evening Post* trumpeted his warnings about the Mesabi's depleted ore reserves and speculated on the future of the steel industry if the war dragged on too long.[51] Senator Harry Truman of Missouri praised Davis' work and criticized the WPB for failing to recognize taconite's potential. Mining companies that once considered Davis "a visionary radical" now regarded him as an important ally, especially after he persuaded the iron range communities to back the repeal of the ad valorem tax.[52]

As the war progressed, Davis' predictions looked increasingly accurate. In 1942, iron ore shipments from the Mesabi topped seventy million tons.[53] While wartime production never again reached that level, it continued at a near-record pace. It was increasingly clear that the Mesabi would begin running out of high-grade ore by the early 1950s if wartime production rates held steady.

In the end, the nation never had to confront the iron ore crisis that might have been. When the war ended, the Mesabi still had millions of tons of high-grade ore available for mining. But those tons would vanish quickly in any postwar construction boom. Mining

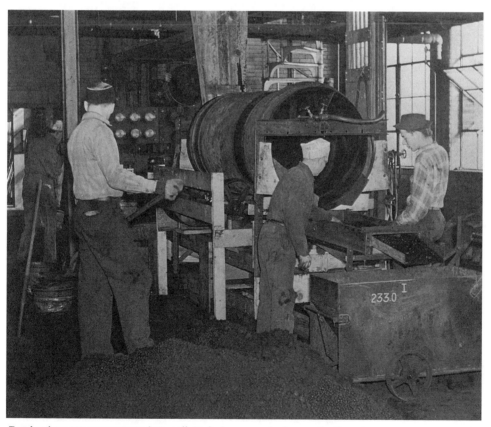

Turning iron ore concentrate into pellets during an early demonstration at the Mines Experiment Station in April 1943.

companies were already positioning themselves to take advantage of the taconite processing advances that Davis and his colleagues at the Mines Experiment Station had made during the previous decade.

In 1945, residents in the North Shore town of Beaver Bay began noticing that someone was buying up land around the bus stop at nearby Silver Bay. Rumors started spreading: a large resort was in the works, or maybe a golf course. A year later, in October of 1946, the truth finally emerged. Reserve Mining Company announced that it planned to build a huge taconite processing plant in Silver Bay and a new taconite mining operation in Babbitt. Suddenly, the glowing predictions of wartime taconite booster Arthur Dudley Gillett didn't seem quite so far-fetched.

If they are successful we shall be able to beneficiate 57 million tons of ore and our Marvelous Mesabi will be active for a thousand years. America will continue to be the outstanding industrial nation of the world. We shall be able to protect democracy against any future Hitlers. Our industrial production will continue to increase. If we keep our people employed our annual production of wealth will surpass our wildest dreams. We shall have both good wages and adequate profits. We shall achieve

The Hull-Rust Mine in Hibbing. In the record-setting year of 1942, Hibbing's mines produced 27 million tons of iron ore.

universal happiness and prosperity. Thus will Dr. E. W. Davis
be vindicated. He will not achieve great wealth for himself; but
we shall record him as one of the benefactors of mankind.[54]

Reserve's Silver Bay plant would produce its first taconite pellets
in 1955. The plant would be known as the E. W. Davis Works.

Sweating Bullets

On the evening of September 19, 1942, the hundreds of night-shift
workers at the Twin Cities Ordnance Plant (TCOP) in New Brighton
were buzzing with anticipation. They had been told to arrive an
hour early so they'd be ready to welcome a very important visitor.
The visitor's identity was a secret. Only those who had to know,
knew. But everybody had an opinion about who the guest might
be. Most employees thought that the VIP was probably a high-
ranking general, come to boost morale at the plant. A few were bet-
ting that he was a big-shot civilian—a senator, maybe. But there
was one thing no one could figure out: what was it about this mystery guest that made it necessary to put a hole in the back wall of
Building 103?

Outside the plant, Charles Horn was growing impatient. Horn
was not used to being made to wait. He was the kind of man who
made others wait for him, who got his own way. Horn had managed
through sheer tenacity to convince the government to let him and
his company—Federal Cartridge Corporation—run what was to be
the biggest government-owned defense plant in the state, and after
landing the contract, he had done things his way: efficiently. Horn
readily admitted that he had no interest in employee relations or
morale.[55] He was concerned only with good product and good
profit. He didn't like to waste money and he didn't like to waste
time. But as he stood outside the plant that evening, that's exactly
what he felt he was doing—wasting time. It was, he would later
write, "the longest hour."[56]

Finally, at about eleven o'clock, a train engine drawing eight
darkened rail cars pulled slowly into the TCOP grounds, coming to a
stop near gate 106A. Moments later, a host of distinguished-looking
people stepped off the train—"so many important personages,"
wrote a reporter for the plant's newsletter, "that there is not a man
alive in the Twin Cities who knows who they all were."[57] But no one
had trouble identifying the man who disembarked last. President
Franklin Roosevelt looked "exactly like I had expected him to look,"

Charles Horn wrote. "A genial smile, the introduction, a hearty hand shake and we were ready for business."[58]

A car was waiting for the president, and he slipped into the front passenger seat. Horn joined Minnesota Governor Harold Stassen in the back. In no time at all, they were passing through the hole in Building 103's back wall and into the heart of the TCOP ammunition works.

Word of the president's arrival spread quickly through the building. Some workers waved as the car inched down the production line. A few cheered. But most, wanting to make a good impression,

TCOP "forelady" Peggy Johlfs presents a package of gold-plated cartridges to President Franklin D. Roosevelt during his tour of the plant on September 19, 1942.

merely stole quick glimpses of the president and then turned back to their work. One worker, Earl Olson, was so oblivious that when the car pulled up to his workbench, he literally dropped his monkey wrench and yelled, "My God, there's the President!"[59]

As the car moved down the line, Charles Horn supplied a running commentary. Governor Stassen could only sit back, listen, and marvel at Horn's determination to keep Roosevelt's attention.

As we entered the plant, the President said, "You've got quite a few women working here." And Mr. Horn said, "Yes, Mr. President. Our only problem is we need more brass, Mr. President. We need more brass for production." We went down a little further and then to turn the car and get into another part of the plant was quite difficult maneuvering the car around. The President said, "Obviously the plant wasn't built for cars to drive through like this," and Mr. Horn said, "No, Mr. President, it wasn't built like that, but we do need more brass, Mr. President. We need more brass." . . . He must have said that five times. And we got the President back down and on to the train, and Mr. Horn turned to me and he said, "You think the President got the point that we need more brass allocation?" I said, "Mr. Horn, if he didn't get that impression, you can't say it was your fault."[60]

Roosevelt's tour of TCOP lasted only an hour, and word of the visit wasn't made public until two weeks later, after he had returned safely to the White House. But to many employees, the president's visit was a high point—"the greatest morale builder the workers have had since Pearl Harbor," in the words of one Federal Cartridge executive.[61] By all accounts, Roosevelt had chosen to come to their plant because of its impressive output. And TCOP was, in fact, one of the most productive defense plants in the nation.

TCOP had its origins in the national military buildup that began in the months before the attack on Pearl Harbor. In 1940, the U.S. government approved plans to create a system of government-owned contractor-operated arms manufacturing plants across the country. Competition for the plants was intense, and many states—including Minnesota—lobbied heavily for them. In early 1941, the Twin Cities region, with its ample labor supply, emerged as a likely location, and the War Department began interviewing potential contractors in the area, including Charles Horn. Horn's firm, Federal Cartridge of Anoka, made ammunition for hunters, and had no experience in the manufacture of military ordnance. Horn could tell that the "army was doubtful that a small company such as Federal Cartridge could do the job,"[62] but he lobbied hard for the contract anyway. In July of 1941, his efforts paid off. Federal Cartridge signed a $30 million contract to operate a small arms plant in New Brighton.[63]

In truth, the plant site was not really in New Brighton; that was merely its mailing address. Technically, the plant was to be built on a slice of what was known as Mound View Township. (After the war, the township was divided into three cities: Mounds View, New Brighton, and Arden Hills, with the plant falling within Arden Hills' boundaries.) The landscape around the plant site was dominated by small farms, marshland, and lakes—many of which attracted summer vacationers. Its boundaries took in a waterfowl refuge established by the Izaak Walton League, a forty-acre arboretum maintained by a University of Minnesota plant pathologist, two taverns, a supper club, and a sand and gravel quarry. Within weeks after the contract with Federal Cartridge was signed, the government had bought them all.[64]

Construction on the plant began in late August, and the first small-caliber bullets rolled off the line in February of 1942. TCOP, as it was now popularly known, was officially in the war business.

About seventy-five thousand men and women applied for jobs at TCOP during the war. Most of them already lived in the Twin Cities area. At times the demand for jobs was so fierce that a line of applicants snaked up the stairs of Minneapolis' Foshay Tower, where Federal Cartridge had its corporate offices. Job-seekers had to meet an array of requirements. They had to be at least twenty-one, U.S. citizens, and healthy. Men had to prove that they held a draft deferment. All applicants were required to take intelligence tests and undergo FBI background checks.[65]

The sudden injection of thousands of workers into what had been the middle of nowhere created traffic congestion beyond imagination. Special bus service from both downtowns was added during the first weeks of production, automated traffic lights went up at major intersections, and highway patrolmen attempted to untangle frequent tie-ups, but the ebb and flow of traffic to and from the plant continued unabated throughout the war. Accidents were common, and sometimes hazardous materials were involved. Carl Holmberg, an ambulance driver assigned to the plant, remembered how trucks carrying gunpowder occasionally got into trouble.

We didn't have any blow-ups, but we had a number of crashes, and of course the powder is packed in isolated compartments and in very cold compartments—they keep it at a very low temperature—and if the powder truck stops along the road and the temperature starts to rise, that's when you could create problems . . . And there was three different times after the plant went [into] production where these powder trucks hauling this powder mix were disabled out on the highway . . . [and] as time was winding up, they recruited the ambulance, and we put the

*powder in the ambulance . . . All we could do was move. So we
put this powder keg in the ambulance and bring it to the arsenal and put it where it belongs.*[66]

Workers at TCOP produced .30-, .45-, and .50-caliber ammunition in five major small arms types: ball, armor piercing, tracer, incendiary, and blanks. The plant itself had three main manufacturing buildings and thirty-five production lines. Employees were
trained for specific tasks, which they performed repeatedly during
their eight-hour shifts. While most workers were paid top wages
(usually more than a dollar an hour),[67] many quickly tired of what
they considered repetitive, mind-numbing work. William Cummings, who worked for about a year as a quality control specialist at
the plant, complained of boredom regularly in his diary.

*My job is so easy it is hard. I really don't do anything. Just pick
up an occasional shell case and look at it. I never find anything
wrong with them.*

*TCOP employees celebrate the fall of Italy's fascist dictator Benito Mussolini
in 1943.*

Out to spend another dreary day at work. So many people quit out here each week and it is no wonder. The work is so very tiresome; the bosses are no good; every one knows there is no future here and one can quit any day and get another job somewhere else right away. I know I would quit if I had something better lined up.[68]

While tedium was common, the explosive nature of the product made for some wild moments. Everett Needels worked in a bunkerlike shop near the firing range where the plant's ammunition was tested. Every once in a while, he and his co-workers had a scare

A woman fires a machine gun while testing shells at the Twin Cities Ordnance Plant.

when a tracer deflected back in their direction. "I'd usually head for the ditch when I heard those coming," he recalled years later. "Everybody around the plant said, 'Don't worry about it, they're just falling.' Then one went through the trunk of my car and buried itself three-quarters of an inch into my spare tire."[69] And it wasn't just employees who had to worry about their safety. In the fall of 1942, a sixty-seven-year-old man was found dead outside his home near Turtle Lake. He had apparently been killed by a stray bullet from the TCOP test range.[70]

But even with the repetitive work and hazardous working conditions, most employees seemed to take pride in being part of an "arsenal of democracy." (Few, if any, considered the term a cliché.) The plant manufactured more than four billion rounds of ordnance—"about ten percent of all the small arms ammunition used by Allied forces during the war."[71] In June of 1943, the army and navy presented TCOP and its employees the "E" award for excellence in war production. Most employees realized that such awards were not all that hard to come by, but many enjoyed wearing their "E" pins nonetheless. "It is an attractive pin," admitted the usually jaded William Cummings.[72]

On August 18, 1945, the War Department officially notified Federal Cartridge that it was terminating the company's contract to operate TCOP. After the ammunition that was in production on V-J Day was inspected and packed, the plant—which had employed about twenty-six thousand people—closed. Soon thereafter, TCOP was mothballed. The army took it over and renamed it the Twin Cities Arsenal. The plant would sit virtually unused for another five years, until it reopened to produce small arms and artillery ammunition for another war—this one in Korea.

Ed Motzko joined the National Guard in 1940, shortly after graduating from high school in his hometown of Clarissa, in central Minnesota. His unit was activated in early 1941, and for the next three years he served in various assignments on the West Coast. Finally, in September of 1944, Motzko shipped out to Europe with the 548th Anti-Aircraft Artillery Battalion. The 548th soon joined the 102nd Infantry Division in the Netherlands and participated in the final push into Germany.

Ed Motzko with two survivors of the Gardelegen massacre

In mid-April of 1945, as the 102nd advanced from the north, word began filtering back to the troops of a horrendous war atrocity that the Germans had committed outside the nearby town of Gardelegen. Knowing that the allied forces were coming, Nazi SS troops had herded hundreds of religious, political, and military prisoners into a masonry barn and set it on fire. After hearing the news from his commanding officer— "You have to see it to believe it, and then after you see, you *still* won't believe it"—Ed Motzko decided he had to see for himself. On April 15, he and a few of his buddies drove out to the farm. Four days later, with the images fresh in his mind, he wrote about what he saw in a letter to his parents in Minnesota.

April 19, 1945 (Germany)
Well, here's something that isn't fit to write home about, but probably by now you have heard and read all about it. All censorship restrictions are released about this terrible incident, so we are able to write about it. This concerns the horrid, gruesome Nazi atrocity that happened at Gardelegen. I saw it, and there aren't words appropriate enough to tell of its terribleness. The

Nazis are every bit as cruel, and even with more beastly habits than we actually realized.

To get on with the Gardelegen Flaming Death House, there were approximately about 1,000 various war prisoners that lost their lives here. They were mostly Russian, Poles, Jews, their own political radicals, and one American Negro soldier has been identified thus far.

To get on with the story, this group of PW's numbered 2,000, which were in Prussia. With the Russians putting on the pressure, they marched this group 1,000 kilometers— or 600 miles— to this front. This journey took about 20 days, with meager food and water rations. Hanover was to be their destination, but with this same city being taken by the 9th Army, Gardelegen was next in line. About 1,000 completed this forced journey. The balance died or were killed en route. During this time they were being guarded by their own fellow prisoners, which were clothed in the Wehrmacht uniform, and equipped with Nazi rifles, etc. They were overseered by the terrible SS troopers, and were to be granted their freedom because of their previous-mentioned duty.

This group was herded to a large brick barn on the outskirts of Gardelegen, which was prepared with two feet of straw, saturated with an inflammable material which covered the entire floor. After all were herded in, they forced in the guards at the last moment, too.

At 6 P.M., Friday, 13th April, a German SS non-com came in and ignited the straw. This attempt was soon beat out. Resorting to their beastly habits now, they opened up with machine gun fire to make them lie down, and during this time they tossed in various grenades, especially those of the incendiary and phosphorus types. There was no quelling the blaze this time. Those who attempted to escape from the four large doors were soon mowed down by machine gun fire.

The fire burned all Friday evening, and the next day, slave laborers were forced to dig large ditches for their burial ground. The burial was well under way, and another Nazi atrocity being covered up, when our division captured this town and found this death house. I visited this horrible scene yesterday, and two piles of human torsos were still smoldering.

We were allowed to take pictures, so I took one whole roll of film, but the memories will vividly portray this ghastly scene with greater meaning to me. It really makes one's blood boil!

Here's practically a miracle that goes with it. Sunday a.m. a Frenchman crawled out from under one of those piles, very much alive to tell of his past experience, which was all torture. We never heard of his exact condition. I don't think there will be words appropriate to describe some of the ghastly scenes inside. Some tried to dig under the dirt, and in their vain efforts, they wore flesh and bone up to the second joints of their fingers, in their futile attempts. Some were blown to pieces by grenades. Phosphorus burns added to the terribleness. There were some that seemed to be so very young, between fourteen and sixteen years old.

This is not the makings of a good letter, so I will end this here. It just goes on to prove that the Nazis need no sympathy whatsoever. No treatment or punishment can be too cruel for these people. They deserve many more hardships than they are now receiving.[1]

5   Minnesota Made

Of all the miniature battles that took place in Minnesota during the war—the fights to secure defense production contracts, the skirmishes over rationed items such as tires, gasoline, sugar, cigarettes, and the like—few were fought as publicly, or with such a sense of urgency, as the battle over the origins of the jeep. The Army's ubiquitous, bouncy, go-anywhere vehicle had earned the respect (some smitten soldiers used the word "love") of U.S. troops around the globe during World War II. In the words of General George Marshall, it was "this country's greatest contribution to the war." Clearly, the jeep had a bright future ahead of it in the postwar world. ("There are few soldiers in the Army today who aren't talking about owning a jeep in post-war years," gushed one company's newsletter.)[1] It promised to emerge from the fighting having earned the kind of brand recognition that marketers long for.

Minneapolis-Moline Power Implement Company (MM) did not make the vehicles most commonly identified as jeeps, but it did hold a certain claim to the name. As the war progressed, the company tried to guarantee that when people thought of jeeps, they also thought of Minneapolis-Moline.

It was a marketing effort doomed to failure.

Minneapolis-Moline's association with the jeep name dated back to the summer of 1940, when the 109th Ordnance Company of the Minnesota National Guard was assigned to try out four UTX "prime movers" manufactured by the Minneapolis firm. Sergeant James O'Brien, a former MM employee, supervised the test runs at Camp Ripley, near Little Falls, and came away impressed. "It wasn't a truck and it wasn't a tractor," he said of the UTX. "Fact of the matter, it wasn't like nothing we'd ever seen, but it could go like a bat out of hell and it could pull anything you hitched to it." After spending a day with the machines, O'Brien and a group of enlisted men concluded that their new vehicle needed a name. Someone suggested "alligator." Another liked "swamp-rabbit." But none of the proposed names seemed quite right. Then O'Brien remembered a doglike character from the popular comic strip *Popeye*: Eugene the Jeep had supernatural powers and could solve almost any problem, sort of like the UTX. Apparently of the opinion that Eugene was not a proper name for a military vehicle, O'Brien suggested the obvious alternative. "Finally I said 'jeep,'" he recalled, "and it stuck."[2]

As word of the UTX jeep's exploits spread, U.S. troops and the U.S. press began applying its catchy unofficial name to a variety of other multipurpose military vehicles, including the machine that eventually appropriated the name—the familiar, boxlike four-by-four produced by Willys-Overland Motors. Minneapolis-Moline's Jeep, which never achieved widespread use, faded from public consciousness, as did the company's hold on the name.

Knowing a promising brand name when he saw one, Minneapolis-Moline's president, W. C. MacFarlane, scrambled to reestablish the Jeep's MM pedigree. He wrote Henry Luce, editor-in-chief of *Time* and *Life* magazines, informing him that "the word 'Jeep' was first given to an Army tractor by the Minnesota National

In 1943 Minneapolis-Moline launched a public relations campaign on behalf of its overlooked military vehicle, with the slogan "Our Light Won't Stay Under the Bushel—The Original Jeep A Child of Minneapolis-Moline."

Guardsmen."[3] When Willys-Overland began using the Jeep name in its advertisements, MacFarlane instructed his lawyers to challenge the practice. In 1944, the Federal Trade Commission jumped into the fray, charging that Willys-Overland's Jeep advertising was intentionally misleading. (The FTC did not, however, try to determine which company could rightfully claim the Jeep name.)[4] The bickering over the Jeep's origins continued into the 1950s, but in the end, Minneapolis-Moline had to accept defeat. In the public's mind, the Willys-Overland Jeep was the real Jeep.[5]

Minneapolis-Moline was just one of dozens of Minnesota firms—and a handful of industries—that hoped to convert their wartime achievements into postwar profits. Many of them ultimately failed to make a smooth transition from a wartime to a peacetime economy, but a few emerged with strengthened product lines and exciting new technologies. For them, World War II was indeed a watershed event.

Miracle Meat

Minnesota's best-known contribution to the war effort was a funny-looking meat product that aroused passions the world over. Spam luncheon meat was just becoming established as a popular consumer item when the Japanese attacked Pearl Harbor. But by the time the war was over, nearly every human being in the United States and Europe knew of Spam. And most of them had an opinion about it. To its detractors, Spam was a twelve-ounce brick of unappetizing processed pork (chopped pork shoulder and ham, to be exact). But to its fans, it was much more: a tasty convenience, an affordable delicacy, and on occasion a godsend.

Spam was the pride and joy of the George A. Hormel Company of Austin, Minnesota. Hormel had introduced Spam in 1937, touting it as a "miracle meat in a can," and consumer response was gratifying. By 1940, nearly three-quarters of the nation's urban dwellers reported eating Spam at one time or another.[6] People liked Spam. They thought it tasted good. They didn't make fun of it.

But then the war came.

During the summer and fall of 1941, the Federal Surplus Commodities Corporation (FSCC) began pressuring U.S. meatpackers, including Hormel, to increase their production of canned meat for Lend-Lease shipments to England and the Soviet Union. (The Lend-Lease Act gave President Roosevelt the power to sell, transfer, exchange, and lend armaments and other goods to any country trying to defend itself against the Axis powers.) At first the agency said it needed four million pounds a week. Then it increased its order to eight million. By November, it was demanding fifteen million pounds. Hormel, which had by that time convinced the FSCC to let it fill much of its Lend-Lease quota with Spam, responded to the challenge by adding new production lines at its Spam plants and by doubling its hours of operation.[7] Soon Spam was pouring into Britain and the Soviet Union by the shipload. By the end of the war, more than one hundred million pounds of it had been sent overseas.[8]

Spam was not the only product that Hormel churned out during the war. In early 1942, Hormel began shifting its focus away from Lend-Lease to concentrate more closely on producing food for American soldiers, sailors, and marines. Unlike the FSCC, the U.S. armed services were most interested in bulk foods. They considered small, consumer-size tins of meat like Spam inefficient for most military uses. So Hormel began packing six-pound tins of luncheon meat, using the same government-approved recipe that other meat-packers used. Unlike Spam, this generic military meat contained no ham and was more heavily cooked and salted. It also suffered from "loose juice"—an unappetizing condition common to many canned meats (but not Spam). It was, in effect, Spam's poor cousin.

The vast difference in quality between Spam and the six-pound tins of military luncheon meat caused headaches for Hormel as the

By the end of 1941, most of the six-pound tins of "defense ham" produced by Hormel came from the company's plant in Austin. The plant was also responsible for a good portion of the firm's Spam output.

war dragged on. It didn't take long for U.S. fighting men to develop a loathing for the inferior-quality luncheon meat that they were served nearly every day (sometimes three times a day). They needed a name for their culinary nemesis, and the name they chose was Spam. It didn't matter that most servicemen were eating a generic meat product with only a casual resemblance to Hormel's twelve-ounce luncheon loaf. As far as they were concerned, they were eating Spam, and they didn't like it.

The GIs' simmering hatred for Spam boiled over in 1943 and 1944 when the publications *Stars and Stripes* and *Yank* published a series of letters, editorials, and articles expressing disdain for Hormel and its increasingly infamous "miracle meat." In one particularly biting piece, the editors of *Yank* told the story of Private Lewis B. Closser, an enterprising GI who had "made the most startling discovery of the war."

> *He has found out that there is not a single can of Spam in the whole U.S. Army . . .*
>
> *Like all the rest of us, Pfc. Closser is pretty well fed up with the Army's steady diet of what we have always called Spam. So he decided to do something about it. He wrote a letter to the Hormel meat packing people, copyright owners of that awful word, and asked them to lay off shipping the stuff overseas for a few weeks at least, even if the boys had to go hungry.*

The article went on to report that in Hormel's letter back to Closser, the company claimed that it had never sold Spam to the army. (A subsequent investigation found that the army had, in fact, received one large shipment in 1942.) The stuff that Closser was complaining about, the letter explained, was actually the ubiquitous bulk luncheon meat that came in six-pound cans. The company accused the army of perpetuating the confusion by continuing to call its generic military meat "Spam." Closser and *Yank* were not impressed with the explanation.

> *All we can say is what Shakespeare once said about a rose:*
> > What's in a name? That which we call Spam
> > By any other name would taste as lousy . . .
>
> *It's not what they call it. It's the frequency with which they throw it into your mess kit. Spam—sorry, we mean luncheon meat—might not be so bad if it was only served at luncheon. But when you get it at breakfast and supper, too, you can't be*

"Whadya mean luncheon meat? I say it's Spam and I say to hell with it!"

From Yank: The Army Weekly, *January 14, 1944*

blamed for getting mad at it. As a matter of fact, it is a wonder the Army selected such a mild and inoffensive term as Spam when it started to call the stuff names.[9]

Hormel had a potential problem on its hands. Spam, which had looked so promising in the years leading up to the war, was now the subject of widespread derision. Hormel executives imagined a nightmare scenario in which hundreds of thousands of Spam-hating servicemen returned home after the war, and refused to let any Hormel products into their homes. Company president Jay Hormel seemed genuinely depressed about the situation when he sat down with a *New Yorker* reporter during the final days of the war:

Mr. Hormel toyed with his drink for a moment, then went on . . . "We didn't even get around to putting Spam on the market until 1937 . . . Sometimes I wonder if we shouldn't have" . . . Mr. Hormel didn't finish the sentence. We got the distinct impression that being responsible for Spam might be too great a burden for any one man. "It's all right," he said defensively in a moment. "Damn it, we eat it in our own home." He shook his head and added, "Trouble is, we eat a lot of things in our home that other people won't eat. My wife is French—I married her after the last war—and she likes calves' brains and stuff like that."[10]

Still, most Hormel executives, including Jay Hormel himself, suspected that Spam's wartime tribulations might actually benefit the company. "Servicemen are giving Spam priceless publicity by griping," said a food researcher with the army's quartermaster corps. "Hormel couldn't buy anything better."[11] As the war came to a close, Jay Hormel was planning to take advantage of that publicity by selling Spam "to new people and new places." He also was preparing to introduce two new products with Spam-like monosyllabic names: a dog food called Arf and a shortening called Spic. If everything went well, the thinking went, Hormel would be known in years to come as the company that made Spic and Spam.[12]

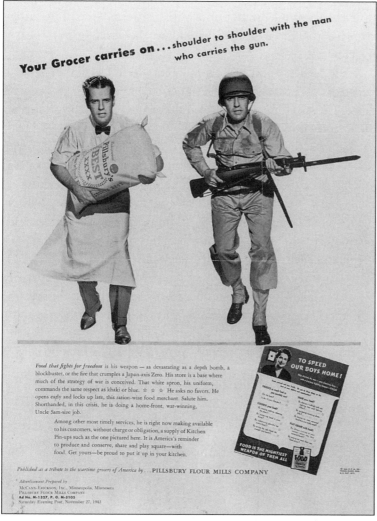

Many Minnesota firms adjusted their marketing strategies to reflect wartime realities. The one shown here appealed directly to the grocers who carried Pillsbury products.

On Autopilot

On the afternoon of November 22, 1944, Oscar Smith, an employee with the U.S. Forest Service, was marking timber in the Superior National Forest near the town of Isabella when an unmistakable sound shattered the silence of the woods. A plane had crashed somewhere nearby. Smith immediately reported what he had heard, and a local ranger rounded up a search team to hunt for the wreckage. A few hours later, when the searchers found the crash site, they were dumbfounded. There, half-buried in the forest floor, was the smoldering hulk of a B-17 Flying Fortress. As the searchers fanned out, they noticed that the huge bomber had shorn off the treetops over a quarter-mile swath before hitting ground. Aircraft parts were strewn across the area. The men did not, however, find any sign of the crew.

As it turned out, the crew members were just fine. They had bailed out over Marion, South Dakota, after one of the B-17's engines failed. The empty plane had stayed airborne for five hours—covering about four hundred miles—before finally running out of fuel.[13]

Earlier in the war, reports of a B-17 flying hundreds of miles with no one at the controls would have caused quite a ruckus. But by November 1944, the story barely made a ripple. As many Americans already knew, U.S. bombers were now equipped with a new electronic device called an automatic pilot. And as many Minnesotans were already aware, the autopilot was a local invention—the product of a company called Minneapolis-Honeywell.

For two years between 1941 and 1943, Minneapolis-Honeywell's automatic pilot had been one of the war's best-kept secrets. Even the company's employee newsletters referred to it only by pronoun.

> *Because of the importance of our product we are prevented by the government from referring to it by name, so its history must refer only to "It." Some months back the Engineering Department at Minneapolis decided they could make a far superior "It" with the use of electronics as only they had developed it. They made an "It" and it worked. In fact, it worked so well that the U.S. Air [Forces] wanted more immediately.[14]*

But by the fall of 1943, the Army Air Forces (AAF) was convinced that the Germans had probably learned all about the top-secret device by examining the wreckage of downed U.S. bombers. There was no longer a reason to keep it secret from the American people.

In a press release, the army and Minneapolis-Honeywell revealed that the c-1 automatic pilot was an electronically controlled mechanism that stabilized planes like the b-17 during bombing runs. "Precision bombing requires a steady platform," a company spokesman said, "because if the plane is tipped or otherwise off its course at the time the bomb is released, this tipping or movement will be imparted to the bomb and cause it to miss the target." The automatic pilot was like a rifleman's tripod, he explained. It held the plane "on the bull's-eye" while the bombs were released. As a result, bombing accuracy increased dramatically.[15]

The revelation of the c-1 changed the way people thought about Minneapolis-Honeywell. Before the war, the company was known primarily as a manufacturer of home thermostats. It had no experience in aviation. But the company was actively trying to expand into the new field of electronics, and in early 1941, it convinced the aaf to look at several electronic devices that it had developed, including a mechanism that controlled cabin temperature in airplanes. While the aaf expressed little interest in those devices, it was

Getting a firsthand glimpse of the Minneapolis-Honeywell C-1 autopilot at the Minnesota Ordnance Show, May 1944.

impressed with the advances Honeywell seemed to be making in the electronics field. It asked the company to develop a system that held cameras steady during reconnaissance flights. Honeywell jumped at the opportunity. The camera mounts that it developed worked extremely well, and as a result, the army hired the company to develop another kind of electronic stabilizing mechanism—one that could hold a plane steady during bombing runs.

The Army Air Forces already had a first-generation autopilot called the AFCE, or Automatic Flight Control Equipment, that worked in conjunction with its state-of-the art Norden bombsight, but it wasn't happy with the device. It tended to cause "exaggerated jerky movements" that made it virtually impossible to keep targets in the bombsight.[16] Honeywell engineers replaced the AFCE's mechanical controls with electronic ones, and by the summer of 1941, they were ready to test the new system in the air. The AAF loaned the company one of its few B-17s (at that time it had less than two dozen), and testing began out of Minneapolis. The modified system performed impressively. No jerky movements. Just smooth flying. In October the AAF renamed the modified system the C-1 autopilot and contracted with Honeywell to produce C-1s for the army's heavy bomber fleet.

Still, pilots were wary. How could an electronic device made by a company with no prior aeronautical experience possibly outperform a human pilot? Honeywell engineer Earl Bower got a chance to change the minds of several skeptical AAF fliers during a simulated bombing run out of Minneapolis on Thanksgiving Day, 1941.

> Well, the big plane was loaded with feed sacks containing lime which would burst on impact and scatter so it could be seen from the plane. On the first run, the bombing was so accurate that aaf personnel on board figured it must have been just luck. So the plane was landed, reloaded with another set of feed sacks, and this entire load was also delivered on target. They were very impressed.[17]

Over the next four years, Minneapolis-Honeywell manufactured thirty-five thousand C-1s for the military. The autopilot, which had operated in secrecy during the first half of the war, was publicly credited with increasing bombing accuracy, reducing pilot fatigue, and saving countless American lives by minimizing the number of follow-up bombing missions. The company, known mainly for its thermostats before the war, was now a leader in aeronautical technology. In the summer of 1945, Honeywell engineers helped bring an end to the war when they traveled to the Marshall Islands to install C-1s on two B-29 Superfortress bombers—the Enola Gay and Bockscar.[18]

Cool Customer

On a fair winter day in early 1945, a crowd of spectators gathered at a parade ground in San Antonio, Texas, to witness a demonstration of one of the most underappreciated military advancements of the war. Soon, overhead, an aerial convoy of C-47 cargo planes disgorged from their holds what seemed like a small army of men and enough canvas-wrapped bundles to fill an entire warehouse. Once the contents of those planes had parachuted safely onto the parade ground, more cargo aircraft appeared overhead, each towing a glider. The gliders were cut loose and within minutes they too were on the parade ground, guided down safely by combat veteran pilots.

And then it was time for lunch.

As the crowd watched, mesmerized, a small contingent of the airborne troops hastily unwrapped food and supplies from the bundles that had floated onto the parade grounds. Another group dragged heavy kitchen equipment from the gliders. In less than an hour, a fully operational field kitchen was serving hot meals to the combat troops who had arrived in the first wave. The kitchen's 50-cubic-foot refrigerator-freezers were keeping a variety of foods fresh at temperatures as low as -18°F.[19]

Many of the invited civilians and military brass were well aware of the significance of what they were seeing. In previous wars, it had been impossible for mess units to keep moving to forward positions during fighting. But that had all changed during World War II. Airborne mess crews now routinely joined combat troops near the front lines, helping to keep America's fighting men well fed. In the sweltering heat of the Pacific, some troops were even treated to an occasional scoop of ice cream or a cold glass of lemonade with ice cubes. These and other advancements in combat cuisine were key components in America's military success, and in many ways they were made possible by the creative thinking of an obscure mechanical genius from Minnesota named Frederick McKinley Jones.

Even before the war had begun, it seemed that Fred Jones had worked on just about every kind of machine there was. The son of an African American mother and an Irish American father, he grew up in the Cincinnati area, often tearing apart toys and watches and kitchen appliances to see how they worked. At the age of twelve, he ran away from the Cincinnati church where he lived (his mother had died when he was very young and his father had abandoned him when he was seven) and embarked on a life of invention. By the time the war broke out, Jones was in his mid-forties and had accumulated patents for dozens of devices including sound track equipment for Hollywood films, a portable X-ray machine, and a radio transmitter. But of all his inventions, none was as successful as the truck refrigerator known as the Thermo King.

Jones had turned his attention to refrigerators during the spring of 1939 while working for Ultraphone Sound Systems, a Minneapolis company that made sound equipment for small movie theaters. The company's president, Joseph Numero, had boasted to one of his golf partners—a trucking executive—that Ultraphone's chief engineer, Fred Jones, could design and build a cooling unit to effectively refrigerate truck trailers. The trucking executive accepted Numero's offer and sent a new 24-foot trailer over to Ultraphone with instructions to "put that refrigeration unit on it that you were bragging about." By this time, Numero suspected that he had promised

For years after the war, Fred Jones remained the only African American member of the American Society of Refrigerating Engineers.

more than he could deliver, but he told Jones to look at the rig anyway. Jones and his crew crawled all over the trailer, taking measure-
ments and making calculations. After about thirty minutes, Jones
announced his conclusion. "We ought to be able to fix up something, Mr. Numero," he said. Jones' design—a 400-pound under-
mounted cooling unit with a self-starting gasoline motor—actually
worked. Jones and Numero patented the design and Ultraphone
suddenly found itself in the truck refrigeration business.

Over the next three years, as the United States prepared for war,
Jones' invention transformed the food transportation and grocery
industry. Producers could now move perishable foods across long
distances without spoilage. Grocers could now offer their customers
fresh fruits, vegetables, meats, and eggs. Frozen foods were suddenly
viable for large-scale marketing. Numero sold Ultraphone to RCA
and created a new company, United States Thermo-Control, to
manufacture and market truck refrigerators. Jones kept improving
on his initial design, eventually mounting the unit high on the
trailer's front, rather than underneath, to protect it from dirt and
debris. By the time the United States entered the war, U.S. Thermo-
Control was the nation's leading truck refrigeration firm. Its front-
mounted Thermo King was the most reliable in the business.

And then the army came calling.

In early 1942, U.S. military planners summoned many of the
country's top refrigeration experts—including Fred Jones—to the
nation's capital to discuss plans for a new generation of field refrigerators. Jones arrived in Washington only to discover that he had
been booked into a "shabby bedroom in an obscure, Jim Crow hotel." All the other refrigeration experts at the conference were staying at one of Washington's finest hotels at government expense. By
this time, however, Jones had hardened himself to the daily indig-
nities he was subjected to as a black man. He spent as little time as
possible at the hotel, immersing himself in the conference. Jones
spent hours discussing designs with his colleagues, and he impressed them with his approach. After several days of presentations
and discussions, the engineers at the conference agreed that Jones'
compact Thermo King unit should be the standard design for all
army and marine field kitchen refrigerators.[20]

During the war, Jones and his colleagues at U.S. Thermo-Control
worked exclusively for the military.[21] They produced a variety of
military food refrigerators—including an ice-cream maker—all
based on Jones' original design. Their units helped save lives by carrying blood and other medical supplies to the front lines, and by

keeping wounded soldiers cool when enemy action grounded hospital planes in sweltering heat. After the war, Brigadier General Georges F. Doriot of the quartermaster corps wrote Joseph Numero to thank him and U.S. Thermo-Control for their contributions to the war effort. "No one realizes more than this office the importance of the time, effort, and skill which have been so fully devoted by your company," he wrote. "We are particularly grateful for the work of Mr. Fred Jones and the other members of your engineering department."[22]

Fred Jones finally started receiving some of the recognition he deserved as U.S. Thermo-Control (later known as Thermo King) took off during the early postwar years. Two national magazines, the *Saturday Evening Post* and *Ebony*, both ran long features on him, and several Twin Cities newspapers followed suit.[23] The articles noted many of Jones' accomplishments, including his World War II contributions, but even the most glowing accounts could not ignore the color of his skin. He was "a self-taught Negro scientist" and a "black Thomas Edison." In fact, Jones was treated until the end of his career as something of a novelty—a brilliant black man in Minnesota's overwhelmingly white business world. Jones never earned more than twelve thousand dollars a year during his long tenure at Thermo King, even after he was promoted to vice president of engineering. He owned no stock in the company. Thermo King retained control of all his patents.[24]

Bright Future

Minnesota Mining and Manufacturing Company was already a corporate institution in the state by the time war broke out in Europe in 1939. 3M, as it was almost universally known, manufactured a myriad of well-respected industrial and consumer products, the best known of which were sandpaper and Scotch brand adhesive tape. But almost all of its products fell into just two broad categories: abrasives and adhesives. By the late 1930s, the company was actively trying to diversify its product lines by devoting more resources to research and development. Among the most promising results was a reflective sheeting called Scotchlite. While Scotchlite was born prior to America's entrance in World War II, it was—perhaps more than any other 3M product—a wartime baby.

The inspiration for Scotchlite dated back to 1937, when a Ramsey County surveyor suggested to a 3M sales executive that the company come up with a way to make highway centerline stripes easier to see at night. The suggestion was intriguing, and soon 3M engineers from a variety of departments were working on the problem. Their solution—a strip of tape coated with tiny glass beads—looked promising, but was ultimately impractical. No matter what the engineers did, they couldn't make the tape stick to asphalt for very long. In one experiment, conducted on Highway 61 near St. Paul's Keller Golf Course, the sight of loosened reflective striping waving in the breeze became so common that motorists dubbed the yet-to-be-named product "3M's friendly tape." The "glass bead project," as it was then called, seemed destined for failure.

But then someone had a bright idea: If it won't work *on* the road, maybe it'll work *beside* the road.[25] Company researchers now focused on developing a reflective sheeting for use on traffic signs. The resulting product—a waterproof backing coated with pigmented lacquer and glass beads—was Scotchlite. Unlike the centerline tape, Scotchlite actually seemed to stay where it was stuck.

On September 1, 1939, the first Scotchlite reflective road signs went up around the new cloverleaf interchange at the junction of Highways 7 and 100 in Minneapolis. Company executives were optimistic about the new product's future, but their excitement was tempered by world events. Hitler's stormtroopers had just invaded Poland. Europe was at war.

Suddenly Scotchlite's future didn't look so bright.

In the months leading up to the Pearl Harbor attack, 3M had channeled an ever-increasing percentage of its production to the nation's military needs. But after the attack, the company threw "its full energy and resources" into the war effort.[26] Unlike many companies, 3M did not drop what it was doing before the war and switch to the manufacture of new wartime products. Instead, it kept making the same abrasives, tapes, and adhesives it had always made, knowing that other wartime manufacturers depended on them. As for Scotchlite, which was still largely untested and unknown, the company's 1942 annual report put it bluntly: "As the product is not essential to defense, only a limited distribution of it will be possible until the end of the war."[27]

To make matters worse, wartime shortages of raw materials threatened to snuff out what little life the Scotchlite project had left. Natural rubber, resins, and pigments—all essential to Scotchlite production—were virtually impossible to obtain, thanks to the government's resource allocation program. If the product was to survive the war, the company's engineers would have to develop a completely new manufacturing process using available raw materials.

That is exactly what they did. 3M's Scotchlite team developed a new formula for the sheeting's main coating material (castor oil and urea formaldehyde), increased its reflecting power to two hundred times that of white paint, and added new colors. It was a classic example of adversity spawning creativity. Far from killing off Scotchlite, the war had actually turned it into a superior product.

Suddenly Scotchlite—the product that once faced almost certain wartime extinction—was "essential to defense." 3M began touting its many military uses: Scotchlite-coated harbor buoys helped guide ships through treacherous waters; airport runway markers faced with Scotchlite guided Allied fliers safely back home; Scotchlited signs led the way to air-raid shelters. And most of all—as its marketing literature indicated—Scotchlite was there to save the lives of airmen downed at sea:

And right there is where Minnesota Mining & Manufacturing steps in with another contribution to the war effort, utilizing

3M produced hundreds of thousands of Scotchlite oar-coating kits for the Army and Navy Air Forces during the war.

one of the newer products to come from its laboratories in an in-
genious manner to give our flying men a much better chance of
being rescued in the dark. The product is "SCOTCHLITE", and
the new use to which this lens-coated material, reflecting light
back to the source of light, is put, is effected by fastening it to
blades of oars. Recently such visible-day-and-night oars have
been made standard equipment in the pneumatic life rafts of
both the Army and Navy Air Forces . . . And so another 3-M
product, originated for peacetime use . . . marches bravely off to
war and does its part in our relentless surge toward Victory.[28]

Of course, the surge toward victory sometimes got bogged down
by arcane realities of military procurement. The first Scotchlite life-
raft paddle kit contained three strips of reflective material cut to
specifications provided by the military. Only after the kits were in
production did 3M learn that U.S. armed forces actually used five
different kinds of oars, and the die-cut reflecting strips only fit one
of them. After making "some hectic adjustments," the company re-
covered from its mistake, and hundreds of thousands of orders began to come in.[29]

Despite its occasional problems, Scotchlite proved itself as an in-
dispensable wartime product and increased its chances of succeed-
ing in the postwar civilian marketplace. The company, which had
publicly downplayed the product's future, now gave Scotchlite its
own division. By 1945, company president W. L. McKnight was sin-
gling out the new product for greatness. Scotchlite, he said, had
reached "the point where it seems evident that it can become an important addition to our line."[30] With the end of the war, scarce raw
materials once again became available, allowing 3M's engineers to
develop new products and expand existing lines, including Scotchlite. "Scotchlite is rapidly finding its place in the advertising field as
well as in the safety field," gushed the company's 1945 annual report.
"Its growing commercial acceptance is emphasized by its recent
adoption by the state of Connecticut for use on license plates of
commercial vehicles, and by indications that it may be adopted in
1946 for use on all automobile license plates within that state."[31]

Unlikely Beginnings

Minnesota's computer industry—indeed, the computer industry as
a whole—might never have developed as quickly as it did if it hadn't
been for one of the Twin Cities' most successful World War II–era

defense contractors. Northwestern Aeronautical Corporation (NAC) was not a technology company in the usual sense, but its short existence set the stage for some remarkable technological advances during the postwar years. The connection between NAC and the computer industry was indirect and was made all the more unlikely by the nature of the company's wartime work.

Northwestern Aeronautical made gliders—motorless aircraft—for the military.

The story of Northwestern Aeronautical is, in many ways, the story of a well-connected East Coast entrepreneur named John E. Parker. Parker was a self-confident, backslapping investment banker with financing experience in the aviation industry. At the time the United States entered the war, Parker was struggling to save a small Kansas City aircraft manufacturer that his investment firm had taken over. After trying unsuccessfully to convince the Army Air

A B-23 bomber tows a glider manufactured by Northwestern Aeronautical Corporation at Wold Chamberlain Field.

Forces to give the company a contract, Parker turned to Northwest Airlines in St. Paul. Parker's firm owned a stake in Northwest, and Northwest—fearing that the war would devastate its normal operations—was looking for military contract work. The investment banker and the airline quickly devised a plan to help each other. Parker formed a new company, Northwestern Aeronautical, investing a thousand dollars of his own money and nine thousand dollars in equipment from the struggling Kansas City firm. Northwest Airlines, in turn, agreed to provide the new company, NAC, with staff, operating space, and advice. Apparently impressed with the arrangement, the Army Air Forces gave Northwestern Aeronautical a contract to produce thirty wooden troop-carrying gliders. Within a few months, it increased its order to three hundred gliders—all due for delivery in 1942.[32]

The army's urgency grew out of the realization that Germany was far ahead of the United States in glider production and strategy. The Nazis had demonstrated the military possibilities of glider warfare in May of 1941 when seventy fully loaded gliders helped pave the way for the invasion of the Greek island of Crete. Now the U.S. AAF was determined to close the glider gap. It contracted with several companies around the country—including NAC—to build gliders based on two basic designs. The CG-4A (CG stood for cargo glider) was made primarily of steel tubes, wood, and fabric. It weighed about a ton and had a wingspan of nearly eighty-four feet. Fifteen fully equipped soldiers (or six soldiers and a jeep) could fit inside. The CG-13A was a larger version of the CG-4A, about four times heavier and wide enough to carry a light truck and thirty troops.

The biggest problem facing John Parker and Northwestern Aeronautical was finding enough qualified glider builders. The demand for other warplanes had already drained the available supply of aircraft workers throughout the country, which meant, reported *National Geographic* magazine, that the company had to hire "anyone who wanted to work."

One of the company's top wing inspectors formerly was a hotel waiter. Two orchestra leaders, a chiropractor, a violin maker, a bond salesman, a music teacher, a minister, a schoolteacher, several cabinetmakers, a former bank president, a civil engineer, and a palm reader took jobs and stuck with them.

The efficient shipping clerk is a bartender. The solemn director of purchases, who now buys two million dollars' worth of materials each month, formerly was a Minneapolis undertaker.[33]

Work on the gliders commenced at four Twin Cities facilities. Engineering and tooling were done at the company's main plant on Minnehaha Avenue in St. Paul. The De Ponti Aviation Company, acting as a subcontractor, took over an old garage on Lyndale Avenue in Minneapolis and built tubular steel airframes for the gliders. Another subcontractor, Villaume Box and Lumber Company, made wooden wings, rudders, and elevators at its plant on St. Paul's west side. Workers put all the pieces together at Northwestern's assembly plant—a series of hangars at Wold-Chamberlain Airport in Minneapolis.

At peak production, NAC manufactured about fifteen gliders a day.[34] The assembly plant at Wold-Chamberlain operated around the clock, and the pace was just as hectic at the other facilities. At Villaume, glider production occupied three-quarters of the company's three-block plant, and the workforce grew more than tenfold. Employees had to put up with less-than-perfect working conditions, including fumes from formaldehyde glue. "Redheads and blondes especially were having problems with skin ailments," one manager recalled.

As the war progressed, Northwestern employees thrilled to news of glider warfare. In July of 1943, a fleet of American gliders led the way in the invasion of Sicily. Eight months later, audacious glider-borne troops established an airfield two hundred miles behind Japanese lines in north-central Burma. And then, on the second day of the Normandy invasion, an armada of four hundred American gliders delivered reinforcements and supplies to the first-wave assault troops who had parachuted and glided into France the day before. As details of the D-Day invasion became known, NAC workers wondered whether their gliders had taken part. John Parker assured the local newspapers that a "great many" had.[35]

By the time the war ended, the employees of Northwestern Aeronautical had turned out around fifteen hundred gliders.[36] The former musicians, palm readers, bartenders, and others who made up its workforce had proven that they could take on technically demanding jobs and excel at them. The question was, what would happen to them now that the war was over? "I felt a great obligation to the staff that I had, these people that were with me during the war," John Parker recalled. "They were very loyal and they were all people that knew they had to find someplace to go and they were all looking to me to see if I possibly couldn't find something to [save their jobs]."[37]

Parker had known all along that the market for troop-carrying wooden gliders would almost certainly dry up once the fighting stopped, and he had been thinking for months about converting the company into a manufacturer of some different kind of product. At one point, he seriously considered turning his main plant on Minnehaha Avenue into a mattress factory,[38] but before he could settle on that, he caught wind of another more intriguing business opportunity.

Even as Parker was pondering his company's future, two naval officers at a top-secret laboratory in Washington, D.C., were trying to figure out how to put their peculiar expertise to peacetime use. Commander Howard Engstrom and Lieutenant Commander Bill Norris oversaw a project called Communications Supplementary Activity–Washington (CSAW, or "seesaw"). Its laboratory was the navy's top code-breaking facility, home to some of the most sophisticated decryption devices ever conceived. Engstrom and Norris were sure that the technology they had helped develop at CSAW would have some sort of postwar business application, they just weren't sure what. Airline reservations? Flight simulators? As the war wound down, they began looking for a partner willing to invest

Troops practice loading and unloading an NAC CG-13A glider.

in a new kind of business—one that specialized in "electronic cal-culators"—but their sales pitch was less than effective. As much as they would have liked to, Engstrom and Norris couldn't say any-thing about their work at CSAW. That information was classified. As a result, their presentations, with their veiled references to sophisti-cated technology, were simply too vague to lure potential investors. The answer was always the same: No, thanks.[39]

That is, until they met John Parker.

Parker had learned from a high-ranking navy friend that a group of naval officers was looking for someone to invest in a highly clas-sified business idea. Intrigued, and still looking for something to re-place NAC's glider business, Parker decided to find out more. The friend put him in touch with Captain Ralph Meader, of the Naval Computing Machine Laboratory in Dayton, Ohio, and that en-counter led to a meeting with Engstrom and Norris. Whatever mis-givings Parker may have had about the naval officers and their neb-ulous business plan vanished after he encountered Admiral Chester W. Nimitz, former commander of the Pacific Fleet. During a short meeting in the admiral's office, Nimitz jabbed a finger at Parker and told him, "There's a job I would like to have you do." The job, of course, was to find a way to build on the technological progress made by CSAW during the war. (Like the others, Nimitz wouldn't say what that work was.) By this time, Parker could tell that the navy was excited about the work being done by the likes of Engstrom, Norris, and Meader—whatever that work was. "I said, 'Aye, Aye, sir,'" Parker recalled. "I had no idea what I was going to do."[40]

In January of 1946, an investment group led by Parker and a technical team headed by Engstrom, Norris, and Meader formed a new company called Engineering Research Associates (ERA). First they had to overcome a potentially debilitating problem: as an untested company, ERA could not legally qualify for major navy contracts, and without a navy contract, it could not survive. That's where Northwestern Aeronautical came in. While NAC was, by this time, largely disbanded, it did have the military operating record that the new firm lacked. If the two companies could be combined somehow, it would solve two problems: ERA would qualify for navy contracts, and Northwestern Aeronautical's remaining employees would keep their jobs—at least for the time being. Parker headed back to the Twin Cities and announced that the two firms would initially share the same management and facilities and would be based in St. Paul.[41] "And when I came back with the ERA, that group of men . . . we had there [at Northwestern] just welcomed me with open arms," he recalled.[42]

Northwestern Aeronautical never made another glider. It survived for another year, making fuel trucks for the aviation industry, and then quietly faded from memory. Engineering Research Associates, however, did more than survive. It thrived. In the years after the war, dozens of young engineers let their imaginations run free in the cavernous old "glider factory"—that's what they called it—on Minnehaha Avenue. Working under a series of military contracts, ERA made some of the most significant advances in early computer technology. In 1951, John Parker sold his majority stake in the firm to Remington Rand, which had recently acquired the company behind the first UNIVAC supercomputer. In the years that followed, Remington Rand merged the Sperry Corporation to form the Sperry Rand Corporation. The computer age was well on its way, thanks—at least in part—to a long-forgotten glider company.

The people of Brainerd had assumed that 1943 would bring a flood of information about the missing men of Company A. The War Department had confirmed the previous December that the Japanese were holding Ernie Miller and Ed Burke as prisoners of war in the Philippines. Surely news of the other Brainerd men would be forthcoming.

But the news did not come.

During the first six months of 1943, the information that had been trickling in from Japan and the Philippines dried up completely. The War Department had no news—good or bad—about Miller and Burke's comrades. The remaining men from Brainerd were still missing in action and presumed captured. Loved ones back home, frustrated by the lack of information, searched for ways to feel useful. The *Brainerd Dispatch* suggested that the city's residents channel their frustrations into the purchase of war bonds:

> *Every dollar loaned in Crow Wing County is a symbol of our pledge to the "Miller Gang." We loan where they gave. We owe to them the right to know that we, their people, are standing firmly at their side. That we, their people, will leave no stone unturned until the Japanese government is wiped completely from the face of the earth. Until every hour these men have suffered in a Japanese prison camp is avenged in a way that the Japanese people will never forget.*[1]

Eleanor Swearingen received this photo of 194th Tank Battalion officers in August 1944. It had been taken eight months earlier. From left to right: Ernie Miller, John Muir, Lyman E. Johnson, Ed Burke, John J. Hummel, Russ Swearingen.

Finally, in June, the Japanese government began releasing more information about the prisoners it was holding, using the International Red Cross as an intermediary. But for the people in Brainerd, much of the early news was devastating. On June 16, Hulda Karlson received a telegram informing her that her son, Staff Sergeant David Karlson, had died while in Japanese custody.[2] That telegram was just the first of several such dispatches that arrived in Brainerd that summer. Third-grader Don Samuelson was at home, waiting for his mother to return from work, when he received a phone call telling him to hurry over to his grandmother's house. "I had a feeling when that call came that something was really up," he recalled years later. When he arrived, he found all his relatives, including his mother, seated at his grandmother's kitchen table. When they told him that his father, Sergeant Walter Samuelson, had died in a Japanese POW camp, he refused to believe it. "As a little kid, even though you're told he's not coming back, somehow you think it's just not true," he said. "He's too strong. He'll be back. So it takes a lot of convincing."[3]

Until this time, all of the information that had come back to Brainerd concerning the men of Company A had been second-hand. No one had received any direct correspondence from the men themselves. Then, in late August, the postman delivered a letter to Ann Miller. It was from her husband, Ernie, the commander of the 194th, at the Zensuji POW camp in Japan:

> I was taken prisoner in Bataan at the time of the surrender on April 9, 1942. I have had no chance of writing home before, but thank God I am now allowed to send this. Have been thinking of you all every minute and wondering if you have remembered my admonition that I will be coming back to you. God speed the day. What a reunion that will be!
>
> I am well although weak from some of the illnesses I have had, but am feeling fine and the doctor assures me I am O.K. I am telling you the absolute truth, my dear, there is nothing for you to worry about as far as I am concerned.
>
> We did our best on Bataan and I'm proud of our record. Scotty [John Muir], [Ed] Burke and [Russ] Swearingen are with me and all in good health.[4]

Soon other Brainerd residents were receiving news from their loved ones. Katherine Porwoll read and reread the short typewritten note that her son, Ken, sent from a POW camp in the Philippines. It was the first word she had received that her son was even alive. Pernina Burke received two similar typewritten cards from her husband, Ed, within a three-week period. But while the letters were nice, they couldn't measure up to the voice messages. That fall, the Japanese government began broadcasting messages from American POWs over shortwave radio. On November 17, Gilbert Swearingen picked up the first broadcast from a member of Company A: his brother, Russ. That same day, Pernina Burke got a phone call from an amateur shortwave operator in Hopkins who said he had recorded a broadcast message from Ed.[5] Such radio messages rarely included substantial news, but the sound of the men's voices eased the torment of the loved ones back home. "That was a marvelous thing that those shortwave operators did," Pernina Burke recalled.

In the twenty-one months since the fall of Bataan, the people of Brainerd had been spared the details of what actually happened to the 12,000 Americans and 78,000 Filipinos who had tried to repel the Japanese invasion of the Philippines. They knew only the most basic facts about the sixty-three Brainerd-area men—all members of Company A, 194th Tank Battalion—who had taken part in the fight. Some of the men had been confirmed dead. Others were prisoners of war. In almost all cases, the circumstances of the men's deaths and the details of their captivity were unknown.

That all changed on January 28, 1944.

On that day, the United States government released, for the first time, documentation of a stunning array of war atrocities perpetrated by the Japanese against American and Filipino prisoners. The information was based in large part on sworn statements from three American servicemen who had escaped from a prison camp in Davao. The men had recounted stories of "unparalleled bestiality" on the part of the Japanese and had described their inhumane treatment during what was soon to become known as the Bataan Death March. In the days after the surrender on Bataan, the Japanese had forced thousands of American and Filipino prisoners to march as far as fifty-five miles to a prison at Camp O'Donnell. The captured troops were repeatedly beaten and denied food and water. Many died of dehydration and heat exhaustion. Many others were executed by their captors. (Later estimates numbered the dead at 24,000).[6]

The people of Brainerd were, like most Americans, outraged. In an editorial titled "The Beast of Asia," *Brainerd Dispatch* editor George Wing threw aside all pretensions of journalistic objectivity.

Reception of the news here among the home-folks of these "Men of Bataan," the story of Japanese atrocities, [was] received with a silent determination to carry through this war against Japan until the very name of Japan will have vanished from the civilized world. There was, happily, a general resentment over the nation directed toward complete elimination of the Japanese as a people and in time, as a race . . .

There must be only one objective—

To wipe Japan and its people from emperor down from the face of the earth![7]

Other Brainerd residents were more diplomatic in their responses. Ann Miller called the revelations of Japanese atrocities "very discouraging" but insisted that she was "not ready to give up" hope that her husband, Ernie, would return safely. George Falconer, whose son, John, was among the prisoners, hoped that the revelations would remind Americans of the grim sacrifices that lay ahead. "Our boys must be avenged," he said. "More

善通寺俘虜收容所規定葉書

3 October, 1943.

Darling Eleanore: I hope this letter reaches you by Christmas end finds you all well. I am wishing you a very Merry Christmas and am hoping to join you in the future Christmas. My health is excellent. Love Russell

Russell S. Sweaninger

The short notes that Brainerd's POWs were allowed to send home rarely contained substantive information, but they were cherished by those who received them.

bonds, more men under arms and more ships at sea will hasten this victory and crush the Japanese nation."[8]

As details of the Japanese army's brutality spread, families in Brainerd clung even more tightly to the cards and letters from the prison camps of the Philippines and Japan. Eleanor Swearingen, for one, took great comfort in the correspondence from her husband, Russ, even though she knew he was not telling her everything. Her son, Don Arm, remembered his stepfather's letters as strangely unfulfilling. "They were told what to send," he said of the prisoners. "If everything wasn't right and he wasn't doing fine, they never would have let him send the letter."[9] Sometimes, though, true emotion slipped past the Japanese censor. In a letter that arrived in August 1944, Russ Swearingen wrote, "Just can't find word to express my relief and gratitude in finding that my family is well and that I have a new baby daughter." Before closing his letter with assurances of his good health ("I weigh 145 pounds"), he added a few comforting words for his stepson. "Donnie must make his grades good and if he will do that I will buy him a new bicycle when I return," he wrote. "I am only awaiting the day when he and I can go fishing and hunting together."[10]

In the fall of 1944, word arrived that two Brainerd POWs had escaped and were heading back home. Sergeant James McComas and Private First Class Joe Lamkin were among eighty-three American prisoners who were rescued after a U.S. submarine sank the Japanese transport ship that was carrying them to another camp in Japan. (Hundreds of other Americans died in the incident.) Upon his arrival in Minnesota, McComas described the pandemonium that broke out after the ship went down. "Those Japs took their guns into their life boats, and cruised around taking pot shots at our struggling men," he said. On November 17, McComas "slipped quietly into town" and was welcomed home by his family. There was no parade, no band playing patriotic tunes. The people of Brainerd knew that many more men still needed to come home. McComas planned to meet with some of the families of his Company A comrades, but more than anything, he wanted his life to return to normal. When asked by a local reporter what other plans he might have, McComas voiced a familiar refrain. His goals were simple, he said: just "some deer hunting and a little fishing."[11]

6 Rumors of War

The mechanics at Mid-Continent Airlines' maintenance facility at Wold-Chamberlain Field in Minneapolis were used to working under pressure, but this was ridiculous. It was the dead of winter—the middle of February 1941—and suddenly the 120-odd mechanics were working around the clock, installing huge auxiliary fuel tanks into two dozen B-25 bombers. The pace was frenzied. The work was difficult. (The 160-gallon collapsible neoprene tanks gave off fumes that gagged the mechanics.) Tempers were fraying. And to top it all off, the bosses were suddenly paranoid about security. "They didn't tell us why we were doing what we were doing," recalled mechanic Roger Poore, "except that we couldn't talk about any of it."[1]

Military police from Fort Snelling now patrolled the area around the Mid-Continent hangar. They were under orders to bar anyone without permission to be there. Reporters, politicians, airport officials—if they didn't have the proper credentials, they weren't allowed anywhere near. In one case, an MP went so far as to fire a warning shot when the airport's manager got too close.

Two weeks after the first B-25s arrived, they were gone again, and the mechanics at Mid-Continent returned to their normal routines. It wasn't until mid-April that they—and the rest of the world—learned the reason for the secrecy.[2]

On April 18, 1942, sixteen B-25s—all modified for long-distance flight by Mid-Continent's Minneapolis mechanics—took off from an aircraft carrier in the mid-Pacific and dropped bombs on the Japanese cities of Tokyo, Osaka, Yokohama, Nagoya, and Kobe. The mission, led by Lieutenant Colonel Jimmy Doolittle, gave Americans a much-needed psychological lift after months of disheartening war news from the Pacific. The United States had finally struck back. "We felt pretty good about all that work we had done on the planes," Roger Poore said.[3]

In retrospect, Doolittle's choice of Mid-Continent for the job made sense. Minneapolis was far from the West Coast—an important consideration given concerns about Japanese spy activity. In

U.S. government agencies regularly exhorted Americans to control the spread of sensitive information such as troop and ship movements.

addition, Mid-Continent's hangar stood at the far south end of the airport, where the fuel tanks could be installed in relative secrecy.

Jimmy Doolittle's bomber modification operation was just one of many military secrets that Minnesotans kept to themselves—or had kept from them—during World War II. Military installations, defense plants, and research institutions around the state clamped down on any information that might be deemed sensitive. "Hush-hush is the byword now," said University of Minnesota President Walter C. Coffey of the numerous wartime projects conducted on campus. "I don't know myself what some of our men are working on."[4] And while relatively few Minnesotans were privy to the kind of information that might be of use to the enemy, most took seriously the government's admonitions to "be smart, act dumb," and button their lips.

Kamikaze Pigeons

Minneapolis Star Journal columnist Cedric Adams, who had a soft spot for animal stories, included an unusual notice in his column for September 2, 1942.

> *Staff members at the University of Minnesota are doing some research on night vision for the war department and they need 25 tame crows. If you have a bird that you'd like to enlist in the war effort for an exceedingly worthy cause, call Main 8177, extension 591 for details or with your crow offer.*[5]

The call for crows was misleading. As Adams may or may not have been aware, the university scientists who asked him to mention their project were not really researching night vision. That was just a ruse meant to hide a rather bizarre truth: they were training birds—pigeons, mostly—to point bombs and missiles at military targets.

"Project Pigeon," as it was known within the War Department, was the brainchild of B. F. Skinner, an up-and-coming assistant professor of psychology at the University of Minnesota. Skinner was the man behind a new and influential psychological research method called operant conditioning. He had proven, through his experiments with rats, that animals could be taught—with reinforcement—to perform relatively complex tasks that they normally wouldn't do (such as dropping a marble down a chute). Skinner was a creature of the laboratory who had never shown much interest in applying his concepts to real-world problems. But in 1940—shortly after joining the Minnesota faculty—Skinner's outlook was beginning to change. Europe was at war and American intervention seemed increasingly likely. Skinner felt compelled to do something for the war effort. Project Pigeon was his contribution.[6]

The idea came to Skinner as he traveled by train to a Chicago conference in April 1940. The war news at the time was depressing. The Nazis had invaded Norway and Denmark. They seemed unstoppable. As the train rumbled toward Chicago, Skinner started thinking about the Germans' bombing of Warsaw. Wouldn't it be wonderful, he thought, if a bomb or missile could destroy Nazi bombers before they destroyed Europe's cities?

> *I was looking out the window as I speculated about these possibilities, and I saw a flock of birds lifting and wheeling in formation as they flew alongside the train. Suddenly I saw them as "devices" with excellent vision and extraordinary maneuverability. Could they not guide a missile? Was the answer to the problem waiting for me in my own backyard?*[7]

Back in Minneapolis, Skinner bought a few pigeons from a poultry store that supplied Chinese restaurants and taught them to peck at bull's-eye targets. When a bird was properly trained, he jacketed it snugly into a man's sock—its head and neck protruding through holes in the toe—and harnessed it to a moveable hoist. He then placed the hoist opposite a bull's-eye and began pushing it toward the target. As the contraption rolled forward, the pigeon moved its head up, down, and sideways to keep the target in sight. Each movement triggered mechanical controls that guided the simulator's direction. And every time the bird "steered" toward the bull's-eye, Skinner reinforced that response with food: a kernel of grain. Before long, Skinner's pigeons were reliably guiding the apparatus to the target as fast as it could go.

Skinner demonstrated his pigeon-guided simulator for physicist John Tate, dean of the university's College of Science, Literature, and Art. Tate was so impressed that he passed along Skinner's plans to Richard C. Tolman, head of the physics department at the California Institute of Technology. Tolman was vice chairman of the National Defense Research Committee (NDRC) and, as such, had the power to give the project a big boost. But while Tolman considered Skinner's idea "a new and unconventional approach," he ultimately rejected it. Skinner thanked Tolman for his time and shelved the project.[8]

It appeared that Skinner's plan was dead. But then, on December 7, the Japanese forced all Americans—including Skinner—to reexamine their priorities. The next day, he returned to his lab and resurrected the pigeon project.

With the help of graduate student Keller Breland, Skinner devised a new training apparatus for his pigeons. This time, the device itself remained stationary while the target rotated and moved from side to side. Once again, the pigeons performed nearly flawlessly. Skinner filmed his pigeons in action and made another bid for support from Tolman and his colleagues at the NDRC. In late March of 1942, Tolman informed him that, after looking over his new reports, the committee still was not "able to justify the use of funds" on the pigeon project. But by this time, Skinner was working full time on his unorthodox guidance system, and he wasn't about to let one more rejection stand in his way. "This has not altered my faith in the plan," he wrote in a letter to John Tate. "I have put aside all other research and am giving all my time exclusively to going on with this work."[9]

After weeks of work with little outside encouragement, an unlikely savior appeared on the scene to rescue Skinner's dream from obscurity. General Mills Company officials had learned of the pigeon project from a local inventor who had recently made Skinner's acquaintance. (The inventor had approached both Skinner and General Mills with plans for a dog-guided torpedo system.) The officials didn't think much of the inventor's ideas, but they were intrigued by Skinner's research and credentials. Like many companies at the time, General Mills was looking for opportunities to contribute to the war effort and gain a share of government contracts. The company gave Skinner a $5,000 grant to develop his pigeon-controlled device "to the point at which support could be obtained from a government agency." It also let him move his lab to the top floor of what was known as the "utility building" of the company's riverside milling complex.[10]

Skinner and his research assistants moved into their new work space on September 1, 1942. After a brief flirtation with crows ("amusing to work with but not very cooperative"),[11] Skinner's team concentrated on the pigeons. Their work produced a new device that required the pigeons to peck at a glass screen on which target images—including an aerial photograph of, inexplicably, Stalingrad—were projected. The birds proved that they could perform admirably under almost any conditions. Noise, vibration, acceleration—it didn't seem to matter. They just kept pecking away at their

Skinner focused his guided missile research on pigeons after deciding that crows, while "remarkable subjects," were too temperamental.

targets. In March of 1943, a pair of NDRC representatives traveled to Minneapolis for a first-hand look at Skinner's pigeons. They came away impressed. Three months later, the NDRC awarded General Mills a $25,000 contract to develop an "organic homing device" under the code name Project Pigeon.[12]

After two years on the fringes of weapons research, it seemed that Skinner and his pigeon project were finally getting some respect. As Skinner and his team focused on the pigeons' training, General Mills engineers tried to refine the mechanical systems that translated the birds' pecking into reliable steering instructions. By September of 1943, they had produced an improved signaling system controlled by four pneumatic valves. Other refinements followed. To improve reliability, the Project Pigeon engineers redesigned the steering apparatus to accommodate three birds instead of just one. "The majority vote of three pigeons offered an excellent guarantee against momentary pauses and aberrations," Skinner wrote.[13] Meanwhile, Skinner and his research assistants designed new "methods for the mass production of trained birds."[14]

By this time the NDRC had provided the Project Pigeon team with some—although not much—information about the missile that the birds might eventually be called on to navigate. The Pelican, as it was called, was actually a winged bomb designed for anti-ship warfare. It still needed a reliable homing device, so the NDRC decided to let Skinner and his team take a stab at it. It gave them rough specifications of the Pelican as well as aerial photographs of its testing site near Toms River, New Jersey. From that point on, Skinner and his team taught their pigeons to peck away at photos of a small slice of the New Jersey coast.

But time was running out for Project Pigeon. By the end of 1943, its $25,000 contract had expired and the NDRC was losing interest again. One NDRC member described the project's data as "not quite good enough to be promising . . . not quite bad enough to throw away." Another was more scathing, ridiculing the project's control mechanism as a "player piano movement type of thing." At a meeting in January 1944, the NDRC voted to cut off funding for Project Pigeon.[15]

Skinner was flummoxed. How could the NDRC scientists dismiss his pigeons' impressive performance? "Every competent person who has familiarized himself with our work has passed from a stage of amused skepticism to a serious belief that the scheme deserves to be

A feathered test subject is placed in a demonstration model of Skinner's pigeon-guided homing device.

tried," he wrote. "It is unfortunate that the final decision always seems to rest with men who have not had the benefit of close contact with the project."[16] But Skinner refused to give up. In March 1944, he convinced the NDRC to give him one last chance. He traveled to Washington to show the committee members a pigeon in action.

Skinner began by touting the advantages of a pigeon-controlled homing device. "We have used pigeons, not because the pigeon is an intelligent bird," he said, "but because it is a practical one and can be made into a machine, from all practical points of view."[17] Then he launched into the demonstration. The pigeon—which had been cooped up in a train's baggage compartment for thirty-six hours— was harnessed in a small black box. It faced a pecking screen on which an image of the New Jersey target site was projected. Skinner had rigged the box with a viewing tube to avoid disturbing the bird, but it soon became clear that the tube was impractical. Skinner took the top off the box so that everyone could watch the pigeon at the same time. Even though the box and screen were flooded with light, the bird performed flawlessly. "It was a perfect performance," Skinner recalled years later, "but it had just the wrong effect:"

The spectacle of a living pigeon carrying out its assignment, no matter how beautifully, simply reminded the committee of how utterly fantastic our proposal was. I will not say that the meeting was marked by unrestrained merriment, for the merriment was restrained. But it was there, and it was obvious that our case was lost.[18]

As Skinner left the meeting, a General Mills executive who had accompanied him to Washington made a perfectly appropriate suggestion: "Why don't you go out and get drunk?" he said.[19]

On April 8, Skinner and the Project Pigeon team received the official word from the NDRC: "Further prosecution of this project would seriously delay others which . . . would have more immediate promise of combat application." Skinner later speculated that the NDRC was alluding to the atom bomb program, but it's more likely that it was referring to recent developments in radar technology.

After three years of on-again, off-again work, Project Pigeon was finished. General Mills withdrew its support and evicted Skinner and his researchers from their flour-mill laboratory. The training device was moved to the basement of the university's psychology building, where it sat unused, gathering dust. Skinner kept about two dozen of the trained birds to see how long they continued to display their reinforced behavior. In the end, he wrote, all he had to show for his three years of work was "a lotful of curiously useless equipment and a few dozen pigeons with a strange interest in a feature of the New Jersey coast."[20]

Most Minnesotans had no idea that a small band of university psychologists had spent a good part of the war training kamikaze pigeons in an old Minneapolis flour mill. Cedric Adams' misleading column about crows and night vision research was apparently the only news item to make even passing reference to the project during the war. Even though some saw it more as a scientific lark than a viable experiment, Project Pigeon was a closely held wartime secret. It remained classified until the late 1950s.

Whirligigs

In the summer of 1944, the residents of Rochester were spending a lot of time looking up at the sky, wondering what was going on up there. Day after day, an Army Air Forces dive bomber took off from the Rochester Airport, climbed to an altitude of about ten thousand feet, and then spun toward the ground in a hair-raising spiral. The plane always came out of the dive without apparent incident, but the people of Rochester couldn't help but wonder what the pilot was trying to accomplish. Did he have a death wish or something? They had no clue that the aerial acrobatic show was part of a secret research operation being conducted in their own backyard—at the Mayo Clinic.

Mayo physicians and scientists had been studying the physiological effects of modern flight since the late 1930s. Their early work focused on the problems pilots encountered at high altitudes—especially the lack of oxygen. But by 1941, a group of Mayo researchers was homing in on another problem: acceleration. In the years since the First World War, planes had become faster and more agile. During tight turns, pilots were subjected to extreme gravitational forces—or g-forces—that sometimes caused them to lose vision (blackout) or consciousness. The Mayo researchers set out to determine what exactly happened to the human body during extreme acceleration and to find ways to help pilots maintain their faculties during high-g maneuvers.

Working under a shroud of secrecy, the acceleration laboratory of the Mayo Aero Medical Unit kicked into high gear in 1942 with the planning and construction of a massive human centrifuge—the first of its kind in the United States. Made of tubular steel, the centrifuge looked something like a long rectangular cage center-mounted on a vertical axel—a simulated cockpit perched on one end. A salvaged Chrysler automobile engine supplied the power, driving two twenty-ton flywheels that had been rescued from an old brewery. Plans called for volunteers to sit in the cockpit while the centrifuge spun, subjecting them to forces as high as nine g. Various instruments would measure the men's vital signs, including breathing, pulse, and blood pressure. The thought of a homemade "whirligig" twirling men at unthinkable speeds on clinic property made some people at Mayo uneasy, and as the centrifuge approached completion, the Board of Governors called in Dr. Charles Code—the man who would supervise the experiments—to reassure them. "They were concerned about safety and so on and they didn't want me to do anything or allow anything to be done that was dangerous," Code recalled years later. "I said to myself, 'There isn't anything about that wheel that isn't dangerous. The whole thing is dangerous!'"[21]

The physicians and scientists of the acceleration laboratory decided early on that they could only ask volunteers to do what they,

The Mayo Aero Medical Unit's human centrifuge, shortly after its completion in 1942

the researchers, had already done themselves. So the researchers be-came their own guinea pigs. Charles Code, Earl Wood, and Ed Lam-bert endured hundreds of experimental "runs" on the centrifuge. (Wood later joked that those runs might have caused "some of our strange behavior during subsequent years.")[22] Once they established that their contraption was safe, dozens of eager volunteers clamored for a chance to take what appeared to be the ultimate thrill ride. At one point, Code was inundated by so many "wild volunteers" beg-ging to go for a spin ("Put me on that wheel, black me out, render me unconscious") that he started turning them down flat. "I had absolutely no use for them," he said.[23] Those who did get to ride didn't always enjoy the experience. "I had only one or two runs at 5 'G,'" wrote one volunteer. "Those two runs almost exceeded my 'merry-go-round tolerance.'"[24]

The data confirmed, among other things, that exposure to ex-treme acceleration restricted blood flow to the head, causing black-outs and loss of consciousness. The findings also suggested that the best way to keep blood flowing to the head was to increase pressure on the arteries in other parts of the body. The question was how best to do that.

Earl Wood was convinced that the answer was the anti-gravity suit. Researchers elsewhere had experimented with garments de-signed to protect pilots from blackout and loss of consciousness, but those suits had proved largely ineffective. Inspired by the early data from the centrifuge experiments, Wood now pictured an inflatable "g-suit" that squeezed the pilot's legs and applied pressure to the ab-domen. The idea was to increase blood pressure at heart level and direct the flow of blood where it was needed most—to the head.

Wood might never have gotten very far with his idea if he had not crossed paths with Dave Clark. Clark owned a small knitting company in Worcester, Massachusetts, and he had begun toying with designs for an anti-gravity suit after seeing the Clark Gable movie *Test Pilot*. Clark had tried for months to interest the army and navy in his designs but had gotten nowhere. Then, at one con-tact's suggestion, Clark wrote to the Mayo Aero Medical Unit about his ideas. To his surprise, he soon received an invitation to Rochester. As he learned later, the researchers at the acceleration laboratory were intrigued with his "unusual skills in knitting and preparing fabrics that would give degrees of elastic support."[25]

For about a year and a half, Earl Wood, Dave Clark, and a hand-ful of other researchers and technicians worked to perfect a g-suit that pilots would actually wear into combat. The first designs, when

tested on the centrifuge, proved very effective at increasing g tolerance, but they were also maddeningly uncomfortable. In the
months that followed, it became increasingly clear to the g-suit
team that comfort was more important than achieving maximum
g tolerance. With this in mind, Wood and Clark pared their design
down to a simple inflatable bladder system that could be built into
a variety of garments. It provided about half as much g-force protection as the first generation of suits, but tests on the centrifuge determined that that was all the protection pilots really needed.

Pilots, however, were not convinced. They didn't want to trust
their lives to a system that had proven itself only on a centrifuge.
They wanted proof that Mayo's g-suit worked where it needed to
work—in the air. But that would not be easy. The Mayo researchers

Charlie Code and Ken Bailey shortly before taking off in the G-Whiz

would first need a plane—and a pilot—capable of safely reproducing the extreme conditions generated by the centrifuge.

The Army Air Forces, which by this time was taking a special interest in Mayo's acceleration studies, was only too glad to help. It sent a brand-new A-24A dive bomber to Rochester and arranged for pilot Captain Kenneth Bailey to fly it. (Bailey was in charge of the Air Transport Command Station at the Rochester Airport, which served as a refueling stop for P-39 combat aircraft on their way to the Soviet Union.) Ed Lambert rigged the plane to supply the same kind of data that the centrifuge did. He called his flying laboratory the "G-Whiz."

As they had during the centrifuge experiments, Lambert, Code, and Wood served as the initial guinea pigs. Other volunteers soon followed. Each test subject sat in the plane's rear seat, wearing a g-suit

In addition to its research on high g-forces, the Mayo Aero Medical Unit spent considerable time studying the biomedical problems faced by pilots during high altitude flights in non-pressurized cockpits. In the fall of 1942, aviation pioneer Charles Lindbergh, a Minnesota native, volunteered to be a test subject in the clinic's high altitude (or low pressure) chamber. Lindbergh made several simulated parachute jumps in the chamber, subjecting himself to the same conditions a pilot would encounter if forced to bail out at forty thousand feet.

(sometimes inflated, sometimes not) and a custom-made plaster helmet with built-in pulse monitors. Bailey (whose g-suit was always inflated) took the plane to ten thousand feet and then dropped it into a death-defying spiral. For fifteen seconds, his passengers struggled to remain conscious—and keep their food down—as they endured g-forces similar to those produced by the centrifuge. Dave Clark took two rides in the G-Whiz, then declined Bailey's offer to take him on a third. "Ken came through on the 'intercom' asking if I was ready for 7 'G,'" Clark recalled years later. "I said, 'there is no point—I'm about sick.'"[26]

The data collected during the G-Whiz experiments over Rochester convinced the army and navy that the Mayo anti-gravity suits worked and that their pilots should wear them. Each service developed its own version and used it extensively. After the war, German aircraft designer Wilhelm Messerschmitt recalled his reaction after seeing a g-suit on a downed American pilot. "We had nothing to match it," he said, "and I knew if American aviation science was so far ahead of us to make such a suit, Germany had lost the war already."[27]

H2X

On New Year's Eve, 1943, hundreds of civilian employees at St. Paul's airport, Holman Field, received a restricted memo from the military officer who oversaw their work. Holman Field was home to the Northwest–St. Paul Modification Center, or "Mod Center," as it was more commonly known. Employees at the Mod Center customized newly minted B-24 Liberator bombers to perform specific duties in specific theaters of war, and their work had always been somewhat hush-hush. But now Captain A. B. Horner, the Army Air Forces' "resident representative," had issued a new directive to employees: to protect the secrecy of the new device that they had begun installing in the big bombers—the device known as H2X.

> *The importance of the H2X project which has recently been put into production at this Modification Center cannot be overemphasized. The part which airplanes equipped with H2X will play during the coming weeks in the combat theaters is of the most vital nature. About the H2X project hangs a major role in the strategy of the Army Air Forces . . .*
>
> *A word of caution, however; this project must be accomplished with the highest secrecy. Don't be concerned about things other than your own particular job. Never mention the project*

*to anyone off these premises and while at work only to those in-
dividuals with whom it is necessary to confer in line of duty.*[28]

Horner's memo confirmed what many employees already knew,
or at least suspected: that H2X was something special—something
so big and so secret that it had its own code name. For the time being, the workers at the Mod Center would go about their jobs, keep
their mouths shut, and let the public and the press think that they
were just continuing to do their usual work.

The Mod Center had never been a secret in the usual sense of the
word. There was, after all, no way to fly hundreds of thundering
B-24s into St. Paul without attracting attention. And since it was impossible to put a lid on the entire operation, the Army Air Forces
had, from the start, made a point of periodically releasing just
enough information to satisfy the public's curiosity.

The need for bomber modification facilities had first become evident in early 1942. The Ford Motor Company's bomber plant at
Willow Run, Michigan, was turning out Liberators at an unbeliev-
able pace—sometimes as fast as one per hour—but to maintain that
pace, Ford could only produce a stripped-down version. The special
equipment that made each plane unique had to be added elsewhere.
The AAF soon began arranging to have civilian contractors operate

A modified B-24 over Holman Field

bomber modification plants at locations around the country. In February of 1942 it contracted with Northwest Airlines to run one such operation at St. Paul's Holman Field.

Northwest faced several daunting challenges in setting up the Mod Center. For one thing, the facilities at Holman Field were limited, to put it mildly. There was an office building belonging to Northwest, an airport administration building, and a National Guard hangar, but that was about it. Moreover, Northwest's employees knew hardly anything about production. The company didn't make things; it offered its customers a service—air travel. But the urgent need for finished bombers outweighed any concerns that Northwest had about doing production work. The first B-24s began arriving in May, and they needed to be customized as soon as possible.

During the first six months of operation, workers at the Mod Center made do as best they could. Mechanics worked on the Liberators wherever they were parked. If the weather turned nasty, they

Thousands of men and women employed by the Northwest–St. Paul Modification Center modified 3,286 aircraft during the course of the war.

threw tarpaulins over the planes so that work could continue. Eventually the company built several wood and canvas "nose hangars" to provide temporary protection from the rain.

In December 1942, the Mod Center took a huge step forward with the addition of a new 600-by-168-foot hangar. A nearly identical hangar, built alongside the first one, opened a few months later. Each could hold thirteen B-24s. The planes moved through the facilities in assembly-line fashion, progressing from one station to another every twenty-four hours. Each bomber was designated for specific duty. Some planes received special radio equipment and antennas. Others were given additional guns or navigation instruments. Aerial tankers were rigged with huge storage tanks. Photo reconnaissance planes had cameras installed.

With the addition of the two hangars, the Mod Center was finally able to keep pace with the production of B-24s coming out of Willow Run. Work continued around the clock. It was, in the words of production scheduling director Ted Gruenhagen, "a hectic period":

> I can remember we didn't miss a production schedule in eleven months, and I didn't have a day off. I worked as much as thirty-six hours at a stretch. Many times, I'd almost meet myself coming and going. Once I fell asleep at the wheel of my car. Still, I was lucky not to be laying out there at the Battle of the Bulge.[29]

During the first year and a half of production, the Mod Center was a kind of open secret. It didn't generate as much news coverage as other war production facilities in the area, such as the Twin Cities Ordnance Plant in New Brighton, but its function was generally understood. Then, in December of 1943, the Mod Center launched the H2X program, and secrecy took on a new urgency. H2X was "the *most* important project ever undertaken at a modification center,"[30] Captain Horner declared, and "it was necessary that care be taken to keep from releasing the fact [of its existence] to the public."[31]

Although most Mod Center employees took the warnings seriously, it didn't take long for details of the H2X to spread across the facility. H2X was military shorthand for high-altitude radar. Planes equipped with this state-of-the-art radar system could essentially "see" through all kinds of cloud cover and could accurately bomb their targets in any kind of weather. U.S. bomber crews had their own name for H2X. They called it "Mickey."

While many workers at the Mod Center assumed that the H2X radar played a key role during the last two years of the war, its full significance did not become clear until after the war was over. The final edition of the Mod Center's monthly newsletter, *Field and Hangar*, unveiled details about the radar project that it had been obliged to keep under wraps for more than a year and half. The H2X project was "by far the most important work" done at the center, the newsletter claimed. Radar-equipped B-24s had played vital roles in the raids on the Ploesti oil fields in Romania in the spring of 1944 and in the bombing campaign that followed the Normandy invasion. In what may have been the ultimate compliment, *Field and Hangar* quoted the general who led the first raid on Ploesti: "If it hadn't been for H2X, the war in Europe probably would still be going on!"[32]

In mid-August of 1945, the Army Air Force officially notified Northwest Airlines that it was shutting down the St. Paul Mod Center. The 130 bombers awaiting modification at Holman Field at the time were designated as surplus and flown to army bases around the country to meet their uncertain fates. During its nearly three and a half years, the Northwest–St. Paul Modification Center had tailored for combat 3,286 aircraft, almost all B-24 Liberators. At its peak production in the summer of 1943, it employed more than five thousand men and women. In an open letter to those employees, Brigadier General E. M. Powers commended the Mod Center for saving the lives of countless American servicemen. "Many more gold stars would be in the windows of American homes," he wrote, "if it had not been for the supply . . . of the B-24s modified at your center."[33]

Raw Deal

In March 1942, dozens of farmers just south of Rosemount, in the area known as Rich Valley, started noticing lines of strange cars "poking their way along the gravel roads."[34] The cars drove slowly back and forth, stopping occasionally as the people inside gazed out their windows at the flat farmland. Rumors started spreading. The country was at war; the government must be looking over land for a military airfield. People began to worry.

But Henry and Margaret Peine were not overly concerned. They owned what the local newspaper called "one of the neatest farms in the state."[35] Rich Valley was a farmer's dream—"sure-crop country," one grower called it.[36] Old-timers swore that the area had suffered only one crop failure in seventy-five years, and that was due to an infestation of chinch bugs.[37] But of all the farms in the area, the Peines' 240-acre spread may have been the most widely admired. "There wasn't a stone on it," Henry Peine recalled. "It was gentle rolling. We had wonderful soil, clay bottom soil . . . That was nice country up this side of Rosemount, level."[38] The Peines hadn't paid much attention to the rumors creeping through Rich Valley during the first few months of the war. An airfield wouldn't eat up that much real estate, they figured. Besides, they were too busy preparing for spring planting to worry about some vague government construction project that might or might not be built. They had work to do.

But soon the rumors gave way to facts. And the facts were devastating.

One day during the last week of March, Henry Peine came home to find a real estate agent waiting for him. The man seemed to know everything about the mystery project that everybody had been whispering about. The government was going to build a huge war plant in Rich Valley, the agent said—not an airfield. All the farmers in the area would have to sell their land and move elsewhere. He rolled out a map showing that the Peines' 240 acres lay at the far south end of the project. The Peines were stunned. Could this be true? Planting season was fast approaching and the government was taking away

Charley Johnson was among the few Rosemount farmers who didn't mind selling his land to the government. "He's 75 years old and was ready to retire anyway," the Minneapolis Star Journal *reported.*

their land? The real agent insisted it was true, and he offered a suggestion. He just happened to have five farms for sale that he'd be glad to show the Peines. Would they be interested in looking? Stunned, the Peines hopped in the agent's car and took a look at the farms he had to offer. None of them came close to matching the quality of the spread they already owned. Before heading on his way, the agent mentioned that the Peines might want to attend a meeting to be held Tuesday in Farmington. Representatives from the government were supposedly going to explain what was going on.[39]

The meeting in Farmington was surprisingly orderly given the tension in the air. The War Department's local real estate manager, J. Wesley White, confirmed that the government planned to build a new arms facility, Gopher Ordnance Works, in Rich Valley and that it was taking ninety-six parcels of land. The site was just what the government was looking for, he said. It was flat, relatively undeveloped, and close to transportation routes and population centers capable of providing plenty of labor. White announced that appraisers would finish their work in about two weeks, at which time landowners would learn how much the government would pay for their property. All farm families should be prepared to move within the month. He asked the landowners to cooperate and to refrain from spreading rumors about the project—rumors that might be "inspired by enemy agents."[40]

Many farmers walked out of the meeting feeling that their world had been upended. Herbert Volkert told a reporter that he was "too blue to talk."[41] Mrs. Otto Boche broke down in tears when asked what she and her husband planned to do. "If they had only told us last fall," she said. "It's such a mess now. Time for seeding and we can't find a place now."[42] "Life was so tranquil and peaceful," recalled Emmet Carroll. "All of a sudden it was just blown to smithereens and we had no foundation; we had no base. It was a horrible feeling."[43]

Like many others, Henry and Margaret Peine began scrambling to find new property, but good farms were in short supply and prices were skyrocketing. A few farmers had acted on the early rumors and had bought up most of the best available land. To make matters worse, the Peines and most Rich Valley farmers had no idea what the government intended to pay for their property. Many assumed it would be well over one hundred dollars an acre, but they couldn't wait to find out. If they wanted to farm that spring, they had to act quickly. Henry Peine convinced a neighbor to sell him 410 acres of decent farmland at about two hundred dollars an acre and secured the sale with a $10,000 down payment. Satisfied that they had done the best they could, the Peines sat back and waited to find out what the government would pay.

The following weeks were exciting and traumatic. Dozens of Dakota County farms changed hands as soon-to-be-evicted farmers raced to find new properties and motivated sellers took advantage of the sudden demand. Hundreds of visitors from around the state milled around Rosemount, hoping to glimpse the site of the new munitions plant. Workmen began remodeling the Rosemount train station to prepare for the increased rail traffic. Government appraisers continued their work while maintaining a strict silence about the impending offers.[44]

In late April, the government began making its offers to individual landowners. As they compared notes, a pattern emerged. To most farmers it was obvious that the government was lowballing them.

About a hundred Rich Valley landowners gathered at a local school to vent their frustrations and plan a strategy. Speakers revealed that the government was offering an average of about sixty dollars an acre (it was actually closer to seventy-five dollars) for about eleven thousand acres of land. The group's co-chairman Julius F. Walkow complained that the offers "smelled to high heaven" and called on the farmers to demand fair prices. "Why should the government take good land for nothing?" he asked. Most of the displaced farmers agreed to reject the offers and approved a proposal to hire legal counsel. The War Department's real estate representative, J. Wesley White, refused to address the farmers' grievances directly; he only said that protests over prices would not delay the construction that would probably start in a matter of days.[45]

Despite their decision to challenge the government's offers, the farmers of Rich Valley knew they had little choice but to move. Those who could moved to new farms. Many others settled in with relatives. Henry and Margaret Peine were among the ones who found themselves in limbo. They thought they had protected themselves by agreeing to buy a new farm, but their offer from the government—seventy-two dollars an acre—was not nearly enough to cover the cost of the new property. Margaret Peine called it "a raw deal."[46] In the end, the deal fell through. The Peines lost their $10,000 down payment and had to settle for another, less expensive, farm in nearby Hampton.

The move out of Rich Valley was heartbreaking for many, including the Peines. "We had to get out, so we went," Margaret Peine

Auction Sale

The government has taken over our farm for a defense plant, we must sell at public auction on the old Joe Peters farm, 6 miles northeast of Farmington, 1¼ miles east of the DeCoster farm, on—

Thurs., April 16

SALE STARTS AT 1 O'CLOCK SHARP

21 HEAD OF LIVESTOCK

4 Guernsey milch cows, 4 beef calves, 1 veal calf

3 HORSES

2 Geldings, 7 and 8 years old
1 Saddle Mare, 6 years old

FARM MACHINERY, ETC.

1 New Ideal manure spreader, 1 feed mill, 1 McCormick-Deering mower, 1 new hay rack, several spools of new barb wire, some new chicken wire.

HOUSEHOLD GOODS

Kitchen stove, circulating heater, kitchen chairs, beds, springs, dressers, tables, day beds, table and floor lamps and many other articles too numerous to mention.

Some corn and 600 pounds of Irish cobbler potatos, certified.

TERMS OF SALE.—Sums of $10.00 and under, cash; over that amount, 6 to 12 months time will be given on notes acceptable to the clerk, bearing interest at 7 percent. Parties desiring credit must make arrangements with clerk before sale, otherwise bidders will be considered cash buyers. Anyone from a distance must make arrangements for credit with their home bank. All property must be settled for before removal from premises.

J. J. Christensen, owner

Frank Byrne, Auctioneer
The First State Bank of Rosemount, clerk

"Minnesota's No. 1 war refugee family." Jonas Christensen and his family had recently moved to Rosemount after being forced to sell their old farm on the site of the Twin Cities Ordnance Plant in New Brighton.

recalled. "Some of our relatives came and helped us move. Some of the neighbors. Everybody felt bad for us, so they helped . . . When we moved over here (to Hampton), I'll never forget it, it was an old broken down house . . . I cried the first night we were there."[47]

By early June, most of the evicted farmers had moved and the transformation of the Rosemount area had begun. A few farm buildings were converted into office space, and many others—houses, barns, silos, granaries, chicken coops, windmills, even out-houses—were auctioned off. Everything else was demolished. New, strangely shaped buildings rose in their place. In downtown Rose-mount, longtime residents shook their heads as a seemingly endless stream of cars and trucks snaked to and from the construction site. South of town, a new trailer court complete with toilet, bath, and laundry facilities sprouted to accommodate the burgeoning population of construction workers and their families.[48]

While some Rosemount residents welcomed the influx of people and excitement, others, including the local rural electrification supervisor, already missed the not-so-old days.

> *Instead of the familiar farm noises there is now only the noise of trucks, excavating machinery, the saw and the hammer. Even the trees will soon be all gone and the ground leveled off without a trace of what was only a few days ago one of the finest farming communities in the state.*
>
> *Instead of the produce from farm and dairies there will be products to be used for the destruction of human life and property. Products which will bring untold misery and sadness to countless homes and ruin the lives of men and women for generations.*[49]

As construction of the powder plant progressed through the summer and fall of 1942, relations between the federal government and the farmers it evicted continued to deteriorate. The government was determined to pay as little as possible for the land it had taken, and when the farmers refused its offers it commenced condemnation litigation. By this time it was clear that the two sides were far apart. The government was offering about seven hundred thousand dollars for nearly eleven thousand acres of property. The farmers claimed the land was worth double that.[50]

By the spring of 1943, the displaced farmers of Rich Valley had a new reason to be outraged. Construction at the Gopher Ordnance Works was months behind schedule. The plant, which was supposed to start production in January, had yet to produce an ounce of cannon or rifle powder. In April, the War Department laid off hundreds of workers in Rosemount and reduced by half the plant's production capacity due to the "present nature of battle and changing requirements at the front."[51] Rumors spread that construction would halt altogether. Three months later the government announced that it was, in fact, putting the Gopher Ordnance Works— along with seven other ordnance plants around the country—on "standby" status. The Gopher plant would remain unfinished. In a letter to the House Military Affairs Committee, Undersecretary of War Robert Patterson tried to head off criticism.

> *The closing of these plants has, no doubt, brought inconvenience and dislocation to local communities, and has directed public attention to idleness which may be inappropriately termed "waste"... Had these facilities not been courageously conceived, planned, and constructed, and had the fortunes of war continued to be adverse, the great destruction and waste of both manpower and money caused by having too little too late would have brought tremendous suffering that the present inactivities fade into insignificance.*[52]

But the evicted farmers of Rich Valley didn't consider the "inactivities" at the Gopher Ordnance Works insignificant at all. The plant that had pushed them off their farms stood unfinished. Much

By 1943, the rich farmland south of Rosemount was covered with train tracks, electrical poles, and massive concrete structures.

of the land they had given up was now unusable. Despite Robert Patterson's claims to the contrary, it did seem like a huge waste—a boondoggle. And to make matters worse, the government was still pressing its lowball offers.

Throughout the summer of 1943, a special three-person condemnation commission held hearings in St. Paul to reappraise seventy disputed properties, with the Justice Department arguing that the government's appraisals were fair and the farmers countering that the offers were too low. In September, the commissioners issued their ruling. They set the value of the land at $941,542—nearly one-third higher than the government's original offer. Most of the farmers were satisfied. The Justice Department was not. The office of the attorney general in Washington directed U.S. Attorney Victor E. Anderson to appeal each case in which the commissioners' appraisal exceeded the government's original offer. The two sides were heading to court.[53]

After several delays, the first of the Rosemount cases went to trial in April 1944. Federal Judge Robert C. Bell heard the cases in batches to expedite what promised to be a long process. Attorney Harold Levander (later Minnesota's governor) represented many of the Rosemount farmers. In his opinion, his clients were "innocent victims" caught in a situation they could not control.[54] Another attorney for the farmers, John McBrien, described an exhilarating atmosphere around the St. Paul courthouse: "The personnel and the clerk's office and the reporters and the bailiffs were all plugging for us and wanting us to do well."[55]

The trials were especially hard on the farmers. The government's lawyers—Victor Anderson, his assistant, Carl J. Eastvold, and Theodore H. Wangensteen of the attorney general's lands division staff—peppered them with questions designed to highlight every one of their farms' flaws. Like many of the growers, Anna Wachter traveled to St. Paul to watch the proceedings and lend moral support. "How they were teased and ridiculed by the government lawyers," she recalled. "It was no fun. So many of them cried. They just broke down and cried."[56]

Henry and Margaret Peine were among the luckier ones. Their case was heard in early June, and they happened to be in court on D-Day. Their lawyer, John McBrien, used the timing to his advantage.

I remember it very vividly, because Judge [Gunnar H.] Nordby had started court with a prayer for the success of the forces . . . I successfully used that as part of my argument to the jury in which I praised the fact that we were living in a country which, when it was engaged in mortal conflict, still had a system of law where the people could go to jury to have their property [valued] . . . I was told it was an effective argument.[57]

The jury awarded the Peines double the government's original offer—an extra $2,200 after attorneys' fees.[58] "From the standpoint of [it being an] increase it was a great victory," McBrien recalled. "From the standpoint of the result it wasn't anything for [the Peines] to be real happy with."[59]

Despite the Peines' victory, neither side really won. When the fight had begun back in 1942, the Rich Valley landowners had claimed that the eighty-four parcels of land that the government took for the Gopher Ordnance Works were collectively worth about $1.5 million, while the government offered about $700,000. By the time all but one of the cases were resolved, in January of 1945, the final number was just over $1 million. The farmers received about $300,000 more than the government originally offered, but $500,000 less than they claimed the land was worth.

In the end, the Gopher Ordnance Works did produce a small amount of cannon powder. The army pulled the project off standby status in the summer of 1944 and placed the plant into production in early 1945. But it never came close to achieving the production goals that were set out for it because, for one thing, it could never attract enough workers. When the final numbers were tallied, the Rosemount facility cost $115 million, making it the government's third most expensive ordnance plant.[60]

Years after the war, Henry Peine still couldn't understand why the government had to take his farm. "They didn't use it," he said. "The government said it was better to have it and not use it . . . But they could've gone at it in a different way. [They just] roust these people out of there and say 'get out and get going,' just as if they didn't pay their taxes . . . I don't think that was ever called for."[61]

DISPATCHES: ROBERT BURNS

About two months after the war ended, Private First Class Robert Burns of Worthington, Minnesota, became one of the first "GI-tourists" to visit the annihilated Japanese city of Hiroshima. Other U.S. soldiers had already inspected the city as part of the official military follow-up to the atomic blast. Burns and his buddies went as sightseers. On October 23, 1945, they spent a Tuesday afternoon walking through a city of ashes, occasionally picking up an undamaged plate or cup to take home as a souvenir. The next day, Burns wrote what today seems a strikingly hard-hearted letter to Artie and Ilma Cale, two friends in Worthington.[1]

Robert Burns (far left) and friends on the outskirts of Hiroshima, October 1945. Radioactivity affected the quality of the film.

October 24, 1945 (Hiro, Japan)

Well, yesterday the Army took us to see what was left of Hiroshima after the atomic bomb visited it. It was a beautiful trip over there as the road followed the bay areas and was very scenic. It was about 25 miles instead of 10. Went through Kure Naval Base and saw what the fire bombs did [to] it and saw the rest of the Jap fleet close up. I'd seen Kure Naval Base before. The Japs had some huge submarines left. They say the largest subs in the world. Lots of war equipment still left along the roads and in caves along the mountains such as airplane and naval parts. Tunnels are filled on either side with equipment they wanted to keep away from the bombs. Hiroshima was a large city (350,000) but now except for about 10 modern buildings like the post office, hospital and a few large concerns . . . everything is absolutely flat. One would have a hard time to tell just where you once lived in the city. The funny part of it is there is very little wreckage around—just powder. All the large buildings that are standing are all burned out inside and [I] suppose off center so will have to be torn down. It's a city that can be planned all over again and all the old mistakes corrected. People have made a few little homes but as a whole don't look any [more] sober than Japs usually do. People still look well [fed] and dress warm enough but it must be pretty heart breaking for the older people. Kids are just as happy and care free as in the U.S. I feel sorry for the old people who have to lug big loads of lumber and junk on their backs. Every one over here works like horses from babies to very old people. The women carry the baby on their back all the time. Of course the baby is happy but it must be a task for the mother. I've seen women lugging 2 railroad ties on their back at one time! Today was a beautiful day and everyone was out pulling big loads of lumber home to improve the place. The Army tore down some barracks so what they didn't want they gave away. The old Nips are ambitious people . . .

I've sure got plenty of souvenirs. Now if I can only get them all home. Will have to make myself a box to carry them in. People have given me lots of them. I picked up 6 or 7 little dishes in the ruins of Hiroshima that I'm taking pains to get home without breaking. Most glassware was all melted but these few escaped without much injury. Here is some of the stuff—several fans, kimono and junk to go with it, trays, babies' sandals, flags, post card, silver dish, chop sticks, a couple wall pictures, couple statues . . . I'll tell you more about [it] when I get home.[2]

7   Matters of Conscience

In the decades following World War II, Harold Stassen consistently took issue with anyone who suggested that Minnesotans were, by nature, isolationists. "My contention always has been that while some [Minnesota] leaders went off in an isolationist direction . . . the people of Minnesota really have never been an isolationist people,"[1] he said. Stassen believed that in the years leading up to the Pearl Harbor attack, Minnesotans' "strong feelings about the rights of people" created "virtual unanimity" that Hitler must be stopped. To back up his contention, Stassen liked to cite figures showing that the percentage of Minnesotans enlisting in the Navy was higher than any other state's. "To think that Minnesotans would be isolationists when you have the highest percentage of enlistments is pretty ridiculous," he said.[2]

But Stassen's faith in the internationalist tendencies of his fellow Minnesotans may have been skewed by his own feelings about the war in Europe. The Republican governor had always leaned in the interventionists' direction, and he officially aligned himself with them in January of 1941, when he threw his support behind President Roosevelt's Lend-Lease bill. In a speech to the Council of State Governments, Stassen called on all Americans to put aside politics and "give united support regardless of geographical location or partisanship to the established foreign policy of the Federal government."[3]

The governor's decision to back the president's interventionist policies put him at odds with almost every other prominent politician in the state. Minnesota's congressional delegation had been leading the isolationist charge even before the war in Europe began in 1939. Representative Harold Knutson, who had voted against U.S. involvement in World War I, warned that "we must not repeat the blunder that we made 22 years ago when we allowed false propaganda to lash us into a fury that ultimately drew us into the war."[4] The state's senior U.S. senator, Henrik Shipstead, promised that he would "cast no vote which [would] imperil . . . America's absolute neutrality in the quarrels of Europe." Congressman August An-

dresen of Red Wing claimed that the American people had no interest in getting involved in what he called the European "mad-
house."[5] Stassen's most reliable interventionist ally in the state's congressional delegation was Senator Joseph Ball, who had been
appointed to his seat by Stassen after the death of Farmer-Labor
Senator Ernest Lundeen in 1940.

Stassen liked to argue that the isolationist attitudes of the state's
politicians did not reflect the sentiments of its voters, but this contention was dubious at best. Ball, who before being appointed to the
Senate was a political columnist for the *St. Paul Pioneer Press*, wrote
that Minnesotans were "overwhelmingly against United States entry into the European war."[6] And while Ball's assessment was based
on his own observations, anecdotal evidence suggested that Minnesotans' opposition to the war was, in fact, widespread. Headlines
from September of 1939 provided a good example. In a span of eight
days, church leaders in St. Paul gathered hundreds of names on a
petition demanding that the United States remain neutral, a group
of Austin businessmen led by Jay Hormel launched a "peace offen-
sive,"[7] and the Minnesota State Federation of Labor called for a con-
stitutional amendment giving voters—not Congress—the right to
declare war.[8] The editor of the *New Ulm Journal* spoke for many
Minnesotans when he questioned Stassen's call for a unified foreign
policy.

> *War is the one foreign policy which Mr. Stassen says we must
> have and which all the people of the State of Minnesota must
> support. Let there be no mistake about it, let the record stand
> forth boldly for all to see and for all to remember . . . Mr. Stassen
> by his oft-repeated statement that we must all support Mr.
> Roosevelt's foreign policy means that we must all be for war.*[9]

Not until 1941 did public opinion about the war begin to coa-
lesce into something resembling the unanimity that Stassen was
convinced he saw. As Germany tightened its grip on Europe and relations between the United States and Japan deteriorated, isolationism began to lose its appeal among Minnesotans. In its place rose an
uncompromising patriotism that discouraged dissent.

In the year after the Pearl Harbor attack, the pressure intensified
to conform to prevailing notions of patriotism. The *Minneapolis
Tribune* reported in October 1942 that the city's school district was
embarking on a program of wartime indoctrination and that "virtual conversion of Minneapolis high schools into military acade-

mies [would] begin immediately."[10] The *Minneapolis Star Journal* told its readers that University of Minnesota President Walter Coffey believed there was "no place on campus" for anyone who didn't consider victory "the most important thing in the world." In St. Paul, W. J. Hickey, the director of the city's speakers' bureau, sent letters to dozens of places of worship, strongly suggesting that they should set aside time during their services for patriotic addresses by "victory speakers." (Several clergymen responded by lecturing Hickey about the boundaries between the secular and the sacred: "By the Constitution of our beloved country Church and State are separated," wrote Pastor W. F. H. Kerl of St. Matthews Evangelical Lutheran Church, "and though the State is at war, the Christian Church as such is not.")[11] And in Crookston, two children were expelled from school after refusing to salute the American flag during a classroom ceremony.[12]

Patriotism was the new ideal—or perhaps an old ideal reanimated. But what made a true patriot? Those who had argued against American intervention insisted that they had always had the

Minneapolis elementary school students were instructed to "extend the left hand, palm upward" when pledging allegiance during wartime.

best interests of their country in mind. Those few who continued to oppose the war after the Pearl Harbor attack believed it was their duty as American citizens to stay true to their principles. As the war progressed, the debate over what it meant to be truly patriotic played itself out in newspapers, in lecture halls, in courts—and in smoke-filled rooms.

America First

Charles Lindbergh, already sensitive to criticism that he was sympathetic to Nazi claims of Aryan superiority, cringed when he was shown to his room at the La Salle Hotel in Minneapolis. "I was given the 'Nordic Suite'!" he wrote in his diary that evening. "What a press story that would make!" Acting the part of the appreciative guest, Lindbergh accepted the room with good grace, happy in the knowledge that "'Nordic' out here doesn't mean what it does in the east. In Minnesota the word 'Nordic' has no anti-Semitic tint."[13]

By May of 1941, Charles Lindbergh—aviation pioneer and fa-

Charles Lindbergh addresses the America First rally at the Minneapolis Auditorium, May 10, 1941.

vorite son of Little Falls, Minnesota—had become one of the most controversial figures in the United States. He had made several trips to Germany during the 1930s and had come away convinced that the Nazi war machine was unstoppable. Lindbergh had returned with a new message—that the United States must, for its own good, steer clear of Germany. Europe's war was its own, he said. America should stay out of it and concentrate on building up its own defenses. He had begun traveling the country on behalf of an isolationist organization called America First, and everywhere he went, he created a huge stir.

Interventionists wasted no time demonizing Lindbergh. The tabloid *PM* called him "the spokesman of the fascist fifth column in America." Columnist Walter Winchell twisted Lindbergh's nickname, "the Lone Eagle," into "the Lone Ostrich." And while President Roosevelt stayed mostly above the fray, a few members of his administration jumped right in. Interior Secretary Harold Ickes, for one, trumpeted the America First Committee's links to "professional fascists and anti-Semites" and labeled Lindbergh "the No. 1 United States Nazi fellow traveler."[14]

But Lindbergh shrugged off the criticism. He kept talking, encouraged by the thousands of cheering supporters who packed venues such as New York's Madison Square Garden and the Arena in St. Louis. By the time he arrived in Minneapolis, his initial trepidation as an America First spokesman was gone.

A "frenzied audience of 12,000 people" roared with approval as Lindbergh took the microphone at the Minneapolis Auditorium. "So wildly enthusiastic was the great throng," marveled the *Minneapolis Tribune and Star Journal*, "that almost every sentence, almost every phrase, in the youthful-looking speaker's speech was interrupted by applause and cheering."[15] Lindbergh peppered his address with tributes to his father, former Minnesota Congressman Charles A. Lindbergh, who had sunk his career by opposing U.S. involvement in World War I. The younger Lindbergh reminded the crowd how his father had warned that the First World War would inevitably lead to a second.

> In this, history has proven he was right. Now you and I, in a new generation, are faced with this choice again. We have seen the result of one European war in which our country took part. Are we to enter a second at this time? Is the destiny of America to be forever merged with that of Europe? Are we to take the policing of the entire world upon our shoulders?[16]

At the conclusion of his speech, the crowd rushed the stage, making it difficult for him to leave. That night, Lindbergh reflected admiringly on his audience. "They averaged a very high type of American,"[17] he wrote.

Lindbergh did not linger in his home state. The next day, over lunch, the chairman of Minnesota's America First chapter asked him to consider running for U.S. senator against the incumbent, Joseph Ball. Lindbergh was appalled at the proposition. "I tried to tell him I was not cut out to be a politician . . . but I could make no impression," he wrote. The former Minnesota boy returned to his room, packed his bags, and hopped a plane for Chicago.[18]

Largely lost in the hubbub surrounding Lindbergh's appearance was the understated opposition of a group known by the ungainly name of the Minneapolis Chapter of the Committee to Defend America by Aiding the Allies. The Committee, as its members liked to call it, had deliberately not picketed the America First rally. Instead, it had placed an ad in the local newspapers, challenging Lindbergh on his antiwar position. "We are convinced that the course which you advocate would lead to the destruction of the democratic way of life," the committee explained. "Knowing your courage, we cannot understand why you are unwilling that we take the risks involved in defending that way."[19] The Committee's challenge to Lindbergh went largely unnoticed by the local press, and Lindbergh never commented publicly about it.

A group dominated by prominent businessmen and community leaders had formed the Minneapolis chapter the previous summer, and while membership never reached the leadership's goal of ten thousand, the organization did eventually enroll nearly four thousand people. It sponsored meetings, sold Give-Aid-to-Britain Christmas cards ("For a Merry Christmas Next Year"), and sent speakers around the state to rally support for U.S. intervention. (One of the members of its speakers' bureau, a young Hubert H. Humphrey, was described in a Committee document as "Spirited but tactful. *Very* good in Q & A.")

Still, the committee struggled to inspire the kind of passionate following that America First enjoyed. In January 1941—four months before Lindbergh's appearance in Minneapolis—the committee held its own rally at the Minneapolis Auditorium and attracted only about four thousand people. Organizers blamed the turnout on the failure of the national committee to send a Hollywood headliner. (Telegrams from Melvyn Douglas and Constance Bennett had to suffice.) "The presence of a movie star does more to fill an auditorium than half a dozen heavy weights," wrote the Minneapolis chapter's chairman, Edgar M. Jaeger, in a letter to the national committee. "You must remember that Minneapolis and St. Paul are probably the heart of the isolationist country."[20]

Even before the Pearl Harbor attack, public opinion in Minnesota began to shift toward the interventionist policies advocated by the Committee to Defend America by Aiding the Allies and away from the isolationism espoused by Charles Lindbergh and America First. Lindbergh himself helped accelerate the shift when, on September 11, 1941, he told the crowd at an America First rally in Des Moines that the British government, the Jews, and the Roosevelt administration were the three "major agitators" for war. His stridency

The national office of the Committee to Defend America by Aiding the Allies worked closely with the Minneapolis unit to build public support for intervention.

offended many Minnesotans, and in an editorial that reflected that sentiment, the *St. Paul Pioneer Press* accused Lindbergh of making "the kind of talk that Hitler or Goebbels would have given."

> *For purposes of his own, he wishes to arouse hatred and preju-dices, set group against group and undermine confidence of the people in their government at a moment when it has been brought to close grips with a powerful and dangerous enemy. The Nazis and others of their kind in this country will now get behind Lindbergh to raise the same smoke screen as the one put up by Hitler when he was leading the German people to their downfall.*[21]

By the eve of the Pearl Harbor attack, Lindbergh had become something of a pariah in Minnesota. "Lucky Lindy" had lost his lus-ter. In what many people took to be a public rebuke, Lindbergh's name was removed from the water tower in his hometown of Little Falls. (The *Little Falls Herald* reported a few years later that the con-tractor hired to repaint the tower omitted Lindbergh's name when he couldn't find anyone willing to paint letters at such a "dizzy height.")[22]

Sedition

Grace Carlson—former job counselor, former psychology instruc-tor, former U.S. Senate candidate, and current state organizer for the Socialist Workers Party—arrived at the federal courthouse in Minneapolis hoping for the best. The Japanese had attacked Pearl Harbor the day before, and the people of Minnesota would likely be looking to take out their anger on someone. Carlson and her co-defendants knew that they made tempting scapegoats, given their conviction just six days earlier on charges of advocating the violent overthrow of the United States government. Would the judge succumb to widespread rage and impose the maximum ten-year sentence?

Federal Judge Matthew M. Joyce looked down on the eighteen convicted defendants and addressed them with a gravity that seemed appropriate for the occasion. He noted that during the course of the trial he had "not once heard a defendant make expres-sion of loyalty or fealty to the flag," although he had heard several of them express hopes that the government would be overthrown. Then he handed down the sentences one by one. "It is the judgment

Among the items confiscated during the raid on the Minneapolis headquarters of the Socialist Workers Party: "several bushels of papers," a party banner, and portraits of Lenin and Trotsky.

of this court," he intoned, addressing the sole female defendant, "that you, Grace Carlson, be confined in an institution to be selected by the attorney general of the United States for sixteen months."[23]

Sixteen months. Not ten years. Decades later, Grace Carlson thought back on her sentencing and its proximity to the Pearl Harbor attack. "Might have been worse," she admitted.[24]

The story of Grace Carlson and her fellow sedition defendants had begun amidst the political machinations of Minneapolis Teamsters Local 544. The Minneapolis Teamsters were led by the Dunne brothers—Vincent, Grant, and Miles—who had consolidated their power after leading a bloody truckers' strike in 1934. The Dunnes were radical Trotskyites who aligned their local with the Socialist Workers Party (SWP) despite the objections of Teamsters national president Dan Tobin. In early June 1941, after years of struggle against Tobin, Local 544 seceded from the Teamsters and the American Federation of Labor (AFL), bolting to the more radical Congress for Industrial Organizations (CIO). Tobin—who had thrown the Teamsters' considerable political clout behind President Roosevelt in the 1940 election—responded by sending a telegram to the president informing him of the Dunne brothers' move. In the telegram, Tobin maintained that the Dunne brothers had refused "to disassociate themselves from the radical Trotskyite organization"—meaning the SWP—and insisted that "these disturbers must in some way be prevented from pursuing this dangerous course."[25]

Two weeks after Tobin sent his telegram to Roosevelt, federal marshals swooped down on SWP headquarters in Minneapolis and St. Paul, confiscating boxes of documents, two red flags, a portrait of Leon Trotsky, "and other allegedly Communistic material."[26] Less than a month later, a federal grand jury indicted twenty-nine people—fifteen party members (including Grace Carlson) and fourteen members of the old Local 544 (including the three Dunne brothers)—on sedition charges. Each indictment contained two counts. The first—based on an 1861 seditious conspiracy statute—charged that the defendants had actually conspired to forcibly overthrow the U.S. government; the second—based on a new law known as the 1940 Smith Act—charged that they had conspired to *advocate* armed revolt against the government.

While the timing of the indictments smelled of political payback (critics charged that Roosevelt had ordered the crackdown on the Trotskyites as a favor to his supporter, Tobin), the government's decision to seek the indictments had just as much to do with patriotic fervor as it did with political favoritism. By the summer of 1941, the

United States was inching closer to war, and many Americans were becoming less tolerant of anti-interventionists such as those in the SWP. The *St. Paul Dispatch*, for one, accused the Trotskyites of engaging in a "campaign of disloyalty" and called the indictments "belated but welcome."[27] Grace Carlson and the others indicted believed that the administration was going after the party in a politically popular effort to stifle dissent. "The Roosevelt Administration knows," claimed codefendant Albert Goldman, "that the S.W.P. is opposed to the war from a principal [*sic*] point of view; that is, we take the position that the war on the part of Britain and the United States is an imperialistic war."[28]

As Carlson and her codefendants awaited trial, others began to weigh in on their behalf. The American Civil Liberties Union (ACLU) telegraphed acting U.S. Attorney General Francis Biddle, urging him to reconsider the crackdown against the SWP. The Justice Department's actions were, according to the ACLU, "dangerous to the preservation of democracy" and calculated to reward supporters of the administration's foreign and domestic policies.[29] Several national publications, including *The Nation* and *The New Republic*, excoriated Biddle and the Roosevelt administration for conducting "prosecutions of opinion."[30] Closer to home, the African American newspaper the *St. Paul Recorder*, while taking no position on the merits of the case against the party, nevertheless threw its support behind the defendants. "The S.W.P. and its leadership . . . have fought anti-Negro programs and racial bigotry wherever they found it," the *Recorder* claimed. "That's enough for us to hope the charges upon which they have been indicted are proven false and that they will be acquitted."[31]

As the trial got under way in Minneapolis in late October, war anxiety was growing. German submarines were attacking U.S. merchant ships in the Atlantic, and United States–Japanese relations were rapidly deteriorating. Many observers recognized that the Minneapolis sedition trial would provide an early test of the nation's "attitude toward free expression of opinion in a time of national crisis."[32] The case against the SWP and the leaders of the former Teamsters 544 was, in the words of the leftist New York newspaper *PM*, "the first peace-time U.S. prosecution for 'seditious opinion' since the tumultuous times of John Adams."[33]

For four weeks, jurors heard evidence about the defendants' allegedly seditious opinions and activities. Most of the government's witnesses were labor activists who opposed the Dunne brothers' control of the local truckers' union. Among other things, prosecutors presented evidence that the SWP had formed a "defense guard" to serve as a precursor to a revolutionary militia. (Conveniently omitted was the evidence that the guards had done little except park cars at a picnic, engage in calisthenics, and take in a strip show.) They also claimed that the party had tried to infiltrate the armed forces and encourage insubordination. The defense, led by defendant Albert Goldman, saw the trial as a rare opportunity to publicize Trotskyite principles, and as such, worth only a half-hearted attempt to counter specific government charges.

In all, eight of the twenty-eight defendants (the twenty-ninth, Grant Dunne, had committed suicide) testified during the trial. Grace Carlson had not planned to be a witness, but she eventually agreed to take the stand. "Goldman said the jurors would just be outraged if they didn't hear a woman report," she later recalled.[34] Newspapers accorded special coverage to Carlson's court appearance in large part because she was the only woman to testify. "Slim, svelte Grace Carlson . . . took the stand in federal court today," the *Minneapolis Times* reported, "to admit frankly that she was a member of the [Socialist Workers] party, in fact state organizer, but to deny that the party's principles, or her own beliefs, called for armed overthrow of the government."[35]

Years later, Carlson described her testimony, and that of the other defendants, as part of "quite a political defense."

> There was a great deal of talk about the question of advocating the forcible overthrow of the government and Goldman's argument was that when the time came for the revolutionary takeover—to use very simple terms—the capitalists would use force and violence against the working masses. Force and violence would occur, and we predicted it would occur, but we didn't advocate it . . . it was a good defense.[36]

When asked during cross-examination whether the SWP had encouraged members to join the army and "sell the party" to soldiers, Carlson made no effort to deny it. "If there are any Socialists in the army, they can talk about Socialism," she said. "We feel that they should be allowed to give their interpretation of Socialist doctrine as well as Democrats or Republicans can talk about their parties."[37]

It took the jury—of eleven men and one woman—about fifty-five hours to reach verdicts for the twenty-three remaining defendants. (Charges against the other five had been dropped earlier.) The jury acquitted all twenty-three defendants on the first charge—

conspiracy to overthrow the government. It convicted eighteen of them, including Grace Carlson, on the second charge of conspiring to *advocate* armed insurrection—specifically, of conspiring to advocate insubordination within the armed forces. It also urged the judge to show leniency in sentencing. After the verdicts were announced, Carlson and the others gathered at the SWP's Minneapolis headquarters to plan their next move. Goldman promised an appeal. "The government has succeeded in winning a verdict of guilty against eighteen members of the Socialist Workers party," he said. "That does not in the least prove that they are guilty of charges leveled against them by the government."[38]

Most of the civil libertarians who had voiced support for the Minnesota Trotskyites just a few months earlier were by that time nowhere to be found. During that first week of December 1941, war seemed increasingly imminent, and few Americans felt compelled to protest the convictions of a small group of "Trotskyite mice."[39] The *Minneapolis Star Journal*, for one, seemed resigned to the fact that times had changed.

> *Naturally, in times when the nation fears for its security, the laws which bear on our civil liberties are stricter, and are more strictly construed, than in times when there are no such fears. It is important that the construction and enforcement of these laws shall not violate the basic freedoms of thought and speech. In this situation "force and violence" are the key words. The jury found in effect, as to those convicted, that force was advocated but not implemented.*[40]

The sentences handed down by Judge Joyce on December 8 went largely unnoticed in the local and national press. The country suddenly had other things to worry about. Grace Carlson and her fellow convicted seditionists challenged their sentences through the federal courts until late 1943 when the U.S. Supreme Court refused to hear their appeals. Then they began doing their time.

Carlson surrendered in Minneapolis during the first week of 1944 and spent most of the rest of the war at a federal prison in West Virginia. By then, hardly anyone was paying attention. "I really miss the comrades, the meetings and the fun," Carlson wrote to a friend after giving herself up. "I used to mix with a much better class of people than I am now dealing with! These god-damn capitalists!"[41]

Bad Memories

Minnesota had embarrassed itself during the last war. In a spasm of wartime overreaction, the 1917 legislature had created a blatantly unconstitutional agency called the Commission of Public Safety (CPS). The agency's seven members interpreted their powers broadly, deciding that their main job was to enforce loyalty throughout the state. As they saw it, "the test of loyalty in war times is whether a man is wholeheartedly for the war and subordinates everything else to its successful prosecution."[42] With no effective checks on its power, the CPS trampled on the civil rights of groups it considered disloyal—including the state's large German American population. Minnesotans of German ancestry were automatically suspect in the eyes of many CPS-inspired patriots. In one notorious case, the German American mayor of New Ulm was forced from office after presiding over a public meeting in which residents protested the nation's draft laws.

Two decades later, in August 1939, the people of New Ulm were wondering whether history might repeat itself. Hitler's troops were

The perils of German heritage. Tired of getting "queer looks" from her neighbors, a victory aid tries to "set people straight" about the loyalty of her dachshund, Otto.

massed on the Polish border and war seemed inevitable. Like most Minnesotans at the time, the majority of New Ulm residents wanted the United States to remain neutral and let the Europeans work out their own problems. But the people of New Ulm were skittish. They remembered what had happened during the last war. As tensions rose in Europe, Tom Conklin, editor of the *New Ulm Daily Journal*, expressed the widespread hope that things would be different this time around.

> *Should there be war, it is our belief that there will be less of the bitter understanding and aroused prejudices that existed during the World War. There are two principal reasons for this supposition. The first is that modern means of news distribution— by press, radio and picture—are not only swifter, but better-organized, and that people will be better able to gain a daily picture of things as they are— not as some biased source wants them to get it.*
>
> *Our second belief is that folks everywhere realize that wars are not the doings of the man in the street, but result from political connivings, greedy commercialism—and that no one really wants war.*[43]

New Ulm's German Americans were in a delicate spot. While many of them agreed with the *Daily Journal* that America should "stay at home and stick to its peaceful pursuits," they didn't want to set themselves up as scapegoats again. As a result, it sometimes seemed that the people of New Ulm went out of their way to convince the rest of the world of their loyalty and patriotism. The *Daily Journal's* assertion "that anyone who doesn't like America better go to whatever country they think is better, and not stay around to complain," typified the lengths to which the community went in its efforts to avoid patriotic backlash.

Every once in a while, anti-German sentiment bubbled to the surface in one Minnesota community or another. In Mankato, a rumor spread: federal agents had taken into custody a local restaurant owner who was suspected of being a "nazi spy." The subject of the rumor, Theodore Holton, had grown up in Germany but had become an American citizen after serving in the U.S. Army during World War I. It turned out that Holton had, in fact, been seen in the car of a government agent, but that the agent was a postal inspector who had simply offered Holton a ride.[44] Sometimes anti-German suspicions led to even sillier overreactions. In a few cases, stores stopped selling the records of New Ulm polka bandleader Whoopee John Wilfahrt after rumors spread that Wilfahrt's drummer was tapping out coded messages to the Nazis.[45]

But those were isolated cases. For the most part, Minnesotans refused to get caught up in the kind of anti-German hysteria that had prevailed during World War I. As the *New Ulm Daily Journal* noted a few days after the Pearl Harbor attack, Governor Harold Stassen had made it clear there would be no Commission of Public Safety this time around. "Regardless of the hysteria which may develop," the *Daily Journal*'s editor wrote, "we are certain he will stick to it."[46]

"Conchies"

Twenty-three-year-old Edward Rassmusson insisted that as a Jehovah's Witness he could not, in good conscience, participate in any way in the war that the United States had just entered. He refused to register with his local draft board in Roseau, as required by the law, and, as a result, now found himself in the courtroom of federal judge Matthew Joyce.

"Have you ever read the Bill of Rights?" the judge asked.

"No," Rassmusson replied.

"You should read it; it would do you some good."

Joyce continued with his questioning. "You are perfectly willing that hundreds of thousands of other American boys should fight to preserve your liberty and your rights as American citizen?"

"Yes."

"And you are not willing to do anything to help?"

"No."

After eliciting a series of mostly one-word responses, the judge decided that he had heard enough. "You have been pretty stubborn about this matter," Joyce said. "I sentence you to serve a year and a day, the place of confinement to be determined by the attorney general."[47]

Trials like that of Edward Rassmusson were more common in Minnesota than many people at the time realized. While reliable figures were hard to come by, a survey of newspaper reports prepared during the fall of 1942 found that only four states—Pennsylvania, New York, New Jersey, and Illinois—had tried more conscientious objector (CO) cases than Minnesota.[48] It was unclear whether Minnesota's high ranking was due to a larger-than-normal population of COs (often referred to derisively as "conchies"), or to a greater-than-normal determination on the part of law enforcement to track down and prosecute draft law violators. Whatever the case, it was clear that not all Minnesotans believed their country was fighting a just war.

In late 1944, an experiment got under way at the University of Minnesota that demonstrated just how far some conscientious objectors were willing to go to remain true to their convictions. Thirty-six COs from around the country had gathered at the university to participate in Dr. Ancel Keys' new "semi-starvation study" (also known as ss-45). Keys was a highly respected physiologist who, in 1939, had designed the army's emergency K-ration. Now he planned to extend his study of human nutrition by putting his ss-45 volunteers through nearly a year of rigorous testing. During the first three months, the men would receive a fairly standard diet to stabilize their weight. During the following six months, they would receive starvation rations designed for severe weight loss. The final three months would be devoted to rehabilitation with slowly increasing rations. Keys hoped that the results of the study would help policy makers plan effective ways to combat hunger and famine in the postwar world.

The ss-45 guinea pigs were all draftees in the Civilian Public Service, the federal government program that gave conscientious objectors an alternative to military service. Most, like volunteer Henry Scholberg, jumped at the opportunity to do something they considered worthwhile. "Here we are in the middle of a war," Scholberg recalled. "Every day we're reading of casualties on both sides, and I thought here are Americans like me dying in the battlefield for their country, and what was I doing? Working in a mental hospital? And here was a chance, I thought, to do something that required sacrifice."[49] Scholberg's fellow volunteer, Kenneth Tuttle, felt the same way. "We had felt restless and frustrated, sweating out the war on the fringes," he said. "This seemed a significant and vital humanitarian service."[50]

At first, during the early weeks of the three-month "standardization" period, it was pretty easy to be an ss-45 volunteer. "This period was wonderful," Tuttle recalled. "All of us had come from isolated hospitals or camps where we worked hard for nine to twelve hours a day. Now we were living in a cultural center where we could go to theaters and concerts, and have dates with the college girls."[51] The guinea pigs were fed a respectable 3,200 calories a day, although, as volunteer Lester Glick wrote in his diary, the menus were "extremely monotonous."[52] The men enrolled in classes at the university and studied foreign languages to prepare themselves for overseas relief work when the war was over. They were required to walk twenty-six miles a week outdoors, and do regular stints on a laboratory treadmill. "We all felt fine," Tuttle said, "and we thought starving for humanity was not a bad proposition at all."[53]

By early February 1945, all of the volunteers had settled into their baseline weight. It was time to start starving. "Tomorrow we start our semi-starvation diet," Lester Glick wrote in his diary on February 11. "Frankly I'm scared!"[54]

Newspapers and magazines caught wind of the project and began chronicling what they considered one of the war's most compelling human interest stories. Now, instead of resorting to derogatory terms like "slacker," reporters began referring to the ss-45 subjects as selfless volunteers whose sacrifice would "benefit famine and war victims throughout the world."[55]

Meals on the first day of semi-starvation seemed "surprisingly large"[56] compared to the nightmare bills of fare that some of the men imagined, but reality soon set in. The men received just two meals a day. Three equally hideous menus rotated daily so that the same meal consumed on Monday evening cruelly reappeared on Thursday. The food was "starchy and unappetizing"—rutabagas, potatoes, beans, dry pancakes with foul-tasting syrup, coarse bread without butter or jelly. "The thought of eating these menus every day for six months is revolting!" Lester Glick wrote just two days

The SS-45 volunteers, pre-starvation

into the semi-starvation phase.[57] Not only did the food taste bad, it was bereft of nutrition. Each man was limited to about 1,800 calories a day.

Within a couple of weeks, the men were becoming much less picky about the food they were served. "By the time you get hungry, you can eat it," said one.[58] Soon, nearly everyone in the experiment was literally licking his plate clean. Even Henry Scholberg, who was initially revolted by the practice, succumbed.[59] Three months into the semi-starvation experiment, the men were treated to a day of special, morale-boosting meals—breakfast with a slice of bacon and an egg; dinner with chicken, mashed potatoes, gravy, and chocolate cake. Several men wept with joy.[60] At another meal, each volunteer received a rare treat: an orange. To the horror of the lab staff, the men inhaled the entire fruit, including the peel.[61]

For a while it appeared that the guinea pigs would stick to their severely restricted diets without much oversight, but then problems began to emerge. One volunteer went on a sudden binge, devouring ice-cream sundaes, one after another, at a succession of local drug stores. The gorged volunteer was immediately dropped from the program and a new buddy system was instituted under which no CO could leave the lab without company. Then chewing gum became a problem. Dr. Keys, in what the men considered a rare act of compassion, had allowed the COs to chew as much Juicy Fruit, Blackjack, and Doublemint as they liked, believing that the habit would have no discernible effect on the experiment. But some volunteers, in a desperate attempt to satisfy their hunger, took their gum-chewing to an extreme, going through as many as forty packs a day. The laboratory staff calculated that this excessive chewing could add about one hundred calories a day to the men's diet. It quickly imposed a new ration: no more than two packages of gum a day.[62]

As the men's weight dropped and their hair thinned and their ribs became visible, their personalities began to change. Many developed obsessions with food. Some hoarded cookbooks and spent hours daydreaming over recipes both simple and exotic. "I don't know what I'd do without my . . . stack of cookbooks," Lester Glick wrote.[63] Others collected kitchen gadgets—toasters, griddles, waffle irons. One volunteer, a mechanical engineer, hunkered down with books on food refrigeration.[64] Before long, many began to lose their tempers—with each other and with people outside the experiment. This lack of control surfaced one day when Glick and a fellow guinea pig ventured out during the fifth month of semi-starvation.

Today Jim and I made a routine visit to a restaurant to watch people eat. We bought our usual black coffee and directed our attention to a well-dressed lady who had ordered a beautiful pork chop dinner. She tinkered with the chop, eating less than half of that wonderful-looking tenderloin. She nibbled at her string beans, embellished with nuts and bacon, which she carefully pushed aside. Her lettuce salad, garnished with carrots and radishes was left half eaten. Finally she ordered a fantastic co-

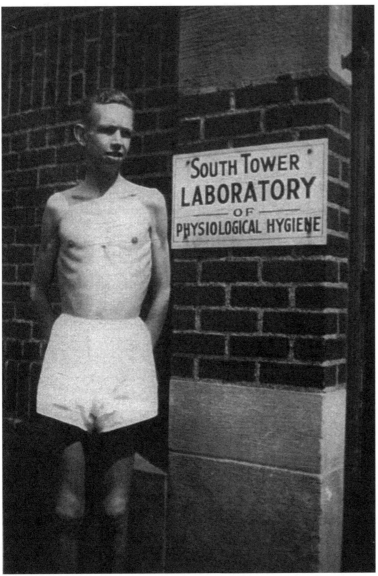

On the last day of starvation, July 29, 1945, Henry Scholberg weighed less than 119 pounds.

conut cream pie, which appeared to us as God's prize creation. She pushed off the wonderful whipped cream on the top, nibbled daintily at the filling, leaving the crust untouched. What a stupid woman! She paid her bill and left the restaurant, with Jim and I close behind. Jim stopped her and proceeded to lecture her on world hunger and how she was contributing to it. She shrieked an exclamation and took off running.[65]

Many of the men were surprised to discover that they no longer had any interest in sex. Henry Scholberg regularly dated one of the young women who worked in the lab, but never tried to kiss her. "The reason we never got around to smooching or kissing was because, due to starvation, we lost our sex drive as well as a lot of weight," he recalled.[66] By early July, Lester Glick was swearing off women as well. "Girls!" he declared in his diary. "At least one less worry!"[67]

Despite the focus on food, or lack of it, the ss-45 volunteers did more than simply reduce their caloric intake. They also had to maintain an exercise schedule designed to burn off many more calories than they took in. They still had to walk twenty-six miles a week, even though their bodies were turning increasingly skeletal. While the long walks outside could be trying at times, it was the treadmill that the men dreaded most of all. In one experiment called the Johnson Test, the guinea pigs had to run for up to five minutes on a treadmill at seven miles an hour. At first, the test didn't seem all that challenging. But as the weeks went by, fewer and fewer of the men could stay on the machine for the full five minutes. By the end of the semi-starvation period, no one in the experiment could last more than a minute without collapsing. It was "grueling torture," a loathsome duty that made starving that much worse.[68]

Dreams turned haunted. In one diary entry, Lester Glick described a particularly difficult night.

I hate my dreams! Last night I dreamed that Dr. Keys took me to a huge building containing hundreds of thousands of beautiful, luscious looking hams, hanging from smoking racks. He opened the locks on the building and told me to go in and help myself. I hesitated and said, "Not me! I'm in starvation." He replied, "That's all past. Go on, eat!" I reached up, delighted, but just as I was ready to sink my teeth into that beautiful ham, I woke up! How frustrating![69]

Kenneth Tuttle had a recurring dream featuring "a bowl of cool, green, shining cabbage just out of my reach." He also reported that, on one occasion, he dreamed of killing everyone on the laboratory staff.[70]

As the final days of the semi-starvation phase approached, the ss-45 volunteers could barely stand to look at themselves in the mirror. Their eyes were fixed in vacant stares. Their skin was scaly, flecked with blackish dots. Noses appeared bony. Lips looked flabby. A swipe of a comb often pulled out tufts of dull, coarse hair. "The bones of my body make me bumpy and ugly," Glick wrote on the final day of starvation. "I can count my ribs in the mirror and my collarbone sticks out as though dislocated. My arm muscles have dwindled so that I can reach around my arm above the elbow with my thumb and third finger."[71]

The first day of rehabilitation was a revelation to some, a "terrific anticlimax" to others. The men were split up into four caloric groups, with the lucky ones receiving 3,400 calories a day—nearly double what they received during the semi-starvation phase. "It looks to me like I am in the top 'consumption group,'" Lester Glick told his diary. "The first meal included real butter, a fruit glass full of milk, and tremendously tasty farina. The second meal included the regular menu plus apple sauce with cinnamon and a pudding dessert. I never tasted such good food in all my life!"[72] Those in the lowest caloric group received just 2,200 calories. "Big deal," Henry Scholberg said years later of his 400-calorie increase. "I was still hungry."[73]

The ss-45 guinea pigs had, on average, lost a quarter of their weight during their six months of semi-starvation. Lester Glick had dropped from 157 pounds to 116, Kenneth Tuttle from 181 to 125. During their three months of rehabilitation, recovery did not come as quickly as they would have liked. "We're seven weeks into rehabilitation and our starvation symptoms have not abated significantly," Glick wrote. "Our looks, our hunger, our minimal weight gain all verify our minimal rehabilitation."[74] But gradually, the guinea pigs began to feel like human beings again. Weights slowly returned to normal. Apathy and inertia subsided. Sex—or at least the thought of sex—regained its appeal after months on hiatus.

The thirty-six conscientious objectors who took part in the study had volunteered with the understanding that, through their sacrifice, they might help millions of hungry and starving people throughout the postwar world. Judged by that goal alone, their efforts were largely in vain. Ancel Keys did not publish the results of the semi-starvation study until 1950—too late to benefit the war victims that the guinea pigs were hoping to help. But the ss-45 volunteers made invaluable contributions to science. Keys' two-volume, 1,385-page report, *The Biology of Human Starvation*, constituted "the most complete record ever of the myriad physiological changes that come with progressive food deprivation."[75] The volunteers also, through their well-publicized ordeal, helped convince at least some Minnesotans to look more kindly on those who opposed the war on moral grounds. ss-45 volunteer Max Kampelman, who would go on to a distinguished career in diplomacy, was especially gratified at the public response. "We have been rather well received in this community and on campus," he wrote. "Many of us have made fine friends here, especially among the faculty and some students."[76] Still, Minnesotans' tolerance for the COs did not automatically lead to admiration. "Most [COs] would willingly die for what they think," the *St. Paul Pioneer Press* noted in an editorial. "Perhaps the real pity is that this is not the kind of world these people dream it to be."[77]

Amalgamation

Minnesota's Republicans seemed like such easy targets. The nation was at war, and many of the state's Republicans—with the notable exceptions of Harold Stassen and freshman Senator Joseph Ball— were prewar isolationists, vulnerable to charges of showing insufficient patriotism. At first glance, it seemed their political futures were in serious doubt.

In fact, they had little to fear. They had no real competition.

The Farmer-Laborites and Democrats who comprised Minnesota's liberal establishment during the war were in a state of suspended political animation. Ever since 1938, when voters swept Stassen into the governor's office and gave him Republican majorities in both houses of the legislature, the state's liberal politicians had been relegated to the fringes of political power. The Farmer-Labor Party had lost much of its previously considerable clout, and the Democratic Party remained what it had been for years: a negligible third party. By 1943, Minnesota's congressional delegation featured only one nominal liberal—Ninth District Representative Harold Hagen, a Farmer-Laborite who would later switch to the Republican camp. Franklin Roosevelt had carried the state in each of the previous three presidential elections, but his margin of victory had shrunk to fewer than fifty thousand votes in 1940.[78] With the 1944 election just a year away, the president's supporters in

Minnesota—and his political strategists in Washington—worried that he could lose the state if, as expected, he ran for a fourth term.

The Farmer-Labor Party had tried to use a "win the war" strategy against the Republicans in 1942 ("your ballot may save an American boy from a bullet").[79] But its efforts had fallen flat, in large part because the Farmer-Laborites themselves had a less than pristine record when it came to supporting the war. (The party, which was strongly influenced by communists sympathetic to the Soviet Union, had gone on record opposing U.S. intervention after Stalin and Hitler signed their nonaggression pact in 1938 and had then switched to a pro-intervention stance after Germany invaded the Soviet Union in the summer of 1940.) The Democrats, who enjoyed little statewide support, had likewise failed to take advantage of the Republicans' perceived vulnerability on the war question.

By 1943, the Farmer-Labor Party and the Democratic Party were so frustrated by their shared inability to make inroads against the Republicans that they began seriously considering an idea that had once seemed anathema to both.

Merger. Or, as party insiders liked to call it, amalgamation.

The two parties had toyed twice before—in 1939 and 1941—with the possibility of merging into one unified liberal party but had never gotten far with the idea. Now, with the outcome of the war still very much in question and Roosevelt's reelection potentially hinging on his showing in Minnesota, events were conspiring to bring the two parties together.

The Farmer-Labor Party, which had always clung fiercely to its independence, now seemed especially keen to see the "fusion" proposition succeed. Its newfound commitment to the proposed merger was directly connected to its relationship with the Communist Party. Communists dominated the Farmer-Labor Party leadership in Minnesota, and, as a result, Farmer-Laborite policies were often indistinguishable from those of the communists. In 1943, the national Communist Party adopted a strategy of cooperation with the national Democratic Party (Roosevelt's reelection was seen as essential to an Allied victory against fascism), and that decision had huge implications for Minnesota's Farmer-Laborites. National communist leaders, believing that Roosevelt's success in Minnesota depended on a unified liberal response, explicitly ordered their underlings in Minnesota "to bring about a merger."[80] At first, many Farmer-Labor leaders, including former governor Elmer Benson, resisted the pressure to merge, but they eventually gave in. "The reactionaries on the home-front as well as the foreign-front are gang-ing up. We can do no less," wrote the Farmer-Labor Association's state secretary, Viena Johnson. "The wedlock may not be lasting, but we might as well enjoy the honey-moon."[81] Before long, Elmer Benson and Farmer-Labor Party chairman Paul Tinge were grandly declaring that the merger would "materially aid our Commander-in-Chief in his great efforts to win a speedy victory and win an enduring people's peace."[82]

Minnesota's demoralized Democratic Party was not as hell-bent on merger as the Farmer-Labor Party was, but its leaders knew a good deal when they saw one. Democratic candidates had performed dismally in the 1942 elections, garnering only half as many votes statewide as Farmer-Labor candidates. By early 1943, Democratic state chairman Elmer Kelm, who had previously responded coolly to the fusion proposition, was beginning to take the idea seriously. After several months of study, he concluded that a merger with the Farmer-Laborites offered the best hope for ensuring Roosevelt's reelection and improving the Democrats' long-term prospects in the state—but only, he insisted, if the Democrats retained control of the newly merged party.[83]

The two parties began seriously negotiating plans for a merger during the fall of 1943. Oscar Ewing, the assistant chairman of the Democratic National Committee, flew from Washington to facilitate the talks. Acting as liaison between the two parties was the brightest star in the state's dimming liberal firmament: former Minneapolis mayoral candidate Hubert H. Humphrey. As the Farmer-Laborites and Democrats repeatedly butted heads, Humphrey's instinctive faith in the power of compromise helped keep the two sides talking. Even when "things looked rough," Humphrey remained convinced that the left-wing Farmer-Laborites (who he later claimed had "parasitically attached" themselves to the Farmer-Labor Party "like a lamprey on a lake trout") were too desperate to let the negotiations fail. "They'll negotiate. They'll come in," he told a Democratic colleague. "There's no doubt about it because it's all for unity, it's all for Roosevelt. As long as the Soviet Union is in the war, this crowd is going to be willing to sell out to anybody—even us."[84]

A few months later, the parties had worked out enough of their differences to officially proceed with the merger. On Friday, April 14, 1944, delegates of the Farmer-Labor Party convened at the Nicollet Hotel in Minneapolis, while nearby at the Radisson the convention of the state Democratic Party was gaveled into session. The highly choreographed proceedings began with the Farmer-Laborites renaming themselves the Fellowship Party—a maneuver that cleared the way for the Democrats to incorporate the Farmer-Labor label into their party's name. Everything looked set for a final merger vote on Saturday. But then an eleventh-hour hitch developed. The old Farmer-Laborites objected to some of the provisions included in the Democrats' new constitution—provisions that, as one reporter put it, leaned "pretty heavily toward control of the amalgamated setup by the Democrats."[85]

What ensued was a madcap exercise in inter-hotel shuttle diplomacy worthy of a Marx Brothers movie. Representatives from both camps were, in the words of Humphrey's aide, Arthur Naftalin, "chasing back and forth between the two hotels," trying to keep the merger from falling apart.[86] One Democratic delegate, Barney Allen of Detroit Lakes, described a scene of longtime rivals jockeying for optimum political position.

> *There was quite a lot of visiting going on among people who were rather long-time Farmer-Laborites or Democrats . . . But it was hard to get the two parties together. One of the things that stood in the way was that the Democrats didn't want to share patronage and this was particularly true state-wide, too . . . Farmer-Laborites and Democrats [were] going back and forth all the time and they'd hang up on some of the damnedest silliest little issues you ever heard of, but it kept on and on and we struggled and struggled and we finally got closer together. Finally, it got late [into the] night and . . . the leftists of the political scene in those days liked to have meetings that would go twenty-six hours in a twenty-four hour period. Everybody was worn out and that was one of their tactics.*[87]

It wasn't until six-thirty on Saturday morning that the two sides finally reached an agreement both could live with. The Democrats reconvened at the Radisson Hotel and approved the revisions to the constitution that had been hammered out that morning. A few hours later they voted to make the merger official by renaming their party the Democratic-Farmer-Labor Party (DFL). "Political history was made," the *Minneapolis Tribune* reported. "Minnesota returned to a two-party state Saturday for the first time in 28 years." With that, the former Farmer-Laborites left their gathering at the Nicollet Hotel and joined their new colleagues at the Radisson for "a great joint jubilee meeting."[88]

The first order of business for the new party was choosing a candidate for governor. Many of the delegates were already placing their hopes on Hubert Humphrey, and on Saturday evening they proposed from the floor of the convention to draft him as the DFL's first candidate. Humphrey, however, had already let it be known that he would not run for governor in 1944, and, as he made clear in an impromptu speech to the convention, the war was the reason. "I want to go into the armed forces if I am acceptable," he declared to the clamoring crowd. "I want to be with those other young men and women in the armed forces, and you can't deny me that privilege."[89] Eugenie Anderson, a delegate from Red Wing, couldn't help but think that the man was destined for great things. "It was a very stirring speech," she recalled years later. "I was sitting beside Frank O'Gorman, my county chairman, and I said, 'That man will be president some day.'"[90] (Humphrey never did serve in the armed forces. Shortly after the convention he learned that he had flunked his navy physical. Democrat Orville Freeman recalled how hard

Minnesota Secretary of State Mike Holm (far right) accepts papers establishing the Democratic-Farmer-Labor Party, April 15, 1944. Left to right: E. M. Kirkpatrick of the Democratic Party; H. J. Griffith of the Farmer-Labor Party; Sander Genis, president of the Minnesota CIO; and Holm.

Humphrey took the news: "I can remember putting him on a train one night when he was just literally crying. He was so frustrated and unhappy and was trying in every way he could to get into the service, and he just couldn't get in.")[91] In the end, the infant party nominated Detroit Lakes' Barney Allen to be its first standard bearer.

Allen eventually lost to the popular Republican incumbent, Edward Thye, but overall the new party performed respectably during its first year. During the general election of 1944, Roosevelt carried the state (albeit by a closer margin than the DFLers would have liked), and DFL candidates gained two congressional seats. The following spring, Hubert Humphrey was elected mayor of Minneapolis. Everything seemed to be going well for the new party. But trouble was brewing.

As the war entered its final months, the far-left wing of the DFL coalition began drifting from its wartime commitment to "liberal unity."[92] The communists and their allies within the party still aligned themselves closely with Soviet policy, and they looked upon the new president, Harry Truman, as a dangerous reactionary of the anti-Soviet sort. As their dissatisfaction with Truman grew, so too did their determination to wrest control of the DFL from the party's more moderate "Humphreyites." They started making plans and waited for the war to end.

Hubert Humphrey was aware of the rumblings from the party's left wing, but he seemed unconcerned about the threat posed by a possible renewal of factional strife. When Elmer Kelm announced plans to step down as DFL chairman, Humphrey dismissed speculation that "the old Farmer-Labor section of the party" would try to replace Kelm with a candidate more to its liking. "This attempt will not be successful," he wrote. He was wrong.[93]

The factional struggle that broke out within the DFL in the months after the war would grind on for nearly three years and would reflect—on the state level—the growing international tensions that defined the postwar years. The DFL's left wing would soon take control of the party in what historian Carl Solberg called "an outright coup." Hubert Humphrey, who during the war had tried "not to become publicly identified with any faction,"[94] would respond by recasting himself as an anti-communist and leading his party away from the far left. The DFL, a party born during World War II, would have to grow up during the Cold War.

In early January, Brainerd residents unfolded their papers to some of the best news they had read in months. U.S. forces under the command of General Douglas MacArthur had invaded the main Philippine island of Luzon—the same island on which the men of Company A, 194th Tank Battalion, had been captured—and were making steady progress in their efforts to liberate the Philippines from the Japanese. Earlier letters had indicated that some Brainerd POWs might still be held in prison camps in the Philippines, and townspeople hoped that the U.S. invasion forces would soon locate and liberate whatever Americans might still be there. Within a few weeks, word arrived that an elite force of U.S. Army Rangers had slipped behind enemy lines on Luzon and rescued more than five hundred Americans from a jungle prison camp near Cabanatuan. The list of liberated Americans included one Brainerd-area soldier: Private First Class Kenneth Gordon of the nearby town of Merrifield. Gordon returned home in early April after a short convalescence in San Francisco, and, like the other two Brainerd prisoners who had come home before him—Jim McComas and Joe Lamkin—he melted back into the community with little fanfare. Gordon was "almost back to normal weight," the *Brainerd Dispatch* reported on his return, and was "almost hysterical with happiness at being at home."[1]

Over the next several months, details about the fate of several other Brainerd men filtered back home—but the news was almost always bad. Claude Gilmer had died in a prison camp. So had Perlie Clevenger and Harvey Finch. Clinton Quinlan, Carroll Guin, Maxwell Dobson, and Arthur Root all had died when the transport ships that were carrying them from the Philippines to Japan were torpedoed. It seemed that another memorial service was being held in Brainerd every week or two.

On August 10, word arrived in Brainerd that another local boy, Roy Nordstrom, had died in a transport ship sinking the previous October. A few days later, the parents of Donald Paine learned that their son had died nearly three years earlier in a Japanese prison camp. The telegrams confirming Nordstrom's and Paine's deaths were the last such messages to arrive in Brainerd during the war. On August 14, Japan accepted the Allies' terms for unconditional surrender. The war was over.

The celebration in Brainerd began with the blowing of the whistle at the Northern Pacific railroad yards. As if on cue, hundreds of automobile horns immediately joined in a chorus of unrestrained blaring. Revelers festooned lampposts and overhead wires with toilet-paper streamers. Homemade confetti littered nearly every horizontal surface. A parade of horn-honking automobiles snaked through town, making it impossible for pedestrians to cross the streets, but the pedestrians didn't care. They were busy with their own impromptu celebrations on the sidewalks. As the evening progressed, the citywide party began to break up. The editor of the *Brainerd Journal Press* was among the many townsfolk who found it difficult to take too much pleasure in the war's end.

> *We came down town for a while and watched the folks celebrate—it was quite a sight to see—but we didn't stay long. We got to thinking about the families who have loved ones that won't be coming back from the war—friends of ours and neighbors of ours—and, well, to make a long story short, we just went home.*[2]

Over the next three weeks, the people of Brainerd waited as patiently as they could for word on the fate of the men of Company A. Making matters worse was the fact that several of the men had earlier sent letters indicating that they were being held at a camp in Hiroshima. The possibility that the Brainerd men, after surviving so long in captivity, might have been caught in an atomic blast was too horrible to contemplate. "I was worried to death," Pernina Burke recalled. It wasn't until late August that the government informed the Brainerd families that the Hiroshima camp was actually located about fifty miles away from the city, well out of the bomb's destructive range. While that news was welcome, it did little to alleviate the frustration of the prolonged official silence on the men's whereabouts.

Then, during the second week of September, the silence broke. Catherine Porwoll received a telegram informing her that her son, Ken, had been liberated and would soon be permitted to communicate with his family. Three days later, the family of Sid Saign got a similar message. The telegrams kept coming. Ed Burke was alive. So were John Muir, Lee MacDonald, Melvin Ahlgrim, and Lawrence Alberg. On September 19, Ann Miller finally received the news that her husband, Ernie, the commander of the 194th Tank Battalion, was likewise alive and free. The telegram confirming his liberation described his condition as only "fair," but Ann could not hide her elation. "I can hardly talk," she said. "He is alive and that is the best news in the world."[3]

In most cases, the returning men of Company A slipped into town quietly, much as the handful of other former prisoners had done. Most were content to forgo a big homecoming. "It didn't bother me any," insisted Henry Peck. "I was just goddamned glad to get home."[4] Ken Porwoll put off his Brainerd homecoming in favor of a side trip to St. Cloud, where his mother now lived. For him, the simplest welcomes were the most memorable.

> *Mother still had my little dog, a rat-tailed spaniel, real curly hair with a skinny tail, and that sucker looked at me, and looked at me, and looked at me, and sniffed me, and looked at me, and he knew that he should know me, but there was something different. But he finally did. He finally turned around and I says, "Hey." And he wagged his tail, and I got licks from him. So that was a pretty good welcome home in that respect.*[5]

Despite the reticence of some of the former prisoners, the people of Brainerd were still eager to commemorate the end of what had been an excruciating ordeal—not just for the men who had spent most of the war in captivity, but for the community itself, which had been forced to endure their absence. After weeks of patience, they finally got their chance. The officers of Company A were on their way home.

On the third weekend of October, Ann Miller, Eleanor Swearingen, and Pernina Burke traveled to Clinton, Iowa, to be reunited with their husbands. (Ernie Miller, Russ Swearingen, and Ed Burke had to undergo tests and treatment at Clinton's Schick General Hospital before returning to Brainerd.) The men were scheduled to arrive at eight o'clock on Sunday morning, and the wives decided to go down a day early to make sure they were there when the train pulled in. They wanted their reunions to be perfect. That evening, Pernina Burke put in a request for a six o'clock wake-up call, climbed into bed, and closed her eyes.

> *I put curlers in my hair of course so I'd be pretty the next morning, and I couldn't sleep. So I turned on the light and read until about one o'clock, and then I did fall asleep. And all of a sudden the phone was ringing, the doorbell was ringing, and this was all in my dreams and I was rushing around trying to stop it, and it was Ann Miller calling me to tell me that the men were there in Clinton and on their way to the hotel. I had slept about twenty minutes. And she said, "They're here!" I said, "Who's here?" She said, "The men. They're in already and they're on their way to the hotel." Oh my goodness. So I had to get up and take the curlers out and before I was half done, Ed was knocking on the door. Oh, God. Unbeliev-*

*able. He was handsome, and he looked great because they had
been traveling for about six weeks since their liberation and they'd
been eating constantly. So they all looked really good. Their arms
and legs were a little thin and they all looked a little pregnant. They
just looked wonderful.*[6]

At breakfast that morning, the three couples joked with each other
about their memorable night. "How did it feel to sleep in a real bed?" Ernie
asked Ed. "Damn good," Ed replied. "No lice, either." At the mention of
lice, Ernie Miller, apparently unconcerned about conventional table man-
ners, pulled up his shirt so that everyone in the diner could see his back.
He still bore the scars of the lice that had feasted on him in the POW camp.
"His back looked like hamburger," recalled Pernina Burke, "hamburger
wrapped in cellophane."[7]

The Millers, the Swearingens, and the Burkes spent a few more days in
Clinton and then headed north to Brainerd. The welcoming parties in their
hometown were small and appropriately subdued. "They respected us
enough not to crowd us when we came in," Pernina Burke recalled.[8] On his
arrival, Ernie Miller spoke with reverence about his home state. "There
were many days when it seemed impossible to believe that I would set foot
on Minnesota soil again," he said. "Perhaps that's why there was such a
reality in the thrill of getting home."[9]

As the newly returned officers settled in, city leaders finalized plans for
a homecoming bash unlike anything the people there had ever seen. There
would be a parade with flags and bunting and marching bands. Governor
Edward Thye was coming from St. Paul to deliver the main address. Minnesota's adjutant general, Major General Ellard Walsh, would award Ernie
Miller the state's highest military honor, the medal of valor. Other guests
of honor would include Miller's fellow officers, Ed Burke and Russ
Swearingen, and ten enlisted men from Company A—Ken Porwoll, Lee
MacDonald, Kenneth Gordon, Robert Swanson, Jim McComas, Clifford
Rardin, Melvin Ahlgrim, Joe Lamkin, Warren Kerrigan, and Glen Nelson. Major Hortense McKay, an army nurse from Brainerd who had been among
the last Americans evacuated from the Philippines in 1942, was also on the
list of honorees.

An estimated twenty thousand people lined the streets of Brainerd to
cheer the men of Company A and the dozens of other World War II veterans
who had gathered for the event. The mile-long procession began outside
the home of Ernie and Ann Miller and proceeded to the armory. About two

thousand marchers took part, including Russ Swearingen's stepson, Don Arm. "[I was] walking down there carrying this big American flag, and [I had] one of those overseas caps on," he recalled years later. "I was—oh, boy—proud."[10]

Of the sixty-two Brainerd-area men who fought in the Philippines with Company A, 194th Tank Battalion, only thirty-two survived, and many of those who returned struggled to feel at home. One member of Company A, long presumed dead, came home to discover that his family had already cashed in his life insurance policy, and that he was no longer welcome. He left Brainerd, reenlisted, and was eventually killed in Korea.[11] Those who stayed in Brainerd often felt that a wall had risen between themselves and their neighbors. "The home people didn't really know how to talk to you," Ken Porwoll recalled. "They were afraid to ask questions for fear that it would trigger some bad memory on you, that you'd flip and become something else. It was kind of like walking on eggshells."[12] Henry Peck remembered how some people treated his stories of Japanese atrocities as outlandish fiction. "They wouldn't believe us, what we told them," he said. "They called us liars. So the men just clammed up. To hell with them."[13]

For the families of the thirty men who did not return, the last months of 1945 were especially painful. "It was tough," recalled Don Samuelson, whose father had died in the camps. "I can remember when [the men] were

About two thousand marchers, including thirteen members of Company A, took part in Brainerd's homecoming parade, October 27, 1945.

going to come back, I wanted to go down to the train station, and my mother said, 'Now remember, he won't be there.' So I guess I knew that, but I didn't want to believe it. It was like, well, he'll come walking off that train."[14] Ken Porwoll remembered how uncomfortable he often felt when he visited the families of his fallen comrades.

> I went to visit to, I suppose, show some sympathy for them or whatever, and the reaction of the dad was, "What did you know that my son didn't know? And why didn't you tell him what you knew, so that he could survive, too?" . . . Or one would say, "Oh, you're one of those that took the easy route out." What do you say to that? Another one would say, "Maybe if you had fought a little harder, the outcome would have been different." . . . And I thought, well, stick it in your ear. I don't need this kind of hassle. So I wouldn't go anymore.[15]

In his history of Brainerd, author Carl Zapffe tried to place into perspective his city's sacrifice during World War II. "Within four months time [after the Pearl Harbor attack]," he wrote, "one out of every 139 of the population of Brainerd was a prisoner of Japan."[16] Brainerd did, in fact, assume a disproportionate burden during the war years—one that few, if any, American cities of comparable size could match. Years after the war, the people of Brainerd elected the late Walt Samuelson's son, Don Samuelson, to represent them in the state legislature. Almost every year, on the anniversary of the fall of Bataan, the younger Samuelson introduced a resolution on the floor of the state senate, commemorating the sacrifice made by the men of Company A. "It was amazing to me . . . how many people didn't know," he said. "They'd come up to me and say, 'Don, I never knew. Wow!' So you've got to keep saying these things if you want that history to be remembered. You've got to keep reminding people."[17]

Spontaneous celebrations broke out on Twin Cities streets and sidewalks as word spread that the war was over.

Conclusion

A middle-aged man careened toward the corner of Fifth and Marquette in downtown Minneapolis, either unaware or unconcerned that cars were speeding past him. He was screaming. Tears poured down his cheeks. He might have been mistaken for a drunk had it not been for the message he had taken upon himself to deliver. "My God," he cried to no one in particular. "My boys are coming home safe!"

The war was over.

Moments later, at 6:08 on the evening of August 14, 1945, the siren perched atop the Northwestern National Bank building began to wail, triggering an eruption of unrestrained joy on the streets below. Crowds coalesced. Traffic came to a halt. Horns blared. Strangers embraced and kissed. Police had decreed earlier that no parades would be allowed in the downtown loop after victory was declared, but nobody had the heart to spoil the fun of the children who spontaneously began marching through the city's streets and sidewalks.[1]

Many Minnesotans were overcome by a mixture of excitement, relief, and anticipation that evening. In St. Cloud, a six-year-old girl scanned a crowd of revelers, fully expecting to see her father emerge from the throng. (He had, after all, promised to "come home when the war was over.")[2] In St. Paul, newspaper vendor Willard Vinitsky sold his entire bundle of five hundred "peace extras" in twelve minutes. "No one waited for their change," he said. "One man gave me two dollars for a paper. Many others handed over a dollar bill and dashed on."[3] At the corner of Fourth and Wabasha, a few young women noticed a soldier who—unlike most of the other servicemen in the area—seemed too shy to join in the celebrations. Before he knew it, the women were planting a flurry of kisses on his blushing face. "He seemed to like it," a reporter observed.[4]

For many other Minnesotans, however, V-J Day was a more solemn affair. At home after home, American flags suddenly appeared, draped over porch railings and hung from windows. Houses of worship filled with parishioners offering prayers of thanks. And here and there, expressions of anger and frustration bubbled to the surface. "What do they think they're celebrating?" muttered a young sailor as he slouched in the seat of a northbound bus.[5] A soldier at the St. Paul USO sipped a cup of coffee and wished that he could feel as happy as everyone else did. "When I think of all the boys who won't be coming back, and I saw plenty of them in Africa and Italy, it makes me almost want to cry," he said.[6] He wasn't alone in feeling that way. More than three hundred thousand Minnesotans had served in the military during World War II. Nearly eight thousand had died, and many more had been wounded.[7] The scars—both physical and psychological—would prove to be deep and lasting.

Even as Minnesotans sorted through their conflicting emotions about the end of the war, they couldn't help but look forward. It

Prayers at a Minneapolis church on V-J Day. Most houses of worship in the Twin Cities stayed open all night.

seemed clear that great things lay ahead for the nation—and for the state. "This world has passed through a time that has been both terrible and great," the *St. Paul Pioneer Press* declared in its first postwar editorial. "We have beaten the terror. We have the greatness in our grasp for the taking."[8] In the months and years that followed, Minnesotans became aware that the postwar world would be—if not great—then at least different.

In economic terms, Minnesota—like much of the rest of the nation—emerged from the war in good shape. Many war contractors including Minneapolis-Moline, Federal Cartridge, Northwest Airlines, and Thermo King thrived by turning their attention back to long-dormant consumer markets. Others, such as Northern Pump, Minneapolis-Honeywell, and Northwestern Aeronautical (soon known as Engineering Research Associates), built on their wartime successes by continuing to rely heavily on government and military contracts. The state's farmers, having met wartime production demands despite severe manpower shortages, continued to increase efficiency and diversify their operations. Among the more notable changes was a dramatic jump in the production of soybeans. (American farmers had begun planting soybeans during the war when the fighting interrupted imports from Asia.)[9] On the iron ranges, communities finally embraced Bud Davis' vision of a taconite future.

On one level, Minnesota's political landscape looked strangely familiar now that the war was over. The Republicans, who had reasserted their dominance with the election of Harold Stassen in 1938, continued to enjoy great success on the statewide level, while the liberal opposition continued to wound itself with factionalism. But on closer examination, the political sands were clearly beginning to shift. The newly formed Democratic-Farmer-Labor Party (DFL)—while rife with internal intrigue—was nonetheless committed to establishing itself as a viable alternative to the Republicans. By 1948, the party's factional struggles would be largely resolved, the far left banished for good. Hubert Humphrey would defeat incumbent Republican Joseph Ball in the race for U.S. Senate (the new party's first statewide victory), and DFL candidates would win four of the state's nine congressional seats. Republicans would continue to do well for several years (the Republican string of governors would last until 1955), but the DFL—a wartime creation—was clearly on the rise.

The social changes after the war were just as profound as those on the economic and political fronts. Thousands of returning vet-

Reading the happy news.

erans went to college and purchased their first homes aided by the
GI Bill of Rights. Thousands of Minnesota women who might never
have considered working outside the home were now—thanks to
their wartime job experiences—at least open to the idea of staying
in the workforce. Many African Americans, inspired by their employment gains during the war, now had much higher expectations
for the future. Few believed that the fight for racial equality would
be easy. In Minneapolis, for example, de facto segregation in the
city's hotels meant that black visitors—even black veterans—often
had a hard time finding a comfortable place to sleep.[10] But now real
progress seemed possible. The war was also a turning point for the

state's Dakota and Ojibwe. Hundreds of Indians had left their reservations during the war to join the armed forces or take high-paying jobs in defense plants. This reservation-to-city migration accelerated considerably once the fighting was over. A similar migration—from farm to city—drained large pools of population from many rural areas. Marshall County, in northwestern Minnesota, for example, lost more than 12 percent of its population between 1940 and 1950, and continued to lose people for decades thereafter. In the first six years after the war, five hundred Jewish refugees resettled in the Twin Cities area.[11]

A month after V-J Day, diarist Alice Brill described how thrilled she was to be able to buy an entire carton of Lucky Strike cigarettes. It was, she wrote, a "great event."

Still, the changes brought by the war and its aftermath were not always obvious to those who experienced them. Few Minnesotans concerned themselves with the economic, political, and social consequences of the war. Most had just one simple wish: for life to return to normal.

For many Minnesotans, normal meant getting married and starting a family. The national baby boom had actually begun in early 1941, about nine months after Congress' introduction of the Selective Service Act triggered a jump in the marriage rate, but only after the war did it really escalate. The state's fertility rate (births per one thousand women of childbearing age), which in 1945 stood at just over eighty-five, began rising steadily as soon as the war ended and continued to hover over one hundred until the late 1960s. For whatever reason, Minnesota's baby boom wound up outpacing and outlasting that of the nation as a whole.[12] Minnesotans clearly longed for what historian William M. Tuttle, Jr., called "the security and fulfillment of family life."[13]

They also longed to return to the days when tires, gasoline, sugar, and meat weren't rationed (in other words, the days before the war)—and when they didn't have to wonder where their next paycheck would come from (as they did during the Great Depression). They wanted to become consumers again. Many Minnesotans, excited over the reappearance of their favorite goods, found it hard to stop spending the money they had saved during years of wartime deprivation. "It sounds odd to have the meat man say, 'What would you like?'" diarist Alice Brill wrote of a trip to her neighborhood butcher. "You can hardly believe your ears. Steak, ham, (ambrosia after such a long wait). Beef tenderloin—and so tender and good."[14] An ad for Northern States Power Company claimed that the typical American woman was eager to equip her postwar home with "a modern de luxe kitchen with all the latest electrical conveniences."[15] Minnesotans' ravenous appetite for consumer goods reached its apex in February of 1946, when thousands of women "stormed" into Dayton's department store in Minneapolis for a chance to buy some of the sixty thousand pairs of nylon stockings that had finally been put on sale. Many laughed off the mob scene at Dayton's as proof that life was returning to normal. Others were less charitable in their assessments. "I think it is appalling to see the crowds of women standing in line waiting for hose," one woman observed with obvious disgust. "When I see such a display of greed I wonder if they have forgotten why we fought this war."[16]

In the end, postwar reality never quite lived up to many citizens' high expectations for it. During the first year after the war, consumer goods were easier to find, but some items—like butter, for example—remained in short supply. A severe housing shortage developed, forcing many families to "double up." A rash of strikes across the nation threatened to undermine reconversion efforts. And perhaps most disconcerting was the fact that the world, with its mushroom clouds and its fast-developing superpower rivalry, now

Crowds began forming outside Dayton's department store in Minneapolis long before the doors opened on its first postwar nylons sale.

seemed more dangerous than ever. On the first anniversary of V-J Day, newspaper editors across the state looked back on the previous year and looked forward to the years to come. Most, including E. T. Edwards of the *Winona Republican-Herald*, expressed mixed feelings about what they saw. "Anyone is free to judge for himself whether the record of the past year justifies the belief that the inspiration which causes people to rise to the occasion and win a war can be aroused to a similar degree to win the peace that follows," Edwards wrote. "But perhaps a year is too short a time to judge."[17]

Notes

Preface

1. John W. Jeffries, *Wartime America* (Chicago: Ivan R. Dee), 1997, 8.

2. Barbara W. Tuchman, *Practicing History* (New York: Alfred A. Knopf), 1981, 48.

3. *We Did Our Job (And We Did It Good): St. Louis County during World War II* (St. Louis County Historical Society), 1986.

Introduction

1. Richard Rainbolt, *Gold Glory* (Wayzata, MN: Ralph Turtinen, 1972), 99.

2. Charles Johnson, "Gophers Tip Badgers, 41–6, Win Big Ten, U.S. Titles," *Minneapolis Tribune and Star Journal*, November 23, 1941.

3. Gareth Hiebert, "Gophers Win Heil 'Trophy' for Hospital," *St. Paul Pioneer Press*, November 23, 1941.

4. D. Jerome Tweton, *Depression: Minnesota in the Thirties* (Fargo: North Dakota Institute for Regional Studies, 1981), 9.

5. Raymond L. Koch, "Politics and Relief in Minneapolis during the 1930s," *Minnesota History* (Winter 1968), 157.

6. Tweton, *Depression: Minnesota in the Thirties*, 7, 53.

7. George A. Barton, "Sportographs," *Minneapolis Tribune*, November 27, 1934.

8. Tweton, *Depression: Minnesota in the Thirties*, 43.

9. U.S. Information Service, Office of Government Reports, *Minnesota: 1941 Defense Supplement*, 1942, 6, Box 8, War History Committee Records, Collected Materials, MHS.

10. U.S. Information Service, *Minnesota: 1941 Defense Supplement*, 2–3.

11. Bernard Swanson, "Smith Wows Them at Heisman Fete," *Minneapolis Tribune*, December 10, 1941.

Brainerd, 1941

1. "Shades of 1917!" *Brainerd Dispatch*, February 20, 1941.

2. Don Arm, interview with the author, February 24, 2003.

3. Ken Porwoll, interview with the author, November 8, 2002.

4. Leonard Strobel, interview with the author, February 24, 2003.

5. Pernina Burke, interview with the author, February 24, 2003.

6. "Farewell and Godspeed," *Brainerd Dispatch*, February 19, 1941.

7. Arm interview.

8. "Manila In Last Ditch Fight," *Brainerd Dispatch*, December 31, 1941.

Chapter 1: Call to Arms

1. "3,522 in County Have Numbers in Lottery Now On," *Brainerd Dispatch*, October 29, 1940.

2. "Westberg Number Is First," *Brainerd Dispatch*, October 29, 1940.

3. Alton D. Smalley, "No. 1 Ramsey Draftees Become 'Minute' Men; Many Watch and Wait," *St. Paul Pioneer Press*, October 30, 1940.

4. J. Garry Clifford and Samuel R. Spencer, Jr., *The First Peacetime Draft* (Lawrence: University Press of Kansas, 1986), 4.

5. "Scenes at Local Recruiting Offices as City Feels Effect of War," *Minneapolis Star Journal*, December 8, 1941.

6. "Enlistments in All Armed Units Set New Mark in City," *Minneapolis Star Journal*, December 9, 1941; "1,500 Seek to Enlist at City Service Centers," *Minneapolis Star Journal*, December 10, 1941.

7. Nat Finney, "Minnesota War Peak to Be 212,500 Men," *Minneapolis Tribune*, October 16, 1942.

8. "Alex Opinion on War Shows a Grim Spirit," *Alexandria Park Region Echo*, December 11, 1941.

9. "Out of Jail to Enter Army," *Alexandria Park Region Echo*, December 19, 1941.

10. "Civil War Veteran Walks 32 Miles to Assist Navy," *Brainerd Dispatch*, January 7, 1943.

11. Pauline Brunette, Naomi Whipple, Robert DesJarlait, and Priscilla Buffalohead, *Ojibway Family Life in Minnesota: 20th Century Sketches* (Coon Rapids, MN: Anoka-Hennepin School District, 1991), 33.

12. Frederick L. Johnson, *Goodhue County, Minnesota: A Narrative History* (Red Wing, MN: Goodhue County Historical Society Press, 2000), 265.

13. "Negro Citizens from All Walks Comment on Japan's Attack on United States," *Minneapolis Spokesman*, December 12, 1941.

14. Cecil Newman, "Five Loyal Men Not Wanted by Army," *Minneapolis Spokesman*, December 12, 1941.

15. David M. Kennedy, *Freedom from Fear: The American People in Depression and War, 1929–1945* (New York: Oxford University Press, 1999), 634.

16. "Only the Strong," *Time*, November 11, 1940, 24.

17. Anne Bosanko Green, *One Woman's War: Letters Home from the Women's Army Corps 1944–1946* (St. Paul: Minnesota Historical Society Press, 1989), 14–15.

18. Ibid., x, xiii.

19. "6,000 See 125 Women Join Service," *St. Paul Pioneer Press*, October 2, 1943.

20. C. H. Russell, "Round Our Town," *Mankato Free Press*, December 8, 1941.

21. Kennedy, *Freedom from Fear*, 633.

22. Marie Kirkevold, interview by Janet Oian, June 27, 1977, tape recording, Northwest Minnesota Historical Center, Minnesota State University, Moorhead, MN.

23. William Ernst, interview by Steve Vatndal, July 11, 1980, tape recording, West Central Minnesota Historical Research Center, University of Minnesota–Morris, Morris, MN.

24. "Army Rejects Fourth of Men Called at Fort," *St. Paul Dispatch*, May 26, 1944.

25. Kennedy, *Freedom From Fear*, 634–35.

26. "Draft to Leave 34,000 between 18 and 29 on Minnesota Farms," *St. Paul Pioneer Press*, January 17, 1945; "Back to the Farm Move Is Ordered," *Minneapolis Star Journal*, October 12, 1942.

27. "Farm Labor Shortage? Some Skeptical Views," *Minneapolis Sunday Tribune and Star Journal*, March 8, 1942.

28. "Draft Delinquents Warned of Penalty," *St. Paul Pioneer Press*, October 25, 1943.

29. "9 Draft Dodgers Get Prison Terms," *St. Paul Pioneer Press*, October 14, 1942.

30. Herbert C. Schultz, "Calendar of Events," Herbert C. Schultz Papers, MHS.

31. Leland Rowberg to Andrew and Marie Rowberg, March 19–24, 1943, Leland Rowberg Papers, MHS.

32. Ibid.

33. Schultz, "Calendar of Events."

34. "Draftees Take Tests," *St. Paul Pioneer Press*, November 26, 1940.

35. Leland Rowberg to Andrew and Marie Rowberg, March 24, 1943, Leland Rowberg Papers, MHS.

36. Dale Francis Becker, "Fort Snelling 1938–1945" (undergraduate paper, University of Minnesota, 1983), 13–14.

37. John Finch, "War Department Personnel Center," *Fort Snelling Bulletin*, June 21, 1946.

38. Stephen E. Osman, "Fort Snelling's Last War," *Roots*, Winter 1989, 19–20.

39. *You Have 1000 Million Friends*, KSTP, November 29, 1942.

40. Leland Rowberg to Andrew and Marie Rowberg, March 25, 1943, Leland Rowberg Papers, MHS.

41. St. Paul Civilian Defense Council, Report of Recreation Committee, January 18, 1943, 2, Box 2, War History Committee Records, Subgroup St. Paul–Ramsey County War History Committee, MHS.

42. "Fitting Men to Invitations Keeps Service Center's Host Hopping," *Minneapolis Sunday Tribune and Star Journal*, July 19, 1942.

43. John Nelson to Cedric Adams, April 19, 1944, Box 12, War History Committee Records, MHS.

44. "Fitting Men to Invitations"; "Soldiers Suckers for Crystal Ball, Dancing," *Minneapolis Times*, July 16, 1942.

Dispatches: Leland Rowberg

1. Leland Rowberg to Andrew and Marie Rowberg, August 12 and 22, September 10, 27, and 30, and October 2, 1944, Leland Rowberg Papers, MHS.

2. "Narrative Account of Interview with Raymond Radke," January 15, 1946, Leland Rowberg Papers, MHS.

3. Marie Rowberg to Leland Rowberg, October 23, 1944, Leland Rowberg Papers, MHS.

Chapter 2: The Home Front

1. "Stassen Asks People to Aid U.S. Defense," *Minneapolis Star Journal*, December 8, 1941.

2. Harold E. Stassen, radio address transcript, December 18, 1941, Box 2, Miscellaneous Records, Civilian Defense Division Records, MHS.

3. "Twin Cities May Be Bombed, Maas Warns," *Minneapolis Star Journal*, January 8, 1942.

4. Alice C. Brill scrapbooks, vol. 1, January 10, 1942, MHS.

5. "Reaction to Maas' Speeches," *Minneapolis Star Journal*, January 12, 1942.

6. Richard Lingeman, *Don't You Know There's a War On? The American Home Front 1941–1945* (New York: Thunder's Mouth Press, 2003), 43.

7. "So You Think Minnesota Can't Be Bombed?" *Minneapolis Daily Times*, February 1, 1942.

8. "Can the Japs Bomb Minneapolis?" and "When You Reach Minneapolis, Consider These Areas Also as Military Objectives," *News Stories of the Northern Pump Company, Minneapolis, Minnesota, from September 24th, 1940–June 11, 1942*, MHS.

9. "The Bull's-Eye," *Commercial West*, February 7, 1942.

10. Mary Proal Lindeke, "The Civilians' Role in the War," *Continuation Course in Medical Social Service* (Minneapolis: University of Minnesota Center for Continuation Study, 1943), 1.

11. Allan Briggs to Red Wing Civilian Defense Council et al., July 2, 1943; Wilbur C. Aronson to Harvey W. Wertz, July 6, 1943, Box 2, Director's General Correspondence and Subject Files, Civilian Defense Division Records, MHS.

12. "Surprise 'Bombing' Here Shows City Unprepared," *Red Wing Republican Eagle*, July 6, 1943.

13. Leo Koll to Allan Briggs, July 10, 1943, Box 1, Director's Correspondence with Local Civilian Defense Councils, Civilian Defense Division Records, MHS.

14. C. A. Zwiener to J. F. Keouhn, April 21, 1942, Box 2, Director's Correspondence with Local Civilian Defense Councils, Civilian Defense Division Records, MHS.

15. Orville E. Lomoe, "Virginia Blackout Success," *Duluth Herald*, July 16, 1942.

16. Gordon Malen, "Blackout Called '99% Perfect' from Air View," *St. Paul Pioneer Press*, July 17, 1942.

17. Neil A Davidson, "Rural Hennepin Can Be Proud," *Minneapolis Tribune*, September 11, 1942.

18. "Report of Area Blackout—Ely, Minnesota: December 14, 1942," Box 3, Director's Correspondence with Local Civilian Defense Councils, Civilian Defense Division Records, MHS.

19. Hildred Long to Frank Long, December 4, 1942, Frank and Hildred Long Papers, MHS.

20. Allan Briggs to Joseph D. Scholtz, May 7, 1943, Box 3, Director's Correspondence with Local

Civilian Defense Councils, Civilian Defense Division Records, MHS.

21. Allan Briggs to L. P. Szarzynski, January 18, 1943, Box 2, Director's Correspondence with Local Civilian Defense Councils, Civilian Defense Division Records, MHS.

22. "Street Lights Glow during Blackout Test in Eveleth," clipping from unidentified newspaper, August 26, 1943, Box 1, Citizens Defense Corps Records, Civilian Defense Division Records, MHS.

23. Gordon B. Clarke to Allan Briggs, August 27, 1943, Box 1, Citizens Defense Corps Records, Civilian Defense Division Records, MHS.

24. Arthur Tomfohr to William J. Meyer, August 26, 1943, Box 1, Citizens Defense Corps Records, Civilian Defense Division Records, MHS.

25. "Surprise State Blackout Called Success Despite Some Violations," *Minneapolis Star Journal*, August 25, 1943.

26. Irwin F. Smith to William J. Meyer, August 30, 1943, Box 1, Director's Correspondence with Local Civilian Defense Councils, Civilian Defense Division Records, MHS.

27. Gus Kleinschmidt to William J. Meyer, August 27, 1943, Box 1, Citizens Defense Corps Records, Civilian Defense Division Records, MHS.

28. "Police Report 82 Blackout Violations," *St. Paul Dispatch*, May 11, 1943.

29. Harvey Kelly to Allan Briggs, September 8, 1943, Box 1, Director's Correspondence with Local Civilian Defense Councils, Civilian Defense Division Records, MHS.

30. F. S. Heaberlin, office memorandum, April 6, 1945, Box 1, *St. Paul Pioneer Press* Records, MHS. Most postwar accounts of the Japanese balloon bomb program indicate that no balloon bombs ever landed in Minnesota. Heaberlin's memo suggests otherwise.

31. Alice C. Brill scrapbooks, vol. 1, December 1942, MHS.

32. "Sale of Ground Horse Meat Reported on Increase Here," clipping from unidentified newspaper, Alice C. Brill scrapbooks, vol. 2, MHS.

33. C. F. Culler, "The Carp for Victory," *Izaak Walton League, Minnesota Division, Bulletin*, Last Quarter 1942.

34. William Cummings diary, April 20, 1942, MHS.

35. Lingeman, *Don't You Know There's a War On?* 235.

36. Ibid., 239.

37. William Cummings diary, July 3, 1943, MHS.

38. Harold Eastlund, interview by Mark Stover,

October 8, 1979, transcription, 8, West Central Minnesota Historical Research Center, University of Minnesota–Morris, Morris, MN.

39. Arthur G. Steffes to Allan Briggs, February 17, 1944, Box 2, Director's General Correspondence and Subject Files, Civilian Defense Division Records, MHS.

40. Lambert S. Gill, interview by Gustavus Loevinger, March 31, 1944, transcription, 25, Box 3, St. Paul–Ramsey County War History Committee Records, War History Committee Records, MHS.

41. Neva Williams, interview, OH 79.16, transcription, 23, MHS.

42. William Cummings diary, April 23, 1942, MHS.

43. Alice C. Brill scrapbooks, vol. 1, May 2, 1942, MHS.

44. "Sugar Books Denied 10% in Minnesota," *Minneapolis Star Journal*, May 6, 1942.

45. Hildred Long to Frank Long, July 25, 1942, Frank and Hildred Long Papers, MHS.

46. Hildred Long to Frank Long, February 21, 1943, Frank and Hildred Long Papers, MHS.

47. W. H. Alderman, "How to Make Our Gardens Produce More," 1944, Box 4, Director's General Correspondence and Subject Files, Citizens Service Corps Records, Civilian Defense Division Records, MHS.

48. Jerome T. Burns to William M. Tuttle, Jr., March 27, 1990, private collection.

49. Alice C. Brill scrapbooks, vol. 2, April 1943, MHS.

50. "Little Squawking by Civilians Found," *St. Paul Pioneer Press*, July 3, 1943.

51. John Lienhard, "Liquid Stocking Situation Confuses Fashion 'Expert,'" *St. Paul Dispatch*, July 28, 1943.

52. Hildred Long to Frank Long, January 20, 1943, Frank and Hildred Long Papers, MHS.

53. Lingeman, *Don't You Know There's a War On?* 267.

54. "Three-Fourths of Retailers Fail to Post Ceiling Prices," *St. Paul Pioneer Press*, June 19, 1942.

55. Marie Kirkevold, interview, June 27, 1977, tape recording, Northwest Minnesota Historical Center, Minnesota State University, Moorhead, MN.

56. "Wanted—1 Cannon," *Minneapolis Star Journal*, September 22, 1942.

57. Carl Narvestad, *A History of Yellow Medicine County* (Granite Falls, MN: Yellow Medicine County Historical Society, 1972), 482.

58. Margaret Entsminger, "St. Peter's Scrap Heap Totals over 250 Tons," *Minneapolis Tribune*, October 1, 1942.

59. "The Battle of Scrap Is On!" *Minneapolis Star Journal*, October 5, 1942.

60. T. Glenn Harrison, untitled history of St. Paul scrap drive, 1942, 20, Box 1, St. Paul–Ramsey County War History Committee Records, War History Committee Records, MHS.

61. "Survey Indicates 7,500-Ton Scrap Harvest for City," *Minneapolis Star Journal*, October 12, 1942; "Water Outlet Proves Too Tough for Diligent Scrapster," *Minneapolis Star Journal*, October 12, 1942.

62. Harrison, untitled history, 22.

63. Alice C. Brill scrapbooks, vol. 2, October 18, 1942, MHS.

64. "Scrap Announcement from MEA," November 19, 1942, Box 23, Collected Materials, War History Committee Records, MHS.

65. "Join the Fat Salvage Campaign," 1942, Box 5, Collected Materials, War History Committee Records, MHS.

66. American Red Cross, Midwestern Area, *The American Red Cross in Minnesota for 1945*, 1945, 1, Box 2, Collected Materials, War History Committee Records, MHS.

67. "League Launches Drive for Deer Hides for War Effort," *Izaak Walton League, Minnesota Division, Bulletin*, First Quarter 1944, 8.

68. "Milkweed Pod Collection Will Start Sept. 15," *Warren (MN) Sheaf*, August 23, 1944; "Swamped by Milkweed Pods," *St. Paul Dispatch*, August 30, 1943.

69. "2 Million Lbs. Of Cattail Fluff," *Holt (MN) Weekly News*, February 11, 1944; "Holt Gets the Cattail Fluff Plant," *Holt (MN) Weekly News*, February 18, 1944.

70. "Fido Joins Army," *Minneapolis Tribune*, March 30, 1942.

71. Alice Lake, "Rejected Dog Gains 40 Pounds in Army," *St. Paul Dispatch*, September 14, 1943.

72. Kennedy, *Freedom from Fear*, 626.

73. A. B. Horner, "Horner Reviews Problems, Achievements," *Field and Hangar*, June 1945, 9, 11.

74. Theodore C. Blegen, *Minnesota: A History of the State* (Minneapolis: University of Minnesota Press, 1963), 545.

Brainerd, 1942

1. Strobel, interview.

2. E. B. Miller, *Bataan Uncensored* (Little Falls, MN: Military Historical Society of Minnesota, 1991), 96–97.

3. "Guard Unit Fights Historic Battle," *Brainerd Dispatch*, January 30, 1942.

4. "Brainerd Area Hardest Hit by Capture of Bataan," *Brainerd Dispatch*, April 10, 1942.

5. "The War Is Very Close to Brainerd," *Brainerd Dispatch*, April 11, 1942.

6. "Company A War Prisoners," *Brainerd Dispatch*, May 14, 1942.

7. "'All's Well on Bataan,' Say Brainerd Soldiers' Long-Delayed Letters," *Minneapolis Tribune*, August 18, 1942.

8. "Army Captain's Wife Pays Tribute to Colonel Miller," *Brainerd Dispatch*, September 3, 1942.

9. Don Samuelson, interview with the author, February 24, 2003.

10. "Lieut. Col. Miller Prisoner of War in the Philippines," *Brainerd Dispatch*, December 7, 1942.

11. "Captain Edward L. Burke Prisoner of the Japanese," *Brainerd Dispatch*, December 14, 1942.

12. Burke, interview.

Chapter 3: Help Wanted

1. Minnesota Department of Education, "Minutes of the Joint Meeting of the Committees on War Production Training and Rural War Production Training and the State Board for Vocational Education," January 18, 1943, 8, Box 13, War History Committee Records, MHS.

2. "Superintendents Study Teacher Shortage Problem," *Minneapolis Times*, April 1, 1942.

3. "'Food Rationing' Is Here! Cafes All Short-Handed," *Minneapolis Tribune*, September 14, 1942; "Acute Labor Shortage in City's Cafes," *Minneapolis Times*, May 13, 1942.

4. Louis Gollop, "17 Bowling Alleys Closed By Pin Setter Shortage," *St. Paul Pioneer Press*, October 16, 1944.

5. "Mechanics Shortage Adds to Auto Problems," *Minneapolis Times*, November 10, 1942; "Pallbearer Shortage Here Blamed on War," *St. Paul Dispatch*, September 22, 1944.

6. "Harvest Hands for Ice Needed," *St. Paul Pioneer Press*, January 7, 1945.

7. Paul E. Miller, "State Set to Mobilize Its Farm Workers," radio script, April 10, 1943, 2, Box 2, Director's General Correspondence and Subject Files, Civilian Defense Division Records, MHS.

8. Paul E. Miller, "Farm Help—The Big Question Mark in 1943 Food Production," radio script, March 11, 1943, 3, Box 2, Director's General Correspondence and Subject Files, Civilian Defense Division Records, MHS.

9. Paul E. Miller, "Minnesota Set to Begin Drive for Farm Help," radio script, February 28, 1943, 2, Box 2, Director's General Correspondence and Subject Files, Civilian Defense Division Records, MHS.

10. Ibid.

11. Minnesota Division of Employment and Security, *Summary of Twin City Labor Market Area Survey*, September 1941, 3, Box 3, Miscellaneous Records, Civilian Defense Division Records, MHS.

12. State Committee on Tolerance, Loyalty, and Unity, *An Appeal to the Citizens of Minnesota*, n.d., Box 2, Miscellaneous Records, Civilian Defense Division Records, MHS.

13. "Stop Order Sought for Smith Talk," *Minneapolis Tribune*, January 16, 1943.

14. Selden Cowles Menefee, *Assignment: USA* (New York: Reynal & Hitchcock, 1943), 101.

15. "Minnesota Indians Do Their Part," *Defense Council Bulletin*, July 1, 1944.

16. Margaret McGillis, interview with the author, August 17, 2003.

17. Ibid.

18. Ibid.

19. "Women Workers Wanted," *Zenith Bulletin*, February 19, 1943.

20. "We Were the First," *Zenith Bulletin*, June 30, 1944.

21. *Remembering the Globe* (Superior, WI: Superior Public Library, n.d.), documentary.

22. "Women Workers Aid Ship Construction in Butler Yards," *News and Views*, October 1944.

23. "By the Ways," *Zenith Bulletin*, May 7, 1943.

24. Larry Oakes, "World War II: 1940–1945," *Minneapolis Star-Tribune*, December 31, 1999.

25. McGillis, interview.

26. Minnesota Department of Education, "Minutes of the Joint Meeting," 9.

27. "Surplus Labor Status Given Twin Cities," *St. Paul Pioneer Press*, June 28, 1943.

28. Minneapolis-Moline Company, *Women Production Workers: Welcome to Minneapolis-Moline*, 1940, 1.

29. Robert C. Vogel and Deborah L. Crown, *The World War II Ordnance Department's Government-Owned Contractor-Operated (GOCO) Industrial Facilities: Twin Cities Ordnance Plant Historic Investigation* (Plano, TX: Geo-Marine, 1995), 42.

30. "First Women Trolley 'Men,'" *St. Paul Pioneer Press*, July 17, 1943.

31. "'Drowning' May Be Popular," *St. Paul Pioneer Press*, May 14, 1943.

32. Moxy Entsminger, "Women Training as Telegraph Operators," *Minneapolis Tribune and Star Journal*, August 9, 1942.

33. Miller, "State Set to Mobilize," 2.

34. Ruthe Rosten, interview by David Ripley, August 15, 1980, tape recording, West Central Minnesota Historical Research Center, University of Minnesota–Morris, Morris, MN.

35. Miller, "Farm Help," 6.

36. Ed Shave, "Women Toil on Farms to Help Win War," *Minneapolis Tribune*, August 12, 1942.

37. Alan Clegg, "A Shipyard Obituary—Without Crepe," *Cargill News*, January 1946.

38. Walter Trost, interview by Sara I. Beckstrand, August 23, 1979, transcript, West Central Minnesota Historical Research Center, University of Minnesota–Morris, Morris, MN.

39. William L. O'Neill, *A Democracy at War: America's Fight at Home and Abroad in World War II* (New York: The Free Press, 1993), 242.

40. Duluth Children's Services, "Community Facilities Application for Lanham Act Funds," n.d., 4, Box 2, Miscellaneous Records, Civilian Defense Division Records, MHS.

41. Minneapolis Children's Services, "Community Facilities Application for Lanham Act Funds, n.d., C-2, Box 2, Miscellaneous Records, Civilian Defense Division Records, MHS.

42. "Granny Now Does Her Bit—Takes Care of the Kiddies," *Twin Cities Ordnance News*, March 10, 1943; Margaret Stukel, "You Can't Shirk Your Children and Work Here," *St. Paul Pioneer Press Magazine*, April 11, 1943, 3.

43. Hilda Rachuy, "A Single Mother and World War II," *Ramsey County History* (Winter 1991), 14.

44. "Working Mothers Here Use Child Care Centers," *St. Paul Pioneer Press*, March 12, 1944.

45. William L. O'Neill, *A Democracy at War: America's Fight at Home and Abroad in World War II* (New York: The Free Press, 1993), 242.

46. Alice C. Brill scrapbooks, vol. 1, June (?), 1942, MHS.

47. "New 'Factory Bob' Giving Women Workers Morale Plus Glamor," *Minneapolis Tribune*, October 26, 1942.

48. Amram Scheinfeld, "Motherhood's Back in Style," *Ladies' Home Journal*, September 1944, 136.

49. Marjorie Bingham, "Keeping At It: Minnesota Women," *Minnesota in a Century of Change* (St. Paul: Minnesota Historical Society Press, 1989), 452; "Many Women Glad to Quit War Jobs," *St. Paul Pioneer Press*, August 17, 1945.

50. Kennedy, *Freedom From Fear*, 779–81.

51. Harry Davis, *Overcoming: The Autobiography of W. Harry Davis*, ed. Lori Sturdevant (Afton, MN: Afton Historical Society Press, 2002), 86–87.

52. Governor's Interracial Commission of Minnesota, *The Negro Worker's Progress in Minnesota*, 1949, 31, 36–37.

53. "Mill City Launches Campaign for Jobs in Local Defense Industry," *Minneapolis Spokesman*, April 18, 1941, 1.

54. "Speakers Claim Negro Defense Role Restricted," *Minneapolis Tribune*, October 10, 1941.

55. "Urges Wider Recognition of Negro in War Jobs," *St. Paul Pioneer Press*, January 11, 1942.

56. "Racial Work Rights Group Formed Here," *Minneapolis Tribune*, August 12, 1942.

57. Cecil Newman, "An Experiment in Industrial Democracy," *Opportunity Magazine*, Spring 1944, 52.

58. "Wash. Sends Man-Power Commission Representative to Check Negro-Barring," *Minneapolis Spokesman*, August 7, 1942.

59. Albert V. Allen, interview, transcript, OH 30.1, MHS.

60. Newman, "Experiment in Industrial Democracy," 53.

61. "Wash. Sends Man-Power Commission Representative to Check Negro-Barring," *Minneapolis Spokesman*, August 7, 1942.

62. Harry Davis, interview with the author, September 5, 2003.

63. Davis, *Overcoming*, 96.

64. Governor's Interracial Commission of Minnesota, *The Negro and His Home in Minnesota*, 76.

65. "Minneapolis Man Objects to 'Special Labeling' of His Blood by Red Cross Bank," *Minneapolis Spokesman*, May 21, 1943.

66. "Turpin Case Is Closed, Defense Committee Reports," *Minneapolis Spokesman*, April 30, 1943.

67. Governor's Interracial Commission, *The Negro Worker's Progress in Minnesota*, 37–38.

68. Davis, *Overcoming*, 99.

69. Davis, interview.

70. "Nab St. Paul Japanese," *St. Paul Dispatch*, December 8, 1941.

71. Kathryn Gorman, "Loyal St. Paul Japs Victims of War," *St. Paul Dispatch*, December 9, 1941.

72. James Hiner, Jr., "Narrative History: War Relocation Authority, Minneapolis District, 1942–1946," 25, Box 14, Minnesota Ethnic History Project, MHS.

73. Michael Albert, "The Japanese," *They Chose Minnesota: A Survey of the State's Ethnic Groups* (St. Paul: Minnesota Historical Society Press, 1981), 558–59.

74. Masaharu Ano, "Loyal Linguists: Nisei of World War II Learned Japanese in Minnesota," *Minnesota History* (Fall 1977), 278.

75. Margaret Zack, "Sentence: Internment Ostracism; Crime: Japanese Ancestry," *Minneapolis Tribune Picture Magazine*, May 13, 1979, 26.

76. Tosh Abe, interview with the author, March 14, 2003.

77. "400 U.S. Japs Resettled in This Area," *St. Paul Pioneer Press*, November 16, 1943; "1,396 Nisei Relocated in State," *St. Paul Dispatch*, November 20, 1944.

78. "A Study of the Relocated Japanese-Americans in Minneapolis," [1944?], Box 14, Minnesota Ethnic History Project, MHS.

79. Ibid.

80. Hiner, "Narrative History," 9f, 16, 20c, 27.

81. Ano, "Loyal Linguists," 283.

82. Al Zdon, "Trained in Minnesota," *Minnesota Legionnaire*, January 2000, 8.

83. Abe, interview.

84. "War Prisoners Available to Minnesota Farmers," *St. Paul Pioneer Press*, June 23, 1943.

85. Miller, "Minnesota Set to Begin," 3.

86. Paul Horn and Hank Peterson, interview by Gloria Thompson, January 11, 1974, transcript, Henry Peterson Records, Northwest Historical Center, Minnesota State University Moorhead, Moorhead, MN.

87. "Prison Labor Opposition Arises," *Moorhead Daily News*, May 23, 1944.

88. "Advance Detail of German War Prisoners Arrives," *Moorhead Daily News*, May 29, 1944; "Additional War Prisoners Arrive," *Moorhead Daily News*, May 31, 1944.

89. Mark Peihl, "POWs Work at Moorhead Truck Farm," *Clay County Historical Society Newsletter*, March/April 1991, 16.

90. Edward J. Pluth, "Prisoner of War Employment in Minnesota during World War II," *Minnesota History* (Winter 1975), 297.

91. Dean B. Simmons, *Swords into Plowshares: Minnesota's POW Camps during World War II* (St. Paul: Cathedral Hill Books, 2000), 1, 27.

92. Horn and Peterson, interview.

93. George H. Lobdell, "Minnesota's 1944 PW Escape," *Minnesota History* (Fall 1994), 113–23.

94. Pluth, "Prisoner of War Employment," 302.

95. "War Captives Cannot Fish in Minnesota," *St. Paul Dispatch*, June 15, 1944.

96. Jerome T. Burns to William Tuttle, March 27, 1990, private collection.

97. Minnesota Public Radio, "We Were the Lucky Ones," May 28, 1985.

98. Peihl, "POWs Work at Moorhead," 16.

99. William Sprung and Faith Evers Sprung, interview, tape recording, Northwest Minnesota Historical Center, Minnesota State University, Moorhead, MN.

100. Pluth, "Prisoner of War Employment," 299.

101. Hermann Massing to Henry Peterson, December 11, 1974, Henry Peterson Records, Northwest Minnesota Historical Center, Minnesota State University Moorhead, Moorhead, MN.

102. Simmons, *Swords into Plowshares*, 48.

103. Hans Johannsen to Henry Peterson, May 10, 1946, Henry Peterson Records, Northwest Minnesota Historical Center, Minnesota State University Moorhead, Moorhead, MN.

Dispatches: Al Hafner

1. Al Hafner to Milly Hafner, various dates, Hafner Family Papers, Olmsted County Historical Society.

Chapter 4: Arsenals of Democracy

1. Ray P. Speer and Harry J. Frost, *Minnesota State Fair: The History and Heritage of 100 Years* (Minneapolis: Argus Publishing Co., 1964), 227–28.

2. Noel E. Allard and Gerald N. Sandvick, *Minnesota Aviation History* (Chaska: Mahb Publishing, 1993), 233–36.

3. "Fair Grounds Plant Called 'Miracle,'" *St. Paul Pioneer Press*, February 29, 1944.

4. Patricia L. Dooley, "Ordnance Works: Condemnation, Construction, and Community Response," *Minnesota History* (Summer 1985), 217–18; U.S. Office of Production Management, *State Distribution of Defense Contract Awards, June 1, 1940 to May 31, 1941*, 1941, Box 2, Correspondence and Miscellaneous Records of State Defense Coordinator, Civilian Defense Division Records, MHS.

5. Francis M. Carroll, *Crossroads in Time: A History of Carlton County, Minnesota* (Cloquet, MN: Carlton County Historical Society, 1987), 295.

6. "$9,000,000 in Factories Entailed in Hemp Fibre Manufacture," *Commercial West*, December 5, 1942, 14; "War Hemp Yield of 1 to 3 Tons an Acre Sighted," *St. Paul Dispatch*, July 15, 1943, 15.

7. "Report of Progress: Defense Industry in the Northwest," *Minneapolis Star Journal*, November 26, 1941.

8. H. J. Miller, *Report on State Efforts to Secure Defense Business for Minnesota Industries*, [1941?], 7.

9. Robert G. Spinney, *World War II in Nashville: Transformation of the Homefront* (Knoxville: University of Tennessee Press, 1998), 19.

10. "King of the Wildcatters," *Time*, June 12, 1944, 115.

11. Robert M. Yoder, "Minnesota's Blitz Producer," *Saturday Evening Post*, February 20, 1943, 20.

12. Ibid.

13. Cedric Adams, "In This Corner," *Minneapolis Star Journal*, May (?), 1942. From the scrapbook "Northern Pump Company News Stories," in Box 16, War History Committee Records, MHS.

14. Philip W. Schulte, "Northern Pump Co. in Fridley Boom with $60,000,000 Defense Contract," unknown newspaper, March (?), 1941.

15. Yoder, "Minnesota's Blitz Producer," 21.

16. "Northern Pump President Replies to Complaint by a Worker's Wife," *Minneapolis Tribune*, April 8, 1942.

17. Yoder, "Minnesota's Blitz Producer," 21.

18. "Northern Pump Finally Ends Discrimination against Negro; Employ Three Men," *Minneapolis Spokesman*, April 3, 1942, 1; "Washington Sends Man-Power Commission Representative to Check Negro-Barring," *Minneapolis Spokesman*, August 7, 1942; "Employment in War Plants in Mpls. Climbing," *Minneapolis Spokesman*, January 8, 1943; "John Hawley Calls French Senegalese Troops N—rs on Radio Program," *Minneapolis Spokesman*, February 12, 1943.

19. Charles W. Washington to Robert C. Weaver, December 6, 1940, Box 3, Correspondence and Miscellaneous Records of State Defense Coordinator, Civilian Defense Division Records, MHS.

20. "John Hawley Calls French Senegalese Troops N—rs on Radio Program," *Minneapolis Spokesman*, February 12, 1943.

21. L. D. Parlin, "'Skinned' of 16 Million Profit, Solons Told by Northern Pump Chief," *St. Paul Dispatch*, June 18, 1943.

22. Yoder, "Minnesota's Blitz Producer," 98.

23. "King of the Wildcatters," *Time*, June 12, 1944, 115.

24. Franklin D. Roosevelt, Annual Message to Congress, January 6, 1942.

25. W. R. Harkins, "Talk before St. Louis County Historical Society," March 26, 1963, Lake Superior Maritime Collections, University of Wisconsin–Superior.

26. Dick Pomeroy, "Superior, Shipbuilding Grew Up Together," *Superior Evening Telegram*, June 30, 1990.

27. Bill Beck and C. Patrick Labadie, *The Pride of the Inland Seas: An Illustrated History of the Port of Duluth—Superior* (Afton, MN: Afton Historical Society Press, 2004).

28. *Remembering the Globe* (Superior, WI: Superior Public Library, n.d.), documentary.

29. Noam Levey, "Ships of Dreams," *Duluth News Tribune*, April 5, 1998.

30. "The Ship That Broke a Record," *Walter Butler News and Views*, January 1944; "Teamwork Wins," *Walter Butler News and Views*, December 1943.

31. Edwin G. Drill, interview, transcript, OH 30.18, MHS.

32. Dick Pomeroy, "World War II Shipbuilders Still at It Today," *Superior Evening Telegram*, March 20, 1982.

33. Drill, interview.

34. "Launch 3 More Vessels at Head of Lakes," *Skillings' Mining Review*, August 15, 1942.

35. *Remembering the Globe.*

36. "The Farmer Goes to Sea," *Time*, September 13, 1943.

37. R. M. Douglas, letter to the editor, *St. Paul Dispatch*, April 3, 1942.

38. Clegg, "Shipyard Obituary," 11.

39. James M. Sutherland, "Cargill's First Navy Tanker Starts down Minnesota River," *Minneapolis Star Journal*, November 5, 1943.

40. Ibid.; Robert Thompson, "Agawam Snakes River, Arrives Here," *St. Paul Pioneer Press*, November 6, 1943.

41. Wayne G. Broehl, Jr., *Cargill: Trading the World's Grain* (Hanover, NH: University Press of New England, 1992), 648.

42. Arthur Dudley Gillett, "The Marvelous Mesabi Will Win the War," MHS.

43. Ibid.

44. E. W. Davis, *Pioneering with Taconite* (St. Paul: Minnesota Historical Society, 1964), 18–19.

45. Davis, *Pioneering with Taconite*, 63.

46. "Range Moves for Legislation to Aid Mining." *Virginia Daily Enterprise*, January 31, 1941.

47. Davis, *Pioneering with Taconite*, 93.

48. "Range Moves for Legislation to Aid Mining," *Virginia Daily Enterprise*, January 31, 1941.

49. E. W. Davis, *Lake Superior Iron Ore and the War Emergency*, 1942, MHS.

50. "Ore Question," *Virginia (MN) Range Facts*, December 24, 1942.

51. "Can Research Save Mesabi?" *Business Week*, May 11, 1946, 19; Warner Olivier, "The Coming Crisis in Iron," *Saturday Evening Post*, November 14, 1942, 22.

52. Olivier, "Coming Crisis in Iron," 122.

53. "Can Research Save Mesabi?" *Business Week*, May 11, 1946, 20.

54. Dudley, "Marvelous Mesabi."

55. Welfare Defense Advisory Committee, "Preliminary Statement Concerning Twin Cities Ordinance [*sic*] Plant," September 17, 1941, Welfare Division Files, Civilian Defense Division Records, MHS.

56. Charles L. Horn, "Mr. Horn's Own Story of President's Visit," *Twin Cities Ordnance News*, October 9, 1942.

57. "Surprise Visit Made at Night September 19," *Twin Cities Ordnance News*, October 9, 1942.

58. Horn, "Mr. Horn's Own Story."

59. "Only Night Shift Here Saw F.R.," *Minneapolis Times*, October 2, 1942; "TCOP Inspected by President Roosevelt," *Twin Cities Ordnance News*, October 9, 1942.

60. Harold Stassen, interview by Deborah L. Crown, September 22, 1994, transcript.

61. "Only Night Shift Here Saw F.R." *Minneapolis Times*, October 2, 1942, 1.

62. Charles L. Horn, "A Letter to Employees from Charles L. Horn," *Twin Cities Ordnance News*, August 28, 1942.

63. Vogel and Crown, *World War II Ordnance*, 28.

64. Ibid., 13, 40.

65. Ibid., 41–42.

66. Carl Holmberg, interview by Deborah L. Crown, September 19, 1994, transcript.

67. Vogel and Crown, *World War II Ordnance*, 31–34, 46.

68. William Cummings diary, November 28, 1942, August 24, 1943, MHS.

69. Neal Gendler, "Uniforms or Not, Their Work Helped Win World War II," *Minneapolis Star-Tribune*, July 31, 1994.

70. "Turtle Lake Man Killed by Bullet," *St. Paul Pioneer Press*, November 12, 1942.

71. Vogel and Crown, *World War II Ordnance*, 34.

72. William Cummings diary, June 15, 1943, MHS.

Dispatches: Ed Motzko

1. Edmund Motzko, interview by Sandy Kilbort, April 20, 1982, transcript, Minnesota Liberators of Concentration Camps Oral History Project, MHS.

Chapter 5: Minnesota Made

1. "Excerpts from Army Times February 5, 1944, Page 11: Jeep was First in the 'Eep' Family," *Minneapolis-Moline Merchandiser*, n.d.

2. "Godfather to the Jeep—Great Mystery Is Solved," *Army Times*, April 17, 1943.

3. "Excerpts from Army Times February 5, 1944, Page 11: Jeep was First in the 'Eep' Family," *Minneapolis-Moline Merchandiser*, n.d.

4. "Jeep Dispute Round Is Won by City Firm," *Minneapolis Tribune*, March 12, 1944.

5. Jim Allen, "Will the Real Jeep Please Stand Up," *Fourwheeler*, March 1996.

6. Carolyn Wyman, *Spam: A Biography* (San Diego: Harcourt, Brace & Company, 1999), 61.

7. "Hormel and the Nation," *The Squeal*, January 1, 1942.

8. Richard Dougherty, *In Quest of Quality: Hormel's First 75 Years* (St. Paul: North Central Publishing, 1966), 198.

9. "What's in a Name?" *Yank, The Army Weekly*, January 14, 1944.

10. "Talk of the Town," *New Yorker*, August 11, 1945.

11. "Spam and the Future," *Fortune*, March 1944.

12. Frances Levison, "Hormel: The Spam Man," *Life*, March 11, 1946, 65.

13. "Fell in Forest," *Virginia (MN) Range Facts*, November 30, 1944.

14. "Modern Magic," *Honeywell Aero*, August 1943.

15. "Now It Can Be Told," *Honeywell Aero*, October 1943.

16. "Researchers Open New Door," *Honeywell World (Centennial Edition)*, 1986.

17. Ibid.

18. J. Michael Stapp, *A History of Honeywell's Aerospace and Defense, 1940–1982*, 1982, 6, Honeywell Corporation Records, MHS.

19. "Big Reach-Ins Fly to Battle with Paratroops," *Air Conditioning & Refrigeration News*," February 26, 1945.

20. "America's Greatest Negro Inventor," *Ebony*, December 1952, 41; Gloria M. Swanson and Margaret V. Ott, *I've Got an Idea: The Story of Frederick McKinley Jones* (Minneapolis: Runestone Press, 1994), 68.

21. The American Society of Mechanical Engineers, *Thermo King Model C Transport Refrigeration Unit: An International Historic Mechanical Engineering Landmark*, October 1996.

22. Georges F. Doriot to J. A. Numero, December 19, 1945, Frederick Jones Papers, MHS.

23. Steven M. Spencer, "Born Handy," *Saturday Evening Post*, May 7, 1949, 31; "America's Greatest Negro Inventor," *Ebony*, December 1952, 41; John Nyberg, "City Inventor Finds Way for GIs to Get Cold Drink," *Minneapolis Star Journal*, January 1, 1945; Jay Edgerton, "Crack Engineer Shuns Praise," *Minneapolis Tribune*, May 4, 1949.

24. Swanson and Ott, *I've Got an Idea*, 78.

25. *Making Roads Safer the World Over*, 1989, 3M Company Records, MHS.

26. Virginia Huck, *Brand of the Tartan: The 3M Story* (New York: Appleton-Century-Crofts, 1955), 227.

27. *A 40-Year History of Reflective Sheeting: A Resource Document*, April 1980, 3M Company Records, MHS.

28. "There'll Be Fewer Blues in the Night," *3M Megaphone*, February 1944.

29. *A 40-Year History of Reflective Sheeting: A Resource Document*, April 1980, 3M Company Records, MHS.

30. "Scotchlite Brightens the Way," *3M Megaphone*, February 1945.

31. *A 40-Year History of Reflective Sheeting: A Resource Document*, April 1980, 3M Company Records, MHS.

32. Erwin Tomash and Arnold A. Cohen, "The Birth of an ERA: Engineering Research Associates, Inc. 1946–1955," *Annals of the History of Computing*, October 1979, 85–86; William H. Nicholas, "Gliders—Silent Weapons of the Sky," *National Geographic*, August 1944, 155.

33. Nicholas, "Gliders," 155.

34. John E. Parker, interview by Arthur L. Norberg, December 13, 1985, and May 6, 1986, transcript, John E. Parker Papers, Charles Babbage Institute, University of Minnesota.

35. "'Many' Invasion Gliders Made in Twin Cities," *St. Paul Pioneer Press*, June 9, 1944.

36. Allard and Sandvick, *Minnesota Aviation History*, 231.

37. Parker, interview.

38. Ibid.

39. Charles J. Murray, *The Supermen: The Story of Seymour Cray and the Technical Wizards behind the Supercomputer* (New York: John Wiley & Sons, 1997), 13–16.

40. Parker, interview.

41. *Engineering Research Associates: The Wellspring of Minnesota's Computer Industry* (St. Paul: Sperry Corp., 1986), 4.

42. Parker, interview.

Brainerd, 1943–1944

1. "To Avenge Bataan," *Brainerd Dispatch*, April 12, 1943.

2. "David Karlson, War Prisoner, Dies in Japan," *Brainerd Dispatch*, June 16, 1943.

3. Samuelson, interview.

4. "Lt Col Miller Proud of Men in Tank Battalion," *Brainerd Dispatch*, August 27, 1943.

5. "Radio Message Received from Japanese Camp," *Brainerd Dispatch*, November 18, 1943.

6. Reuel S. Moore, "Japs Torture American Prisoners," *Brainerd Dispatch*, January 28, 1944.

7. "The Beast of Asia," *Brainerd Dispatch*, January 29, 1944.

8. "Brainerd Seething over News about War Prisoner Atrocities," *Brainerd Dispatch*, January 28, 1944.

9. Arm, interview.

10. "Prisoner of War in Japan Greets New Daughter," *Brainerd Dispatch*, August 12, 1944.

11. "Tired, Happy McComas Home," *Brainerd Dispatch*, November 18, 1944.

Chapter 6: Rumors of War

1. Don Boxmeyer, "Pearl Harbor Counterstrike Was Aided Here," *St. Paul Pioneer Press*, June 2, 2001.

2. Allard and Sandvick, *Minnesota Aviation History*, 227–29.

3. Boxmeyer, "Pearl Harbor Counterstrike."

4. Bob Speer, "'U' War Projects So Secret Even Coffey Doesn't Know," *Minneapolis Times*, August 26, 1942.

5. Cedric Adams, "In This Corner," *Minneapolis Star Journal*, September 2, 1942.

6. James H. Capshew, "Engineering Behavior: Project Pigeon, World War II, and the Conditioning of B. F. Skinner," in Laurence D. Smith and William R. Woodward, *B. F. Skinner and Behaviorism in American Culture* (Bethlehem: Lehigh University Press, 1996), 133.

7. B. F. Skinner, *The Shaping of a Behaviorist* (New York: Alfred A. Knopf, 1979), 241.

8. Capshew, "Engineering Behavior," 133.

9. Skinner, *Shaping of a Behaviorist*, 256.

10. Ibid., 258; Gail B. Peterson, "Days of Great Illumination: B. F. Skinner in the Gold Medal Flour Mill," lecture, Mill City Museum, Minneapolis, MN, April 1, 2004.

11. Ibid., 260.

12. Capshew, "Engineering Behavior," 135–36.

13. B. F. Skinner, "Pigeons in a Pelican," *American Psychology* 15 (1960): 31.

14. Ibid., 32.

15. Capshew, "Engineering Behavior," 138–39.

16. Ibid., 139.

17. Ibid., 141.

18. Skinner, "Pigeons in a Pelican," 34.

19. Ibid.

20. Ibid.

21. *History of Mayo Aeromedical Unit* (Rochester: Mayo Foundation, 1995), 36.

22. Earl H. Wood, *Charlie Code*, 1975, Mayo Historical Suite, Mayo Foundation, Rochester, MN.

23. *History of Mayo Aeromedical Unit* (Rochester: Mayo Foundation, 1995), 37.

24. Dave Clark, *The E. J. Baldes I Knew*, 1979, Mayo Historical Suite, Mayo Foundation, Rochester, MN.

25. *History of Mayo Aeromedical Unit* (Rochester: Mayo Foundation, 1995), 20–21.

26. Clark, *E. J. Baldes I Knew*.

27. *Reaching New Heights: Secret Stories of the Mayo Clinic Aero Medical Unit* (Rochester, MN: Mayo Clinic, 2002), documentary.

28. A. B. Horner to Northwest Airlines Modification Center Employees, December 31, 1943, Box 16, War History Committee Records, MHS.

29. Allard and Sandvick, *Minnesota Aviation History*, 238.

30. Memo, A. B. Horner to Northwest Airlines Modification Center Employees, December 31, 1943, War History Committee Records, MHS.

31. A. B. Horner, "Horner Reviews Problems, Achievements," *Field and Hangar*, September 1945.

32. "Center Closes with Brilliant Record," *Field and Hangar*, September 1945.

33. Ibid.

34. "Many Farms Change Hands," *Dakota County Tribune*, April 10, 1942.

35. Ibid.

36. George Hellickson, "Rosemount Community Is Set Back on Its Heels by Arms Plant News," *Minneapolis Sunday Tribune and Star Journal*, April 5, 1942.

37. "Many Farms Change Hands," *Dakota County Tribune*, April 10, 1942.

38. Henry Peine and Margaret Peine, interview by Nancy Pilgrim and Helen Davis, July 15, 1976, transcript, MHS.

39. Ibid.

40. "Farmers Hear They Must Vacate," *Dakota County Tribune*, April 3, 1942.

41. Hellickson, "Rosemount Community."

42. Ibid.

43. Emmet C. Carroll, interview by Teresa Seliga and Helen Davis, June 22, 1976, transcript, MHS.

44. "90 Farmers Awaiting U.S. Offers," *Dakota County Tribune*, April 17, 1942; "Rail Activity Starting at Rosemount This Week," *Dakota County Tribune*, April 24, 1942.

45. "Farmers Fight U.S. Offers for Area Farm Land," *Dakota County Tribune*, May 8, 1942.

46. Peine and Peine, interview.

47. Ibid.

48. "Arms Plant to Be Larger Than Originally Planned," *Dakota County Tribune*, June 5, 1942; "Project Buildings Offered for Sale," *Dakota County Tribune*, June 12, 1942; "Rosemount Powder Plant Workers Homeward Bound," *Dakota County Tribune*, July 3, 1942.

49. C. H. Gelder, "C. H. Gelder, R.E.A. Manager, Tells How Farm Land Has Changed into Big Project," *Dakota County Tribune*, July 31, 1942.

50. "War Plant Land Values Hiked 31%," *St. Paul Dispatch*, September 22, 1943.

51. "Unions Here Protest Gopher Plant Layoffs," *St. Paul Pioneer Press*, April 12, 1943.

52. "Rosemount Plant to Be Idle under Army 'Standby' Order," *St. Paul Dispatch*, July 20, 1943.

53. Patricia L. Dooley, "Gopher Ordnance Works: Condemnation, Construction, and Community Response," *Minnesota History* 49 (Summer 1985), 222.

54. Harold Levander, interview by Teresa Seliga and Helen Davis, July 6, 1976, transcript, MHS.

55. John McBrien, interview by Tom Copeland and Nancy Pilgrim, June 29, 1976, transcript, MHS.

56. Anna E. Wachter, interview by Helen Davis and Nancy Pilgrim, June 23, 1976, transcript, MHS.

57. McBrien, interview.

58. Peine and Peine, interview.

59. McBrien, interview.

60. Dooley, "Gopher Ordnance Works," 228.

61. Peine and Peine, interview.

Dispatches: Robert Burns

1. "Hiroshima," *Worthington Daily Globe*, June 30, 1983.

2. Robert Burns to Artie and Ilma Cale, October 24, 1945, Artie M. Cale Papers, MHS.

Chapter 7: Matters of Conscience

1. Harold Stassen, interview by Alec Kirby, June 1991, transcript, OH6, MHS.

2. Harold Stassen, interview by Deborah L. Crown, September 22, 1994, transcript.

3. Ivan Hinderaker, "Harold Stassen and Developments in the Republican Party in Minnesota, 1937–1943" (master's thesis, University of Minnesota, 1949), 638.

4. Ibid.

5. "Petition Sent Minnesota Solons," *St. Paul Dispatch*, September 19, 1939.

6. Hinderaker, "Harold Stassen," 628.

7. "Rotary Asks Peace," *St. Paul Pioneer Press*, September 20, 1939.

8. "Preserve Old Neutrality Act," *Minnesota Union Advocate*, September 28, 1939.

9. Hinderaker, "Harold Stassen," 631.

10. "High Schools Will Be War Academies," *Minneapolis Tribune*, October 16, 1942.

11. W. F. H. Kerl to W. J. Hickey, December 7, 1942, Box 3, St. Paul–Ramsey County War History Committee Records, MHS.

12. "High Court Asked to Reverse Flag Ruling," *St. Paul Pioneer Press*, June 23, 1943.

13. Charles A. Lindbergh, *The Wartime Journals of Charles A. Lindbergh* (New York: Harcourt Brace Jovanovich, 1970), 485.

14. A. Scott Berg, *Lindbergh* (New York: G. P. Putnam's Sons, 1998), 409, 418.

15. M. W. Halloran, "12,000 Roar Approval as Lindbergh Demands America Keep Out of War," *Minneapolis Sunday Tribune and Star Journal*, May 11, 1941.

16. "Text of Lindbergh Speech," *Minneapolis Sunday Tribune and Star Journal*, May 11, 1941.

17. Lindbergh, *Wartime Journals*, 485.

18. Ibid., 487.

19. "Addressed to Mr. Lindbergh," *Minneapolis Star Journal*, May 10, 1941.

20. George W. Garlid, "Minneapolis Unit of the Committee to Defend America by Aiding the Allies," *Minnesota History* 41 (Summer 1969), 272.

21. "Imitator of Hitler," *St. Paul Pioneer Press*, September 13, 1941.

22. "Lindbergh's Name to Be Repainted on Water Tower," *Little Falls Herald*, August 21, 1942.

23. "Vince Dunne, 11 Others Get 16-Month Terms," *Minneapolis Daily Times*, December 8, 1941.

24. Grace Carlson, interview by Carl Ross, transcript, MHS.

25. Thomas L. Pahl, "G-String Conspiracy, Political Reprisal or Armed Revolt: The Minneapolis Trotskyite Trial, *Labor History* (Winter 1967), 37.

26. "Socialist Worker Party Offices Here Raided by U.S. Marshals," *Minneapolis Tribune*, June 28, 1941.

27. "A Move against Disloyalists," *St. Paul Dispatch*, June 28, 1941.

28. Pahl, "G-String Conspiracy," 38.

29. Ibid., 42–43.

30. Ibid., 45.

31. "Leaders O.K. by Us," *St. Paul Recorder*, August 1, 1941.

32. Kenneth G. Crawford, "Dunne Brothers Wait to See If 1941 Will Be Another Red-Hunting Year," *Louisville Courier-Journal*, July 27, 1941.

33. James A. Wechsler, "First Peace-Time Sedition Trial in 150 Years Opens," *PM*, October 20, 1941.

34. Carlson, interview.

35. "Woman Denies SWP Planned Armed Revolt," *Minneapolis Times*, November 25, 1941.

36. Carlson, interview.

37. Ben Holstrom, "Plot Denial Ends SWP Testimony," *Minneapolis Star Journal*, November 25, 1941.

38. "18 Guilty of Plot to Disrupt Army, They and 5 Others Freed of Sedition," *New York Times*, December 2, 1941.

39. "Mice Apprehended," *Time*, December 15, 1941, 29.

40. "The SWP Verdict," *Minneapolis Star Journal*, December 2, 1941.

41. Grace Carlson to Evelyn Anderson, January 7, 1944, Grace Carlson Papers, MHS.

42. Carol Jensen, "Loyalty as a Political Weapon," *Minnesota History* 43 (Summer 1972), 46.

43. Tom Conklin, "Column Left," *New Ulm Daily Journal*, August 24, 1939.

44. "Restaurant Man Victim of 'Fifth Column' Rumors," *Mankato Free Press*, June 26, 1940.

45. Robert Franklin, "No Longer Enemies—Just People," *Minneapolis Star-Tribune*, October 2, 2002.

46. "Some Thoughts on This War," *New Ulm Daily Journal*, December 10, 1941.

47. "'Conscientious Objector' Draws Year and a Day," *Fergus Falls Daily Journal*, January 9, 1942.

48. "Statistical Chart of C.O. Cases Reported in Newspapers to Date, September 15, 1942," Box 22, War History Committee Papers, MHS.

49. Henry Scholberg, interview with the author, October 29, 2002.

50. Kenneth Tuttle, "'U' Test Volunteer Describes 'Famine,'" *Minneapolis Star Journal*, [1946?].

51. Ibid.

52. Lester J. Glick, "'I Was Hungry . . .'" *Builder Magazine*, December 1994, 6.

53. Tuttle, "'U' Test Volunteer.'"

54. Glick, "I Was Hungry," 6.

55. Gladys Wood, "'Conchies at U on Starvation Diet, Test War, Famine Effect," *St. Paul Dispatch*, March (?), 1945.

56. Tuttle, "'U' Test Volunteer."

57. Glick, "I Was Hungry," 7.

58. Virginia Arne, "CO War Starvation Diet to End in Late July," May (?), 1945.

59. Scholberg, interview.

60. Kenneth Tuttle, "'Guinea Pigs' Lose Interest in Life as Hunger Grows," *Minneapolis Star Journal*, [1946?].

61. Scholberg, interview.
62. Tuttle, "'Guinea Pigs' Lose Interest."
63. Glick, "I Was Hungry," 9.
64. Tuttle, "'U' Test Volunteer."
65. Glick, "I Was Hungry," 11.
66. Scholberg, interview.
67. Glick, "I Was Hungry," 10.
68. Tuttle, "'Guinea Pigs' Lose Interest."
69. Glick, "I Was Hungry," 10.
70. Tuttle, "'Guinea Pigs' Lose Interest."
71. Glick, "I Was Hungry," 13.
72. Ibid., 14.
73. Scholberg, interview.
74. Glick, "I Was Hungry," 17.
75. David Brown, "Keys of Nutrition: When America Was Hungry to Understand the Science of Diet, Ancel Keys Stepped Up to the Plate," *Washington Post*, October 22, 2002.
76. Max Kampelman to Elias Lieberman, April 2, 1945, Box 1, Max Kampelman Papers, MHS// Bibliography: Kampelman, Max. Papers. MHS.]
77. "Conscientious Objector," *St. Paul Pioneer Press*, April 1, 1942.
78. Theodore C. Blegen, *Minnesota: A History of the State* (Minneapolis: University of Minnesota Press, 1963), 538.
79. State Farmer-Labor Women's Committee, *The War and the Election*, 1942, campaign brochure, MHS.
80. John Earl Haynes, *Dubious Alliance: The Making of Minnesota's DFL Party* (Minneapolis: University of Minnesota Press, 1984), 113.
81. Vienna P. Johnson to Susie Stageberg, Dec. 15, 1943, Box 8, Farmer-Labor Association Papers, MHS.
82. Paul Tinge and Elmer Benson to Elmer Kelm, January 7, 1944, Box 18, Elmer Benson Papers, MHS.
83. Haynes, *Dubious Alliance*, 107.
84. Hubert H. Humphrey, *The Education of a Public Man: My Life in Politics* (New York: Doubleday & Company, 1976), 84–85.
85. M. W. Halloran, "Hannegan Asks Unity on Fusion," *Minneapolis Star Journal*, April 14, 1944.
86. Byron G. (Barney) Allen, interview by Arthur Naftalin, August 10, 1978, transcript, Hubert Humphrey Oral History Project, MHS.
87. Allen, interview.
88. M. W. Halloran, "After 28 Years State Gets Back to 2 Parties," *Minneapolis Tribune*, April 16, 1944.
89. Lewis Mills, "Humphrey Bars His Nomination," *Minneapolis Tribune*, April 16, 1944.
90. Eugenie Moore Anderson, interview by Arthur Naftalin, July 14, 1978, transcript, Hubert Humphrey Oral History Project, MHS.
91. Orville L. Freeman, interview by Arthur Naftalin, January 16, 1978, transcript, Hubert Humphrey Oral History Project, MHS. Humphrey was not the only high-profile Minnesota politician to appreciate the personal and political ramifications of military service. In April 1943, Governor Harold Stassen resigned his office to accept a commission as lieutenant commander in the U.S. Navy. His decision to give up the governorship sparked debate among Minnesotans—some applauded his patriotism and others believed he had accepted a carefree naval assignment for political gain. Stassen went on to serve with distinction. As a flag officer under Admiral W. F. Halsey he played a major role in the United Nations charter conference in San Francisco and led a mission to liberate thousands of U.S. and Allied POWs in the days preceding Japan's formal surrender.
92. Haynes, *Dubious Alliance*, 126.
93. Carl Solberg, *Hubert Humphrey: A Biography* (New York: W. W. Norton & Company, 1984), 112.
94. Ibid.

Brainerd, 1945

1. "Merrifield Soldier Tells of Prison Camp Release," *Brainerd Dispatch*, April 4, 1945.
2. "Off the Editor's Chest," *Brainerd Journal Press*, August 17, 1945.
3. "Lt. Col. Miller Liberated from Japanese Camp," *Brainerd Dispatch*, September 19, 1945.
4. Henry Peck, interview with the author, February 24, 2003.
5. Porwoll, interview.
6. Burke, interview.
7. Ibid.
8. Ibid.
9. "Col. Miller Due to Arrive at His Brainerd Home Today," *Brainerd Dispatch*, October 25, 1945.
10. Arm, interview.
11. Porwoll, interview.
12. Ibid.
13. Peck, interview.
14. Samuelson, interview.
15. Porwoll, interview.
16. Carl Zapffe, *Brainerd, Minnesota, 1871–1946: Seventy-Fifth Anniversary* (Brainerd: Brainerd Civic Association, 1946), 163.
17. Samuelson, interview.

Conclusion

1. "Minneapolis Goes Wild with VJ Joy," *Minneapolis Tribune*, August 15, 1945.

2. "Prayers, Confetti Mark Peace Here," *St. Cloud Daily Times*, August 15, 1945.

3. "Newsboy Chalks Up 500 Sales in 12 Minutes as Extras Flood Loop," *St. Paul Pioneer Press*, August 15, 1945.

4. "Scenes of Solemnity and Jollity," *St. Paul Pioneer Press*, August 15, 1945.

5. "Prayers, Confetti Mark Peace Here," *St. Cloud Daily Times*, August 15, 1945.

6. "Servicemen's Center Hails Jap Surrender," *St. Paul Pioneer Press*, August 15, 1945.

7. Theodore C. Blegen, *Minnesota: A History of the State* (Minneapolis: University of Minnesota Press, 1963), 543; U.S. War Department, *World War II Honor List of Dead and Missing: State of Minnesota*, 1946, iii; U.S. Navy, *State Summary of War Casualties [Minnesota]*, 1946, 1.

8. "Grandeur of Victory," *St. Paul Pioneer Press*, August 15, 1945.

9. Theodore C. Blegen, *Minnesota: A History of the State*, 564.

10. "Discrimination," *Minneapolis Spokesman*, April 19, 1946.

11. "500th Jewish DP Arrives in St. Paul," *Keynoter*, October 1951.

12. Minnesota Department of Health, *1999 Minnesota Health Statistics Annual Summary—Overview*, 1999, 2, www.health.state.mn.us/divs/chs/99annsum/overview.pdf.

13. William M. Tuttle, Jr., *"Daddy's Gone to War": The Second World War in the Lives of America's Children* (New York: Oxford University Press, 1993), 27.

14. Alice Brill scrapbooks, vol. 7, March (?), 1946, MHS.

15. "What Do Women Want?" *Northfield Independent*, November 9, 1944.

16. "Screaming Mobs Rush Dayton's Nylon Sale," *Minneapolis Star Journal*, February 6, 1946.

17. E. T. Edwards, "A Year Ago and Now," *Winona Republican-Herald*, August 14, 1946.

Bibliography

"2 Million Lbs. of Cattail Fluff." *Holt (MN) Weekly News*, February 11, 1944.

3M Company. Records. MHS.

———. *A 40-Year History of Reflective Sheeting: A Resource Document*, 1980.

———. *Making Roads Safer the World Over*, 1989.

"9 Draft Dodgers Get Prison Terms." *St. Paul Pioneer Press*, October 14, 1942.

"18 Guilty of Plot to Disrupt Army, They and 5 Others Freed of Sedition." *New York Times*, December 2, 1941.

"90 Farmers Awaiting U.S. Offers." *Dakota County Tribune*, April 17, 1942.

"400 U.S. Japs Resettled in This Area." *St. Paul Pioneer Press*, November 16, 1943.

"500th Jewish DP Arrives in St. Paul." *Keynoter*, October 1951.

"1,396 Nisei Relocated in State." *St. Paul Dispatch*, November 20, 1944.

"1,500 Seek to Enlist at City Service Centers." *Minneapolis Star Journal*, December 10, 1941.

"6,000 See 125 Women Join Service." *St. Paul Pioneer Press*, October 2, 1943.

"$9,000,000 in Factories Entailed in Hemp Fibre Manufacture." *Commercial West*, December 5, 1942.

Abe, Tosh. Interview by Dave Kenney. March 14, 2003.

"Acute Labor Shortage in City's Cafes." *Minneapolis Times*, May 13, 1942.

Adams, Cedric. "In This Corner." *Minneapolis Star Journal*, May (?) 1942.

———. "In This Corner." *Minneapolis Star Journal*, September 2, 1942.

"Additional War Prisoners Arrive." *Moorhead Daily News*, May 31, 1944.

"Addressed to Mr. Lindbergh." *Minneapolis Star Journal*, May 10, 1941.

"Advance Detail of German War Prisoners Arrives." *Moorhead Daily News*, May 29, 1944.

Albert, Michael. "The Japanese." In *They Chose Minnesota: A Survey of the State's Ethnic Groups*, edited by June Drenning Holmquist, 558–64. St. Paul: Minnesota Historical Society Press, 1981.

"Alex Opinion on War Shows a Grim Spirit." *Alexandria Park Region Echo*, December 11, 1941.

Allard, Noel E., and Gerald N. Sandvick. *Minnesota Aviation History*. Chaska, MN: Mahb Publishing, 1993.

Allen, Albert V. Interview by Carl Ross. June 17, 1981.

Allen, Byron G. (Barney). Interview by Arthur Naftalin. August 10, 1978.

Allen, Jim. "Will the Real Jeep Please Stand Up." *Fourwheeler*, March 1996.

"'All's Well on Bataan,' Say Brainerd Soldiers' Long-Delayed Letters." *Minneapolis Tribune*, August 18, 1942.

American Red Cross, Midwestern Area. *The American Red Cross in Minnesota for 1945*, 1945.

American Society of Mechanical Engineers. *Thermo King Model C Transport Refrigeration Unit: An International Historic Mechanical Engineering Landmark*, 1996.

"America's Greatest Negro Inventor." *Ebony*, December 1952.

Anderson, Eugenie Moore. Interview by Arthur Naftalin. July 14, 1978.

Ano, Masaharu. "Loyal Linguists: Nisei of World War II Learned Japanese in Minnesota." *Minnesota History* 45 (Fall 1977): 273–87.

Arm, Don. Interview by Dave Kenney. February 24, 2003.

"Arms Plant to Be Larger Than Originally Planned." *Dakota County Tribune*, June 5, 1942.

"Army Captain's Wife Pays Tribute to Colonel Miller." *Brainerd Dispatch*, September 3, 1942.

"Army Rejects Fourth of Men Called at Fort." *St. Paul Dispatch*, May 26, 1944.

Arne, Virginia. "CO War Starvation Diet to End in Late July." Publication unknown, May (?) 1945.

"Back to the Farm Move Is Ordered." *Minneapolis Star Journal*, October 12, 1942.

Barton, George A. "Sportographs." *Minneapolis Tribune*, November 27, 1934.

"The Battle of Scrap Is On!" *Minneapolis Star Journal*, October 5, 1942.

"The Beast of Asia." *Brainerd Dispatch*, January 29, 1944.

Beck, Bill, and C. Patrick Labadie. *The Pride of the Inland Seas: An Illustrated History of the Port of Duluth—Superior*. Afton, MN: Afton Historical Society Press, 2004.

Becker, Dale Francis. "Fort Snelling 1938–1945." Undergraduate paper, University of Minnesota, 1983.

Benson, Elmer. Papers. MHS.

Berg, A. Scott. *Lindbergh*. New York: G.P. Putnam's Sons, 1998.

"Big Reach-Ins Fly to Battle with Paratroops." *Air Conditioning & Refrigeration News*, February 26, 1945.

Bingham, Marjorie. "Keeping At It: Minnesota Women." In *Minnesota in a Century of Change*, edited by Clifford E. Clark, 433–71. St. Paul: Minnesota Historical Society Press, 1989.

Blegen, Theodore C. *Minnesota: A History of the State*. Minneapolis: University of Minnesota Press, 1963.

Bofman, Albert. *Maladministration and Human Relations in a Federal Prison*. Philadelphia: J. W. Reilly, 1948.

Boxmeyer, Don. "Pearl Harbor Counterstrike Was Aided Here." *St. Paul Pioneer Press*, June 2, 2001.

"Brainerd Area Hardest Hit by Capture of Bataan." *Brainerd Dispatch*, April 10, 1942.

"Brainerd Seething over News about War Prisoner Atrocities." *Brainerd Dispatch*, January 28, 1944.

Brill, Alice C. Scrapbooks. MHS.

Broehl, Wayne G., Jr. *Cargill: Trading the World's Grain*. Hanover, NH: University Press of New England, 1992.

Brown, David. "Keys of Nutrition: When America Was Hungry to Understand the Science of Diet, Ancel Keys Stepped Up to the Plate." *Washington Post*, October 22, 2002.

Brunette, Pauline, Naomi Whipple, Robert DesJarlait, and Priscilla Buffalohead. *Ojibway Family Life in Minnesota: 20th Century Sketches*. Coon Rapids, MN: Anoka-Hennepin School District, 1991.

"The Bull's-Eye." *Commercial West*, February 7, 1942.

"By the Ways." *Zenith Bulletin*, May 7, 1943.

Cale, Artie M. Papers. MHS.

"Can Research Save Mesabi?" *Business Week*, May 11, 1946.

Capshew, James H. "Engineering Behavior: Project Pigeon, World War II, and the Conditioning of B. F. Skinner." In *B. F. Skinner and Behaviorism in American Culture*, edited by Laurence D. Smith and William R. Woodward. Bethlehem: Lehigh University Press, 1996.

"Captain Edward L. Burke Prisoner of the Japanese." *Brainerd Dispatch*, December 14, 1942.

Carlson, Grace. Interview by Carl Ross. June 14 and 17, 1987.

Carroll, Emmet C. Interview by Teresa Seliga and Helen Davis. June 22, 1976.

Carroll, Francis M. *Crossroads in Time: A History of Carlton County, Minnesota*. Cloquet, MN: Carlton County Historical Society, 1987.

"Center Closes with Brilliant Record." *Field and Hangar*, September 1945.

"Civil War Veteran Walks 32 Miles to Assist Navy." *Brainerd Dispatch*, January 7, 1943.

Clark, Dave. "The E. J. Baldes I Knew." Mayo Historical Suite, Mayo Foundation, Rochester, MN, 1979.

Clegg, Alan. "A Shipyard Obituary—Without Crepe." *Cargill News*, January 1946.

Clifford, J. Garry, and Samuel R. Spencer, Jr. *The First Peacetime Draft*. Lawrence: University Press of Kansas, 1986.

Code, Charles, and Edward H. Lambert, H. Frederic Hemholz, Joseph H. Szursewski, and Earl Wood. "History of Mayo Aeromedical Unit." Transcribed discussion, Mayo Foundation, Rochester, MN, 1995.

"Col. Miller Due to Arrive at His Brainerd Home Today." *Brainerd Dispatch*, October 25, 1945.

"Company A War Prisoners." *Brainerd Dispatch*, May 14, 1942.

Conklin, Tom. "Column Left." *New Ulm Daily Journal*, August 24, 1939.

"Conscientious Objector." *St. Paul Pioneer Press*, April 1, 1942.

"'Conscientious Objector' Draws Year and a Day." *Fergus Falls Daily Journal*, January 9, 1942.

Crawford, Kenneth G. "Dunne Brothers Wait to See If 1941 Will Be Another Red-Hunting Year." *Louisville Courier-Journal*, July 27, 1941.

Culler, C. F. "The Carp for Victory." *Izaak Walton League, Minnesota Division, Bulletin*, Last Quarter, 1942.

Cummings, William. Diaries. MHS.

"David Karlson, War Prisoner, Dies in Japan." *Brainerd Dispatch*, June 16, 1943.

Davidson, Neil A. "Rural Hennepin Can Be Proud." *Minneapolis Tribune*, September 11, 1942.

Davis, E. W. *Lake Superior Iron Ore and the War Emergency*, 1942.

———. *Pioneering with Taconite*. St. Paul: Minnesota Historical Society, 1964.

Davis, Harry. Interview by Dave Kenney. September 5, 2003.

———. *Overcoming: The Autobiography of W. Harry Davis*, edited by Lori Sturdevant. Afton, MN: Afton Historical Society Press, 2002.

"Discrimination." *Minneapolis Spokesman*, April 19, 1946.

Dooley, Patricia L. "Gopher Ordnance Works: Condemnation, Construction, and Community Response." *Minnesota History* 49 (Summer 1985): 215–28.

Dougherty, Richard. *In Quest of Quality: Hormel's First 75 Years*. St. Paul: North Central Publishing, 1966.

Douglas, R. M. Letter to the editor. *St. Paul Dispatch*, April 3, 1942.

"Draft Delinquents Warned of Penalty." *St. Paul Pioneer Press*, October 25, 1943.

"Draft to Leave 34,000 Between 18 and 29 on Minnesota Farms." *St. Paul Pioneer Press*, January 17, 1945.

"Draftees Takes Tests." *St. Paul Pioneer Press*, November 26, 1940.

Drill, Edwin. Interview by Carl Ross. October 14, 1987.

"'Drowning' May Be Popular." *St. Paul Pioneer Press*, May 14, 1943.

Duluth Children's Services. "Community Facilities Application for Lanham Act Funds," n.d.

Eastlund, Harold. Interview by Mark Stover. October 8, 1979.

Edgerton, Jay. "Crack Engineer Shuns Praise." *Minneapolis Tribune*, May 4, 1949.

Edwards, E. T. "A Year Ago and Now." *Winona Republican-Herald*, August 14, 1946.

"Employment in War Plants in Mpls. Climbing." *Minneapolis Spokesman*, January 8, 1943.

"Enlistments in All Armed Units Set New Mark in City." *Minneapolis Star Journal*, December 9, 1941.

Entsminger, Margaret. "St. Peter's Scrap Heap Totals over 250 Tons." *Minneapolis Tribune*, October 1, 1942.

———. "Women Training as Telegraph Operators." *Minneapolis Tribune and Star Journal*, August 9, 1942.

Ernst, William. Interview by Steve Vatndal. July 11, 1980.

"Excerpts from Army Times February 5, 1944, Page 11: Jeep Was First in the 'Eep' Family." *Minneapolis-Moline Merchandiser*, n.d.

"Fair Grounds Plant Called 'Miracle.'" *St. Paul Pioneer Press*, February 29, 1944.

"Farewell and Godspeed." *Brainerd Dispatch*, February 19, 1941.

"Farm Labor Shortage? Some Skeptical Views." *Minneapolis Sunday Tribune and Star Journal*, March 8, 1942.

"The Farmer Goes to Sea." *Time*, September 13, 1943.

Farmer-Labor Association. Papers. MHS.

"Farmers Fight U.S. Offers for Area Farm Land." *Dakota County Tribune*, May 8, 1942.

"Farmers Hear They Must Vacate." *Dakota County Tribune*, April 3, 1942.

"Fell in Forest." *Virginia (MN) Range Facts*, November 30, 1944.

"Fido Joins Army." *Minneapolis Tribune*, March 30, 1942.

Finch, John. "War Department Personnel Center." *Fort Snelling Bulletin*, June 21, 1946.

Finney, Nat. "Minnesota War Peak to Be 212,500 Men." *Minneapolis Tribune*, October 16, 1942.

"First Women Trolley 'Men.'" *St. Paul Pioneer Press*, July 17, 1943.

"Fitting Men to Invitations Keeps Service Center's Host Hopping." *Minneapolis Sunday Tribune and Star Journal*, July 19, 1942.

"'Food Rationing' Is Here! Cafes All Short-Handed." *Minneapolis Tribune*, September 14, 1942.

Franklin, Robert. "No Longer Enemies—Just People." *Minneapolis Star-Tribune*, October 2, 2002.

Freeman, Orville L. Interview by Arthur Naftalin. January 16, 1978.

Garlid, George W. "Minneapolis Unit of the Committee to Defend America by Aiding the Allies." *Minnesota History* 41 (Summer 1969): 267–83.

Gelder, C. H. "C. H. Gelder, R.E.A. Manager, Tells How Farm Land Has Changed into Big Project." *Dakota County Tribune*, July 31, 1942.

Gendler, Neal. "Uniforms or Not, Their Work Helped Win World War II." *Minneapolis Star-Tribune*, July 31, 1994.

Gillett, Arthur Dudley. "The Marvelous Mesabi Will Win the War," [1943?].

Glick, Lester J. "'I Was Hungry . . .'" *Builder Magazine*, December 1994.

"Godfather to the Jeep—Great Mystery Is Solved." *Army Times*, April 17, 1943.

Gollop, Louis. "17 Bowling Alleys Closed by Pin Setter Shortage." *St. Paul Pioneer Press*, October 16, 1944.

Gorman, Kathryn. "Loyal St. Paul Japs Victims of War." *St. Paul Dispatch*, December 9, 1941.

Governor's Interracial Commission of Minnesota. *The Negro and His Home in Minnesota*, 1947.

———. *The Negro Worker's Progress in Minnesota*, 1949.

"Grandeur of Victory." *St. Paul Pioneer Press*, August 15, 1945.

"Granny Now Does Her Bit—Takes Care of the Kiddies." *Twin Cities Ordnance News*, March 10, 1943.

Green, Anne Bosanko. *One Woman's War: Letters Home from the Women's Army Corps 1944–1946*. St. Paul: Minnesota Historical Society Press, 1989.

"Guard Unit Fights Historic Battle." *Brainerd Dispatch*, January 30, 1942.

Hafner, Al, and Milly Hafner. Papers. Olmsted County Historical Society, Rochester, MN.

Halloran, M. W. "12,000 Roar Approval as Lindbergh Demands America Keep Out of War." *Minneapolis Sunday Tribune and Star Journal*, May 11, 1941.

———. "After 28 Years State Gets Back to 2 Parties." *Minneapolis Tribune*, April 16, 1944.

———. "Hannegan Asks Unity on Fusion." *Minneapolis Star Journal*, April 14, 1944.

Harkins, W. R. "Talk before St. Louis County Historical Society," March 26, 1963.

"Harvest Hands for Ice Needed." *St. Paul Pioneer Press*, January 7, 1945.

Haynes, John Earl. *Dubious Alliance: The Making of Minnesota's DFL Party*. Minneapolis: University of Minnesota Press, 1984.

Hellickson, George. "Rosemount Community Is Set Back on Its Heels by Arms Plant News." *Minneapolis Sunday Tribune and Star Journal*, April 5, 1942.

Hiebert, Gareth. "Gophers Win Heil 'Trophy' for Hospital." *St. Paul Pioneer Press*, November 23, 1941.

"High Court Asked to Reverse Flag Ruling." *St. Paul Pioneer Press*, June 23, 1943.

"High Schools Will Be War Academies." *Minneapolis Tribune*, October 16, 1942.

Hinderaker, Ivan. "Harold Stassen and Developments in the Republican Party in Minnesota, 1937–1943." Master's thesis, University of Minnesota, 1949.

Hiner, James, Jr. "Narrative History: War Relocation Authority, Minneapolis District, 1942–1946."

"Hiroshima." *Worthington Daily Globe*, June 30, 1983.

Holmberg, Carl. Interview by Deborah L. Crown. September 19, 1994.

Holstrom, Ben. "Plot Denial Ends SWP Testimony." *Minneapolis Star Journal*, November 25, 1941.

"Holt Gets the Cattail Fluff Plant." *Holt (MN) Weekly News*, February 18, 1944.

Honeywell Corporation. Records. MHS.

"Hormel and the Nation." *The Squeal*, January 1, 1942.

Horn, Charles L. "A Letter to Employees from Charles L. Horn." *Twin Cities Ordnance News*, August 28, 1942.

———. "Mr. Horn's Own Story of President's Visit." *Twin Cities Ordnance News*, October 9, 1942.

Horn, Paul, and Hank Peterson. Interview by Gloria Thompson. January 11, 1974.

Horner, A. B. "Horner Reviews Problems, Achievements." *Field and Hangar*, June 1945.

Hubert Humphrey Oral History Project. Records. MHS.

Huck, Virginia. *Brand of the Tartan: The 3M Story*. New York: Appleton-Century-Crofts, 1955.

Humphrey, Hubert H. *The Education of a Public Man: My Life in Politics*. New York: Doubleday & Company, 1976.

"Imitator of Hitler." *St. Paul Pioneer Press*, September 13, 1941.

"Jeep Dispute Round Is Won by City Firm." *Minneapolis Tribune*, March 12, 1944.

Jeffries, John W. *Wartime America*. Chicago: Ivan R. Dee, 1997.

Jensen, Carol. "Loyalty as a Political Weapon." *Minnesota History* 43 (Summer 1972): 42–57.

"John Hawley Calls French Senegalese Troops N—rs on Radio Program." *Minneapolis Spokesman*, February 12, 1943.

Johnson, Charles. "Gophers Tip Badgers, 41–6, Win Big Ten, U.S. Titles." *Minneapolis Tribune and Star Journal*, November 23, 1941.

Johnson, Frederick L. *Goodhue County, Minnesota: A Narrative History*. Red Wing, MN: Goodhue County Historical Society Press, 2000.

Jones, Frederick. Papers. MHS.

Kennedy, David M. *Freedom from Fear: The American People in Depression and War, 1929–1945*. New York: Oxford University Press, 1999.

"King of the Wildcatters." *Time*, June 12, 1944.

Kirkevold, Marie. Interview by Janet Oian. June 27, 1977.

Koch, Raymond L. "Politics and Relief in Minneapolis during the 1930s." *Minnesota History* 41 (Winter 1968): 153–70.

Lake, Alice. "Rejected Dog Gains 40 Pounds in Army." *St. Paul Dispatch*, September 14, 1943.

Lake Superior Maritime Collections, University of Wisconsin–Superior.

"Launch 3 More Vessels at Head of Lakes." *Skillings' Mining Review*, August 15, 1942.

"Leaders O.K. by Us." *St. Paul Recorder*, August 1, 1941.

"League Launches Drive for Deer Hides for War Effort." *Izaak Walton League, Minnesota Division, Bulletin*, First Quarter 1944.

Levander, Harold. Interview by Teresa Seliga and Helen Davis. July 6, 1976.

Levey, Noam. "Ships of Dreams." *Duluth News Tribune*, April 5, 1998.

Levison, Frances. "Hormel: The Spam Man." *Life*, March 11, 1946.

Lienhard, John. "Liquid Stocking Situation Confuses Fashion 'Expert.'" *St. Paul Dispatch*, July 28, 1943.

"Lieut. Col. Miller Prisoner of War in the Philippines." *Brainerd Dispatch*, December 7, 1942.

Lindbergh, Charles A. *The Wartime Journals of Charles A. Lindbergh*. New York: Harcourt Brace Jovanovich, 1970.

"Lindbergh's Name to Be Repainted on Water Tower." *Little Falls Herald*, August 21, 1942.

Lindeke, Mary Proal. "The Civilians' Role in the War." *Continuation Course in Medical Social Service*. Minneapolis: University of Minnesota Center for Continuation Study, 1943.

Lingeman, Richard. *Don't You Know There's a War On? The American Home Front 1941–1945*. New York: Thunder's Mouth Press, 2003.

"Little Squawking by Civilians Found." *St. Paul Pioneer Press*, July 3, 1943.

Lobdell, George H. "Minnesota's 1944 PW Escape." *Minnesota History* 54 (Fall 1994): 113–23.

Lomoe, Orville E. "Virginia Blackout Success." *Duluth Herald*, July 16, 1942.

Long, Frank and Hildred Long. Papers. MHS.

"Lt. Col. Miller Liberated from Japanese Camp." *Brainerd Dispatch*, September 19, 1945.

"Lt Col Miller Proud of Men in Tank Battalion." *Brainerd Dispatch*, August 27, 1943.

Malen, Gordon. "Blackout Called '99% Perfect' from Air View." *St. Paul Pioneer Press*, July 17, 1942.

"Manila in Last Ditch Fight." *Brainerd Dispatch*, December 31, 1941.

"Many Farms Change Hands." *Dakota County Tribune*, April 10, 1942.

"'Many' Invasion Gliders Made in Twin Cities." *St. Paul Pioneer Press*, June 9, 1944.

"Many Women Glad to Quit War Jobs." *St. Paul Pioneer Press*, August 17, 1945.

Mayo Clinic. *Reaching New Heights: Secret Stories of the Mayo Clinic Aero Medical Unit*. Rochester, MN: Mayo Clinic, 2002, documentary.

McBrien, John. Interview by Tom Copeland and Nancy Pilgrim. June 29, 1976.

McGillis, Margaret. Interview by Dave Kenney. August 17, 2003.

"Mechanics Shortage Adds to Auto Problems." *Minneapolis Times*, November 10, 1942.

Menefee, Selden Cowles. *Assignment: USA*. New York: Reynal & Hitchcock, 1943.

"Merrifield Soldier Tells of Prison Camp Release." *Brainerd Dispatch*, April 4, 1945.

"Mice Apprehended." *Time*, December 15, 1941.

"Milkweed Pod Collection Will Start Sept. 15." *Warren (MN) Sheaf*, August 23, 1944.

"Mill City Launches Campaign for Jobs in Local Defense Industry." *Minneapolis Spokesman*, April 18, 1941.

Miller, E. B. *Bataan Uncensored*. Little Falls, MN: Military Historical Society of Minnesota, 1991.

Miller, H. J. *Report on State Efforts to Secure Defense Business for Minnesota Industries*, [1941?].

Miller, Paul E. "Farm Help—The Big Question Mark in 1943 Food Production," March 11, 1943. Minnesota Civilian Defense Division Records. MHS.

———. "Minnesota Set to Begin Drive for Farm Help," February 28, 1943. Minnesota Civilian Defense Division Records. MHS.

———. "State Set to Mobilize Its Farm Workers," April 10, 1943. Minnesota Civilian Defense Division Records. MHS.

Mills, Lewis. "Humphrey Bars His Nomination." *Minneapolis Tribune*, April 16, 1944.

Minneapolis Children's Services. "Community Facilities Application for Lanham Act Funds," n.d.

"Minneapolis Goes Wild with VJ Joy." *Minneapolis Tribune*, August 15, 1945.

"Minneapolis Man Objects to 'Special Labeling' of His Blood by Red Cross Bank." *Minneapolis Spokesman*, May 21, 1943.

Minneapolis-Moline Company. *Women Production Workers: Welcome to Minneapolis-Moline*, 1940.

Minnesota Citizens Defense Corps. Records. MHS.

Minnesota Citizens Service Corps. Records. MHS.

Minnesota Civilian Defense Division. Records. MHS.

Minnesota Department of Education. "Minutes of the Joint Meeting of the Committees on War Production Training and Rural War Production

Training and the State Board for Vocational Education," January 18, 1943. Minnesota War History Committee. Records. MHS.

Minnesota Department of Health. "1999 Minnesota Health Statistics Annual Summary—Overview," 1999, http://www.health.state.mn.us/divs/chs/99annsum/overview.pdf.

Minnesota Division of Employment and Security. *Summary of Twin City Labor Market Area Survey*, September 1941.

Minnesota Ethnic History Project. Records. MHS.

"Minnesota Indians Do Their Part." *Defense Council Bulletin*, July 1, 1944.

Minnesota Liberators of Concentration Camps Oral History Project. Records. MHS.

Minnesota Public Radio. "We Were the Lucky Ones," May 28, 1985.

Minnesota State Committee on Tolerance, Loyalty, and Unity. *An Appeal to the Citizens of Minnesota*, n.d.

Minnesota Welfare Defense Advisory Committee. "Preliminary Statement Concerning Twin Cities Ordinance [*sic*] Plant," September 17, 1941.

"Modern Magic." *Honeywell Aero*, August 1943.

Moore, Reuel S. "Japs Torture American Prisoners." *Brainerd Dispatch*, January 28, 1944.

Motzko, Edmund. Interview by Sandy Kilbort. April 20, 1982.

"A Move against Disloyalists." *St. Paul Dispatch*, June 28, 1941.

Murray, Charles J. *The Supermen: The Story of Seymour Cray and the Technical Wizards behind the Supercomputer.* New York: John Wiley & Sons, 1997.

"Nab St. Paul Japanese." *St. Paul Dispatch*, December 8, 1941.

Narvestad, Carl. *A History of Yellow Medicine County.* Granite Falls, MN: Yellow Medicine County Historical Society, 1972.

"Negro Citizens from All Walks Comment on Japan's Attack on United States." *Minneapolis Spokesman*, December 12, 1941.

"New 'Factory Bob' Giving Women Workers Morale Plus Glamor." *Minneapolis Tribune*, October 26, 1942.

Newman, Cecil. "An Experiment in Industrial Democracy." *Opportunity Magazine*, Spring 1944.

———. "Five Loyal Men Not Wanted by Army." *Minneapolis Spokesman*, December 12, 1941.

"Newsboy Chalks Up 500 Sales in 12 Minutes as Extras Flood Loop." *St. Paul Pioneer Press*, August 15, 1945.

Nicholas, William H. "Gliders—Silent Weapons of the Sky." *National Geographic*, August 1944.

Northern Pump Company. "News Stories of the Northern Pump Company, Minneapolis, Minnesota, from September 24th, 1940–June 11, 1942."

"Northern Pump Finally Ends Discrimination against Negro; Employ Three Men." *Minneapolis Spokesman*, April 3, 1942.

"Northern Pump President Replies to Complaint by a Worker's Wife." *Minneapolis Tribune*, April 8, 1942.

"Now It Can Be Told." *Honeywell Aero*, October 1943.

Nyberg, John. "City Inventor Finds Way for GIs to Get Cold Drink." *Minneapolis Star Journal*, January 1, 1945.

Oakes, Larry. "World War II: 1940–1945." *Minneapolis Star-Tribune*, December 31, 1999.

"Off the Editor's Chest." *Brainerd Journal Press*, August 17, 1945.

Olivier, Warner. "The Coming Crisis in Iron." *Saturday Evening Post*, November 14, 1942.

O'Neill, William L. *A Democracy at War: America's Fight at Home and Abroad in World War II.* New York: The Free Press, 1993.

"Only Night Shift Here Saw F.R." *Minneapolis Times*, October 2, 1942.

"Only the Strong." *Time*, November 11, 1940, 24.

"Ore Question." *Virginia (MN) Range Facts*, December 24, 1942.

Osman, Stephen E. "Fort Snelling's Last War." *Roots* 17 (Winter 1989): 16–21.

"Out of Jail to Enter Army." *Alexandria Park Region Echo*, December 19, 1941.

"Pacifism and Conscientious Objectors." *Hibbing Daily Tribune*, July 23, 1942.

Pahl, Thomas L. "G-String Conspiracy, Political Reprisal or Armed Revolt: The Minneapolis Trotskyite Trial." *Labor History* (Winter 1967): 30–51.

"Pallbearer Shortage Here Blamed on War." *St. Paul Dispatch*, September 22, 1944.

Parker, John E. Interview by Arthur L. Norberg. December 13, 1985, and May 6, 1986.

———. Papers. Charles Babbage Institute, University of Minnesota.

Parlin, L. D. "'Skinned' of 16 Million Profit, Solons Told by Northern Pump Chief." *St. Paul Dispatch*, June 18, 1943.

Peck, Henry. Interview by Dave Kenney. February 24, 2003.

Peihl, Mark. "POWs Work at Moorhead Truck Farm." *Clay County Historical Society Newsletter*, March/April 1991.

Peine, Henry, and Margaret Peine. Interview by Nancy Pilgrim and Helen Davis. July 15, 1976.

Peterson, Henry. Records. Northwest Minnesota Historical Center, Minnesota State University Moorhead, Moorhead, MN.

"Petition Sent Minnesota Solons." *St. Paul Dispatch*, September 19, 1939.

Pluth, Edward J. "Prisoner of War Employment in Minnesota during World War II." *Minnesota History* 44 (Winter 1975): 290–303.

"Police Report 82 Blackout Violations." *St. Paul Dispatch*, May 11, 1943.

Pomeroy, Dick. "Superior, Shipbuilding Grew Up Together." *Superior Evening Telegram*, June 30, 1990.

———. "World War II Shipbuilders Still at It Today." *Superior Evening Telegram*, March 20, 1982.

Porwoll, Ken. Interview by Dave Kenney. November 8, 2002.

"Prayers, Confetti Mark Peace Here." *St. Cloud Daily Times*, August 15, 1945.

"Preserve Old Neutrality Act." *Minnesota Union Advocate*, September 28, 1939.

"Prison for Preachers." *Fairmont Daily Sentinel*, May 19, 1942.

"Prison Labor Opposition Arises." *Moorhead Daily News*, May 23, 1944.

"Prisoner of War in Japan Greets New Daughter." *Brainerd Dispatch*, August 12, 1944.

"Project Buildings Offered for Sale." *Dakota County Tribune*, June 12, 1942.

Rachuy, Hilda. "A Single Mother and World War II." *Ramsey County History* (Winter 1991): 12–17.

"Racial Work Rights Group Formed Here." *Minneapolis Tribune*, August 12, 1942.

"Radio Message Received from Japanese Camp." *Brainerd Dispatch*, November 18, 1943.

"Rail Activity Starting at Rosemount This Week." *Dakota County Tribune*, April 24, 1942.

Rainbolt, Richard. *Gold Glory*. Wayzata, MN: Ralph Turtinen, 1972.

"Range Moves for Legislation to Aid Mining." *Virginia Daily Enterprise*, January 31, 1941.

"Reaction to Maas' Speeches." *Minneapolis Star Journal*, January 12, 1942.

Remembering the Globe. Superior, WI: Superior Public Library, n.d.

"Report of Progress: Defense Industry in the Northwest." *Minneapolis Star Journal*, November 26, 1941.

"Researchers Open New Door." *Honeywell World (Centennial Edition)*, 1986.

"Restaurant Man Victim of 'Fifth Column' Rumors." *Mankato Free Press*, June 26, 1940.

Roosevelt, Franklin D. *Annual Message to Congress*, January 6, 1942.

"Rosemount Plant to Be Idle under Army 'Standby' Order." *St. Paul Dispatch*, July 20, 1943.

"Rosemount Powder Plant Workers Homeward Bound." *Dakota County Tribune*, July 3, 1942.

Rosten, Ruthe. Interview by David Ripley. August 15, 1980.

"Rotary Asks Peace." *St. Paul Pioneer Press*, September 20, 1939.

Rowberg, Leland. Papers. MHS.

Russell, C. H. "Round Our Town." *Mankato Free Press*, December 8, 1941.

St. Paul Civilian Defense Council. "Report of Recreation Committee." January 18, 1943.

St. Paul Pioneer Press. Records. MHS.

St. Paul–Ramsey County War History Committee. Records. MHS.

Samuelson, Don. Interview by Dave Kenney. February 24, 2003.

"Scenes at Local Recruiting Offices as City Feels Effect of War." *Minneapolis Star Journal*, December 8, 1941.

"Scenes of Solemnity and Jollity." *St. Paul Pioneer Press*, August 15, 1945.

Scheifeld, Amram. "Motherhood's Back in Style." *Ladies' Home Journal*, September 1944.

Scholberg, Henry. Interview by Dave Kenney. October 29, 2002.

Schultz, Herbert C. Papers. MHS.

"Scotchlite Brightens the Way." *3M Megaphone*, February 1945.

"Screaming Mobs Rush Dayton's Nylon Sale." *Minneapolis Star Journal*, February 6, 1946.

"Servicemen's Center Hails Jap Surrender." *St. Paul Pioneer Press*, August 15, 1945.

"Shades of 1917!" *Brainerd Dispatch*, February 20, 1941.

Shave, Ed. "Women Toil on Farms to Help Win War." *Minneapolis Tribune*, August 12, 1942.

"The Ship That Broke a Record." *Walter Butler News and Views*, January 1944.

Sibley, Mulford Q. *Conscription of Conscience*. Ithaca: Cornell University Press, 1952.

Simmons, Dean B. *Swords into Plowshares: Minnesota's POW Camps during World War II*. St. Paul: Cathedral Hill Books, 2000.

Skinner, B. F. "Pigeons in a Pelican." *American Psychology* 15 (1960): 28–37.

———. *The Shaping of a Behaviorist*. New York: Alfred A. Knopf, 1979.

Smalley, Alton D. "No. 1 Ramsey Draftees Become 'Minute' Men; Many Watch and Wait." *St. Paul Pioneer Press*, October 30, 1940.

"So You Think Minnesota Can't Be Bombed?" *Minneapolis Daily Times*, February 1, 1942.

"Socialist Worker Party Offices Here Raided by U.S. Marshals." *Minneapolis Tribune*, June 28, 1941.

Solberg, Carl. *Hubert Humphrey: A Biography*. New York: W. W. Norton & Company, 1984.

"Soldiers Suckers for Crystal Ball, Dancing." *Minneapolis Times*, July 16, 1942.

"Some Thoughts on This War." *New Ulm Daily Journal*, December 10, 1941.

"Spam and the Future." *Fortune*, March 1944.

"Speakers Claim Negro Defense Role Restricted." *Minneapolis Tribune*, October 10, 1941.

Speer, Bob. "'U' War Projects So Secret Even Coffey Doesn't Know." *Minneapolis Times*, August 26, 1942.

Speer, Ray P., and Harry J. Frost. *Minnesota State Fair: The History and Heritage of 100 Years*. Minneapolis: Argus Publishing Co., 1964.

Spencer, Steven M. "Born Handy." *Saturday Evening Post*, May 7, 1949.

Sperry Corporation. *Engineering Research Associates: The Wellspring of Minnesota's Computer Industry*. St. Paul: Sperry Corp., 1986.

Spinney, Robert G. *World War II in Nashville: Transformation of the Homefront*. Knoxville, TN: University of Tennessee Press, 1998.

Sprung, William, and Faith Evers Sprung. Interview.

Stapp, J. Michael. *A History of Honeywell's Aerospace and Defense, 1940–1982*, 1982.

Stassen, Harold. Interview by Deborah L. Crown. September 22, 1994.

———. Interview by Alec Kirby, June 1991.

———. Radio address, December 18, 1941.

"Stassen Asks People to Aid U.S. Defense." *Minneapolis Star Journal*, December 8, 1941.

State Farmer-Labor Women's Committee. *The War and the Election*. Campaign brochure, 1942.

"Stop Order Sought for Smith Talk." *Minneapolis Tribune*, January 16, 1943.

Strobel, Leonard. Interview by Dave Kenney. February 24, 2003.

"A Study of the Relocated Japanese-Americans in Minneapolis," [1944?].

Stukel, Margaret. "You Can't Shirk Your Children and Work Here." *St. Paul Pioneer Press Magazine*, April 11, 1943.

"Sugar Books Denied 10% in Minnesota." *Minneapolis Star Journal*, May 6, 1942.

"Superintendents Study Teacher Shortage Problem." *Minneapolis Times*, April 1, 1942.

"Surplus Labor Status Given Twin Cities." *St. Paul Pioneer Press*, June 28, 1943.

"Surprise 'Bombing' Here Shows City Unprepared." *Red Wing Republican Eagle*, July 6, 1943.

"Surprise State Blackout Called Success Despite Some Violations." *Minneapolis Star Journal*, August 25, 1943.

"Surprise Visit Made at Night September 19." *Twin Cities Ordnance News*, October 9, 1942.

"Survey Indicates 7,500-Ton Scrap Harvest for City." *Minneapolis Star Journal*, October 12, 1942.

Sutherland, James M. "Cargill's First Navy Tanker Starts down Minnesota River." *Minneapolis Star Journal*, November 5, 1943.

"Swamped by Milkweed Pods." *St. Paul Dispatch*, August 30, 1943.

Swanson, Bernard. "Smith Wows Them at Heisman Fete." *Minneapolis Tribune*, December 10, 1941.

Swanson, Gloria M., and Margaret V. Ott. *I've Got an Idea: The Story of Frederick McKinley Jones*. Minneapolis: Runestone Press, 1994.

"The SWP Verdict." *Minneapolis Star Journal*, December 2, 1941.

"Talk of the Town." *New Yorker*, August 11, 1945.

"TCOP Inspected by President Roosevelt." *Twin Cities Ordnance News*, October 9, 1942.

"Teamwork Wins." *Walter Butler News and Views*, December 1943.

"Text of Lindbergh Speech." *Minneapolis Sunday Tribune and Star Journal*, May 11, 1941.

"There'll Be Fewer Blues in the Night." *3M Megaphone*, February 1944.

Thompson, Robert. "Agawam Snakes River, Arrives Here." *St. Paul Pioneer Press*, November 6, 1943.

"Three-Fourths of Retailers Fail to Post Ceiling Prices." *St. Paul Pioneer Press*, June 19, 1942.

"Tired, Happy McComas Home." *Brainerd Dispatch*, November 18, 1944.

"To Avenge Bataan." *Brainerd Dispatch*, April 12, 1943.

Tomash, Erwin, and Arnold A. Cohen. "The Birth of an ERA: Engineering Research Associates, Inc. 1946–1955," *Annals of the History of Computing* (October 1979): 83–87.

Trost, Walter. Interview by Sara I. Beckstrand. August 23, 1979.

"Turpin Case Is Closed, Defense Committee Reports." *Minneapolis Spokesman*, April 30, 1943.

"Turtle Lake Man Killed by Bullet." *St. Paul Pioneer Press*, November 12, 1942.

Tuttle, Kenneth. "'Guinea Pigs' Lose Interest in Life as Hunger Grows." *Minneapolis Star Journal*, [1946?].

———. "'U' Test Volunteer Describes Famine." *Minneapolis Star Journal*, [1946?].

Tuttle, William M., Jr. *"Daddy's Gone to War": The Second World War in the Lives of America's Children*. New York: Oxford University Press, 1993.

Tweton, D. Jerome. *Depression: Minnesota in the Thirties*. Fargo: North Dakota Institute for Regional Studies, 1981.

"Twin Cities May Be Bombed, Maas Warns." *Minneapolis Star Journal*, January 8, 1942.

"Unions Here Protest Gopher Plant Layoffs." *St. Paul Pioneer Press*, April 12, 1943.

"Urges Wider Recognition of Negro in War Jobs." *St. Paul Pioneer Press*, January 11, 1942.

U.S. Information Service. Office of Government Reports. *Minnesota: 1941 Defense Supplement*, 1942.

U.S. Navy. *State Summary of War Casualties [Minnesota]*, 1946.

U.S. Office of Production Management. *State Distribution of Defense Contract Awards, June 1, 1940, to May 31, 1941*, 1941.

U.S. War Department. *World War II Honor List of Dead and Missing: State of Minnesota*, 1946.

"Vince Dunne, 11 Others Get 16-Month Terms." *Minneapolis Daily Times*, December 8, 1941.

Vogel, Robert C., and Deborah L. Crown. *The World War II Ordnance Department's Government-Owned Contractor-Operated (GOCO) Industrial Facilities: Twin Cities Ordnance Plant Historic Investigation*. Plano, TX: Geo-Marine, 1995.

Wachter, Anna E. Interview by Helen Davis and Nancy Pilgrim. June 23, 1976.

"Wanted—1 Cannon." *Minneapolis Star Journal*, September 22, 1942.

"War Captives Cannot Fish in Minnesota." *St. Paul Dispatch*, June 15, 1944.

"War Hemp Yield of 1 to 3 Tons an Acre Sighted." *St. Paul Dispatch*, July 15, 1943.

"The War Is Very Close to Brainerd." *Brainerd Dispatch*, April 11, 1942.

"War Plant Land Values Hiked 31%." *St. Paul Dispatch*, September 22, 1943.

"War Prisoners Available to Minnesota Farmers." *St. Paul Pioneer Press*, June 23, 1943.

"Washington Sends Man-Power Commission Representative to Check Negro-Barring." *Minneapolis Spokesman*, August 7, 1942.

"Water Outlet Proves Too Tough for Diligent Scrapster." *Minneapolis Star Journal*, October 12, 1942.

"We Were the First." *Zenith Bulletin*, June 30, 1944.

Wechsler, James A. "First Peace-Time Sedition Trial in 150 Years Opens." *PM*, October 20, 1941.

"Westberg Number Is First." *Brainerd Dispatch*, October 29, 1940.

"What Do Women Want?" *Northfield Independent*, November 9, 1944.

"What's in a Name?" *Yank, The Army Weekly*, January 14, 1944.

Williams, Neva Welty. Interview by James E. Fogerty. January 25, 2000.

"Woman Denies SWP Planned Armed Revolt." *Minneapolis Times*, November 25, 1941.

"Women Workers Aid Ship Construction in Butler Yards." *News and Views*, October 1944.

"Women Workers Wanted." *Zenith Bulletin*, February 19, 1943.

Wood, Earl H. "Charlie Code." Mayo Historical Suite, Mayo Foundation, Rochester, MN, 1975.

Wood, Gladys. "'Conchies' at U on Starvation Diet, Test War, Famine Effect." *St. Paul Dispatch*, March (?), 1945.

"Working Mothers Here Use Child Care Centers." *St. Paul Pioneer Press*, March 12, 1944.

Wyman, Carolyn. *Spam: A Biography*. San Diego: Harcourt, Brace & Company, 1999.

Yoder, Robert M. "Minnesota's Blitz Producer." *Saturday Evening Post*, February 20, 1943.

Zack, Margaret. "Sentence: Internment Ostracism; Crime: Japanese Ancestry." *Minneapolis Tribune Picture Magazine*, May 13, 1979.

Zapffe, Carl. *Brainerd, Minnesota, 1871–1946: Seventy-Fifth Anniversary*. Brainerd: Brainerd Civic Association, 1946.

Zdon, Al. "Trained in Minnesota." *Minnesota Legionnaire*, January 2000.

Index

PHOTO CREDITS

For institutional listings, the name of the photographer, when known, is given in parentheses, as is additional information about the source of the item.

Toshio W. Abe: Page 90. Served four years, seven months, and eleven days in the Army in China, Burma, and India. Used with permission.

Don Arm: Page 12. Used with permission.

Pernina Burke: Page 11. Used with permission.

Crow Wing Historical Society: Pages 8, 226. Used with permission.

W. Harry Davis: Page 83. Courtesy of W. Harry Davis from *Overcoming: The Autobiography of W. Harry Davis* (Afton Historical Society Press).

Federal Cartridge Company: Pages ii, 128. Used with permission.

Harvard University Archives: Pages 170 and 171. Used with permission.

Lake Superior Maritime Collections at University of Wisconsin–Superior: Page 73. Used with permission.

Mayo Historical Suite: Pages 174, 176, 177. By permission of the Mayo Foundation for Medical Education and Research. All rights reserved.

Minneapolis Photo Collection/Minneapolis Public Library: Pages i, 43, 77 (top), 131, 132, 228

Minnesota Historical Society Collections: Pages 1 (*Minneapolis Journal*); 2, 4, 5, 6, 7; 15, 29 (From the Herbert C. Schultz World War II Albums);

16-17, 64, 80, 196, 202, 207, 220, 233, 235 (*Minneapolis Star and Tribune* News Negative Collection); 18, 154 (Photos by George Luxton); 20, 47, 54, 63 (*St. Paul Dispatch-Pioneer Press*); 21, 22, 25, 30, 31, 32, 34; 36, 62 (Minnesota State Archives Collection); 42 (1992.287.3, Civilian Defense Council); 49, 51, 55, 56, 59, 60, 61; 66 (T. J. Strasser); 77 (bottom; *Minneapolis Tribune*); 91, 92; 94 (Photo by *St. Paul Dispatch*); 100 (Photo by Roy Swan); 108 (Photo by Doug Hoffman for George Ryan Studios); 110, 111, 114; 118 (Photo by Rubel); 43, 120, 183 (Photo by *Minneapolis Star Journal*); 123, 125; 126 (Photo by Roleff); 138, 140, 143, 145, 148, 152; 157 (Photo by Bruce Sifford Studio); 166, 179, 180; 186 (From the Farmington *Dakota County Tribune*, April 10, 1942); 188, 191, 197, 200, 230, 232.

Edmund Motzko: Page 134. Used with permission.

Northwest Minnesota Historical Center: Pages 96-97 (Henry Peterson Collection, Northwest Minnesota Historical Center, Moorhead, Minnesota. Used with permission.)

Olmsted County Historical Society: Page 102. Used with permission.

Henry Scholberg: Pages 211, 213. Used with permission.

Leonard Strobel: Page 65. Used with permission.

Eleanor Swearingen: Pages 160, 163. Used with permission.

Minnesota Goes to War was designed by Will Powers at the Minnesota Historical Society Press. Typesetting was done by Judy Gilats at Peregrine Graphics Services, St. Paul. This book was printed by Edwards Brothers, Ann Arbor.